D0429075

RECEIVED

APR 0 4 2006
DOUGLASS-TRUTH LIBRARY

Praise for Janet Langhart Cohen's *From Rage to Reason*

"*Janet Langhart Cohen has written a remarkable memoir about her life's journey, which began in the segregated projects of Indianapolis. Frank, thoughtful, and exceedingly hopeful, Janet has written not only her story, but also a haunting story about America as well.*"   —The Honorable William Jefferson Clinton
The 42nd President of the United States

"*Janet Langhart Cohen's direct, no-nonsense look at her amazing life perfectly parses the age-old question of race in America with refreshing honesty, unyielding optimism and powerful, often transcendent emotion. A moving story.*"
—Ken Burns

"*From Rage to Reason imbues the singular life of a remarkable woman with the richness of a novel—at once impassioned, wry, angry and wise. True to the character of its author, the book sees clearly, and pulls no punches. With grace and honesty, Janet Langhart Cohen admits us into the life of a black woman in contemporary America and by doing so, illuminates both what has changed, and what still must change. This is a moving and wonderful book.*"   —Richard North Patterson

"*The gloriously beautiful Janet Langhart Cohen recounts her life story which will break your heart and lift your spirits. In immensely readable prose she illuminates the American dream made real, lived by a woman who is a genuine patriot. This is a book that will be a classic. And, by the way, From Rage to Reason would make a great movie.*"   —Jack Valenti, Chairman and CEO,
Motion Picture Association of America

"*Janet Langhart Cohen's life story is compelling and inspirational. She has much to say and we should all listen.*"   —Tom Brokaw

"*Janet Langhart Cohen is a remarkable person, with whom I have had the privilege and pleasure of having a valued friendship for many years. Aside from her stunning physical beauty, Janet has a quick, inquisitive and thoughtful mind, and a wonderful vocabulary. She also has the courage of a lion when she sees bullies or hypocrites in action hurting someone, and can set them down—hard—with a few well-chosen phrases. The substance of this book is important, and well worth the read. If there are any others out there who have the credentials to write this story, they are few. I believe that history will judge this effort to be a definitive work.*"   —F. Lee Bailey

"*A riveting, piognant saga of a poor little black girl in a single parent home who made it to the top of our schizoid, white-on-black society against formidable odds. Growing up under the cruel, dead hand of segregation, Janet Cohen recounts ever so movingly a fascinating journey through a racial/racist minefield. She shocks and awes—with admiration.*"   —Arnaud de Borchgrave, Director,
Transnational Threats Initiative
Center for Strategic & International Studies,
Editor-at-Large, *The Washington Times* and UPI

"*Janet has written about her life with customary frankness, boldness and self-confidence. A remarkable story of her triumph over poverty, adversity and racism.*"
—Edward W. Brooke, former U.S. Senator, and
Massachusetts Attorney General

"*This absorbing book shows Janet Langhart Cohen at close range—a luminous woman of great warmth and high purpose who has led a fascinating and often inspiring life.*" —Michael Beschloss

"*A truly inspiring story by a truly lovely woman.*" —Christopher Buckley

"*Janet Langhart Cohen has lived in both the white world and the African-American world; she understands both, has flourished in both and has written a poignant and powerful story of her fascinating life. The reader cries with her, laughs with her, worries with her and celebrates with her; From Rage to Reason is a riveting book by a remarkable woman.*" —Al Hunt, *The Wall Street Journal*

"*Janet Langhart Cohen's story provides a powerful lesson for every white person who didn't have to go through what she did, but is not as good looking as Janet, so didn't have that enormous advantage either.*" —Al Franken, # 1 *New York Times* Bestselling author of *Lies: and the Lying Liars Who Tell Them . . . A Fair and Balanced Look at the Right*

"*Janet and I share a collective memory of oppression. My weapon was music to overcome the rage; Janet's weapon was her sheer determination to speak truth to power. This is a must read.*" —Quincy Jones, Emmy and Grammy Award-winning composer and producer, best-selling author, and CEO, Quincy Jones Media Group

"*Told with unflinching honesty and unwavering patriotism, From Rage to Reason is more than just a memoir, it is the story of one woman's courage to stand up in the face of discrimination while still serving the country she loves. Janet Langhart Cohen's story is the coming-of-age story of our country.*" —Vernon E. Jordan, Jr., Senior Managing Director of Lazard Freres & Co. LLC and *New York Times* Bestselling author of *Vernon Can Read! A memoir*

"*'You go girl' is what black women in America are once again cheering for Janet Langhart Cohen. We are happy that she has documented her life's journey so that future generations can learn about the responsibilities that are required of sustained success. And we are very proud that beyond the beauty, brilliance and accomplishments, Janet still remains a 'do right sista' at heart and in reality.*" —Cathy Hughes, Founder/Chairperson, Radio One/TV One, Inc.

"*I have followed Janet Langhart Cohen's career since the late 1970s when she was on TV in Boston. I initially was struck by her beauty, poise and intellect. Having gotten to know her in more recent years, I have found that she is also honest, curious and outspoken. All these traits come through in From Rage to Reason. As do all African American professional women, Janet has had to be successful in two worlds. She and her wonderful husband, Bill Cohen, are a true example of what the American dream can be once race and prejudices are put behind us. Her story is a must read for anyone trying to find their place in this crazy world of ours.*" —Debra L. Lee, President and COO, Black Entertainment Television

"*This is a quintessential American story of an extraordinary woman who confronted adversity and triumphed by her strength of will and character.*" —Senator John McCain

From Rage to Reason

My Life in Two Americas

Janet Langhart Cohen

with Alexander Kopelman

KENSINGTON PUBLISHING CORP.
http://www.kensingtonbooks.com

Some of the names have been changed
in order to protect the privacy of the individuals.

DAFINA BOOKS are published by

Kensington Publishing Corp.
850 Third Avenue
New York, NY 10022

Copyright © 2004 by Janet Langhart Cohen

All rights reserved. No part of this book may be reproduced in any form or by any means without the prior written consent of the Publisher, excepting brief quotes used in reviews.

All Kensington titles, imprints and distributed lines are available at special quantity discounts for bulk purchases for sales promotion, premiums, fund-raising, educational or institutional use.

Special book excerpts or customized printings can also be created to fit specific needs. For details, write or phone the office of the Kensington Special Sales Manager: Kensington Publishing Corp., 850 Third Avenue, New York, NY 10022. Attn. Special Sales Department. Phone: 1-800-221-2647.

Dafina Books and the Dafina logo Reg. U.S. Pat. & TM Off.

Library of Congress Card Catalogue Number: 2003112541
ISBN 0-7582-0393-4

First Printing: May 2004
10 9 8 7 6 5 4 3 2 1

Printed in the United States of America

To the memory and spirit of my beloved mother,
Louise Gillenwaters Stamps,
who taught me
love, tolerance, and faith.

One ever feels his two-ness, an American, a Negro: two souls, two thoughts, two unreconciled strivings; two warring ideals in one dark body, whose dogged strength alone keeps it from being torn asunder.

—W.E.B. DuBois
The Soul of Black Folks
(1903)

ACKNOWLEDGMENTS

I am indebted to many people for the inspiration and assistance they provided in helping me to reach back into the past to retrieve memories and experiences that have been both painful and liberating.

First and foremost, there is my husband, Bill, the love of my life, who encouraged me—no insisted—that I tell of the people, times, and events that shaped my life. His discipline, drive, creative talent, and persistence pushed me to complete this book. Throughout our years together, he has listened to me reminisce about my experiences. His total recall was truly astonishing. He really was listening!

I thank Alex Kopelman for the many hours he spent recording my recollections and helping to capture their essence.

To my agent, Mel Berger, who introduced me to Karen Thomas, my editor at Kensington Publishing. Karen's infinite patience, insights, and probing questions were instrumental in providing clarity and coherence to the final manuscript.

I was fortunate to have had Jed Lyons, a friend from Bill's political days, read a first draft of the manuscript and persuade me that to speak of reason as much as of rage and that people, good and bad, had lessons to offer.

Melvin Murphy brought to this project the same level of commitment to accuracy and excellence as he did in serving our country as a member of the United States Marine Corps.

From my days in Boston to the present, Tony Staffieri has always been there to remind me of an individual's or event's significance.

I thank Sheila Weidenfeld, who with her husband, Edward, first welcomed me to Washington. Sheila advised me to keep a diary and chronicle important moments. While I didn't always make formal entries, I kept many of the most precious and memorable times under lock and key.

University of Maryland professor and writer Dr. Ronald Walters, thank you for the time you devoted to helping me further understand the human condition and to be prepared to provide answers to the questions I've raised. For assuring me that the Almighty would give me the temerity to tell this story with boldness and not bitterness, I thank Gloria Whitted.

I am indebted to Sidney Poitier, Quincy Jones, Vernon Jordan, and Colin Powell, whose life stories inspired me to write of my own and to know that the path to success and enlightenment has been paved with hope as well as hardship.

To Donna Britt, whose columns and counsel reinforced the need for me to speak the truth.

Finally, I will remain eternally grateful to Kari Lidgett, my executive assistant, for her support and sacrifice. Kari gave up her nights and weekends to research, toil, and type the countless drafts of manuscripts. She is a young woman, wise beyond her years, who lent a sympathetic ear and critical eye to my story as it unfolded. I treasure her friendship.

PREFACE

"Be sure to wear your red dress tonight," said the voice on the machine. The caller was my husband, Bill Cohen, who was serving as Secretary of Defense. While his message lasted only seconds, I wasn't sure of its significance. Tonight was going to be a very special occasion to be sure. President Bill Clinton was going to deliver his final State of the Union address to the American people, and I had been invited by the White House to sit in the section reserved for the President's family and guests.

My husband had always complimented my choice in clothes, and I knew that a red dress I had designed was his favorite. I thought perhaps he was sending me a subliminal message that I was the rose in his life and he wanted all of those in attendance to know it. He had such flashes of romanticism, I thought, laughing. But the brevity of the message hinted that something more might have motivated his call. Its ambiguity left me both intrigued and troubled. Generally I don't like surprises, particularly at public events.

But on that night, I received the surprise of my life when President Clinton during the course of his address singled out my contribution to the men and women who serve in our armed forces. "No one has traveled farther or worked harder on behalf of those who defend our nation . . ." I was stunned as the members of Congress burst into sustained applause with a standing ovation. "Stand up, Janet, stand up," someone shouted. I stood and brought both hands to my face to stem the flood of tears that had erupted.

The President of the United States had publicly acknowledged all of the hundreds of thousands of miles I had traveled with Bill to express America's support and gratitude to those who wear our nation's uniform. It was, without a doubt, one of the sweetest moments of my life, one that is still trapped in the amber of my mind. However, the very memory of that moment stirs deeper and darker recollections of a past that was filled with racial prejudice and hatred that remain a stain on the soul of America.

Just a few decades ago, Black people were being lynched, beaten, fire-hosed, and bombed for demanding nothing more than the Constitutional rights promised to every other American. In noting the prominence and success of African-Americans in our society today, it is frequently said that, "Black people have come a long way." I'd say it another way. It is White people who have come a long way, for Blacks have always had the ability to excel in any endeavor. It was Whites who denied us the opportunity to share in the blessings of freedom during most of our years in America. The truth and irony is that we the oppressed, by demanding our rights, have enlightened the oppressor. And because of that enlightenment, it is America that has traveled the greatest distance.

During the span of my years, I have lived in a world of two Americas: one Black, one White; one segregated, one integrated; one divisive, one decent; one old, one new.

I have known a country of profound prejudice, but one of equal promise. While I continue to burn whenever I see evidence of bigotry and injustice, I also know that America is the only country that is willing to expose and openly confront its failures and seek to overcome them.

My story is but one of millions where, through sheer determination and luck, many people of color have been able to overcome discrimination and hardship to achieve their goals. The real story, however, is how America has been willing to grow and evolve into a nation worthy of its ideals. I love this country, despite its faults and because of its promise. I love America for its willingness to reach toward the light in search of an ever-higher humanity.

—*Janet Langhart Cohen*

1

Learning My Colors

"You're pretty for a colored girl."

Beauty is said to reside in the eye of the beholder. In this case the beholder was a twelve-year-old White girl who was occupying the hospital bed next to mine. We were both the same age and recovering from tonsillectomies at Indianapolis's Charity Hospital, Marion County General.

Her observation was intended as a compliment, an offering of friendship. But it was the kind of compliment that landed with a left hand. She was too young to comprehend the implicit assumption of the White race's entitlement to physical beauty. But I was not too young to comprehend that beauty transcends color. Nonetheless, her words remained etched in my mind.

Incredibly, more than forty years later, a United States senator, in praising me to my husband, Bill Cohen, asked, "Which one of Janet's parents is White?"

"Why do you ask?"

"Well, she's so intelligent."

Once again, there was no hint of malice in the words, but this time, they hit like stones. The audacity that Blacks were considered to have been bred only for brawn not beauty and surely not for brains, I found offensive. After all, for so many years, we were regarded as only three-fifths human and unlikely to close the gap on the evolutionary ladder. His ignorance and sense of superiority allowed him to believe my intelligence must have been the product of a White man who had crawled into my ancestral bed.

African-Americans have led America far since the days of slavery, lynchings, Jim Crow segregation and miscegenation laws, Dixiecrat politics, Bull Connor fire hoses, attack dogs, and church bombings. That road of hatred has been marked with the gravestones of heroes of all colors. Black people now occupy seats of power in government and corporate boardrooms. Black athletes now dominate the sports world and Black actors appear on the big screen in roles other than chauffeurs, maids, thugs, and prostitutes. However, in the Academy Award's seventy-four-year history, only three Black people have received the film industry's highest tribute for best actor, the Oscar, while countless Europeans have repeatedly realized that unique American dream.

While it's important to recognize our progress, it's hard to ignore the invidious assumptions that still linger in the hearts and minds of those who dwell at all levels of American society. It's also hard to ignore that the Ku Klux Klan, along with kindred race-hating groups such as the Council of Conservative Citizens, has slithered its way into the twenty-first century.

In 2003, the Supreme Court had to rule on whether the KKK has the Constitutional right to continue its ritual of cross burning—the most virulent practice of racism. Hooded violence masquerading as an expression of mere speech in the land of freedom! The very appearance of the Klan on the Supreme Court's docket forced me to think back to my childhood and my remote encounter with a people who barely tolerated us by day and organized to terrorize and torture us at night.

I was just four years old and, at the time, I had no concept that skin color could generate such profound fear and hatred in a civilized world. In 1945, my mother, a single parent, and I frequently lived in boardinghouses or with family members. On some occasions she would find work as a domestic, working and living in the homes of White people. It was called "living on the place." Since there were just the two of us, I was allowed to live with her in the home of Mr. and Mrs. Camon just outside of Indianapolis.

The Camons had two daughters, Sally who was ten and Jane who was twelve years old. They were friendly and looked after me while my mother tended to her daily chores. Even now, whenever moments of bitterness and rage well up inside me at the racist injustices that I see or encounter, I look back upon their genuine care and kindness toward me and know that there exists the "better angels of our nature."

One Indian summer, late in the afternoon, we were playing in the yard and saw a parade of cars drive by. Not the aerodynamically and indistinguishable clones of today, but big, beautiful black cars with running boards and bug-eyed lamps. Cars whose grills looked like human faces. Cars with real character.

"Let's go see where they're all going," said Jane, the older sister. "Maybe they're having a picnic!"

The Camons's home was located in a quiet suburban neighborhood, and we had some latitude to wander around as long as we didn't stray too far away. So we left the yard and followed the cars down the road. Eventually, we cut into a dirt path with strands of trees and came upon a large clearing where the cars were gathering.

There were dozens of people milling about at what looked to be a large family picnic. There were men talking in small groups, while women sat on the cars' running boards and children ran around playfully. All of it seemingly pleasant and social, except for one strange thing—almost everyone was wearing a white robe.

We were up on a slope, looking down on the glade. Sally and Jane laid down on their stomachs and pulled me down between them.

Jane said, "Janet, we've got to be very, very quiet. We can't make any noise because we will get into really big trouble for having you here."

I thought she meant that they would get in trouble for taking me so far away from the house. I had no idea what was unfolding in front of us—that all of these laborers, merchants, and churchgoers had gathered here to reinforce their sick, twisted notions of superiority and their hatred of people like me!

Dusk was turning to evening. As the light started to fade, a cross that was set in the ground at the far end of the clearing burst into flames. It was awesome and, to my eyes, beautiful. Like most children, I was fascinated by the fire and was always being shooed away from the stove by my mother. To see this huge, shooting flame was incredible. My first instinct was to clap my hands and yell with delight. But my companions' admonition to remain quiet had been delivered with such intensity, that I knew I had to constrain my excitement.

Then the people in the robes began to put on their heads what looked like pillowcases with holes cut in them so they could see and breathe. They gathered in the formation of a cross and began chanting something unintelligible. It was a ritual that I found both mysterious and strangely exciting.

When the first stars began to appear overhead, Sally and Jane knew it was time for us to get home. They pulled me up to my feet, signaling for me to be quiet. The ominous sound of the chanting followed us as we stole away.

We arrived home late for dinner. I joined my mother in the kitchen while the sisters ran upstairs to wash. I played with a coloring book until my mother finished serving the family their dinner and then we sat down for our meal together. Sensing that I would get into trouble for straying so far from the house, I decided not to disclose my evening's adventure. Years later, after seeing a Klan rally on television, I described to her the eerie gathering that I had witnessed.

Mother, of course, was horrified, her face reflecting fear, rage, and fierce determination.

"Oh, sweetheart, you shouldn't have had to see that."

Indeed. None of us—White or Black—should ever have to see that. Not then. Not now. Not ever again. Cowards who pass for Christians by day and terrorists by night make a mockery of the Constitution when they claim that they're entitled to express their hate-filled voices freely at our expense. A burning cross is not about freedom of expression. It's a naked appeal to violence that tries to wrap itself up in the red, white, and blue of the American flag. It's a voice from the bowels of hell, exhorting hooded racists to commit mayhem and murder against innocent people in the name of God. They had betrayed America's creed of "equality for all" and replaced it with oppression and hate.

In ways that I did not appreciate at the time, my mother had been trying her best to protect me against people who hated me because of the pigmentation of my skin. Protect and prepare me at the same time.

Next door to Mrs. Camon lived an elderly White widow. She was frail and spent most of her time in her upstairs bedroom. During the summer, she would sit by an open window, looking at the birds and squirrels gathered around the feeders. Whenever she saw me, she would call out in a kind voice, "Hello, little angel. How are you today?" I would look up, giving my best smile for her.

One day, after we exchanged our usual greeting, she said, "I have a treat for you." With that she called me over to the fence that separated the yards and threw a chocolate bonbon to me. Now chocolate is not quite the value of gold, but for me, not far from it. I picked up the treat from the grass, gobbled it down, and I thanked her.

"Would you like another, honey?" she asked.

"Yes, please." I nodded emphatically. And just as the second piece of brown gold was sailing my way, my mother stepped out into the yard.

"Janet!" she called out to me in a stentorian voice that she usually reserved for when I had done something out of line. "Come in the house and have your lunch!"

I picked up the chocolate and expressed my thanks to the neighbor and rushed inside, thinking that my mother was angry because I was eating sweets before lunch.

"How dare she!" my mother exclaimed as I sat down at the kitchen table. "Just because you're a little colored girl, she thinks that she can throw things out the window at you! How dare she?"

I was confused. To me it was simply a case of a kind old woman who liked feeding goodies to birds, squirrels, and little girls. I thought my being "colored" had little to do with her generosity. I ate my sandwich in silence.

"I know you love sweets, Janet," Mother said after she had time to settle down. "I just want you to remember that you don't ever have to eat them off the ground from anyone—ever!"

It was a lesson that Mother, through her actions, had demonstrated before. I remember once while Mother was doing general housekeeping for a Mrs. Gertrude Bauer, I was playing underneath the ironing board that had been set up in a room near the kitchen. Mrs. Bauer came into the room and began speaking to my mother in a loud voice. She didn't like the way Mother was pressing the laundry.

Mother did not apologize or say "yes, ma'am." She simply said, "I'm pressing it the same way I always do, Mrs. Bauer."

I looked up, sensing that something was about to happen. Mrs. Bauer, furious that my mother had spoken back to her, raised her right hand and tried to slap my mother's face. Mother, who was pressing the laundry with her right hand, used her left arm to block the blow and shoved Mrs. Bauer's hand away. "Don't you ever try to strike me again, especially in front of my child!" she practically shouted.

Mrs. Bauer was stunned that a Black woman had the audacity to touch her. Mother didn't hesitate for a moment. She slammed the iron down, reached down and pulled the iron's cord from the wall socket, and grabbed me by the arm. Together we walked straight out of the house.

At the time, I couldn't understand why Mrs. Bauer was so angry over laundry, but I remember feeling a great sense of pride that my mother was not afraid of her. I wanted to be just like her, unafraid of anyone, ready to defend her against anyone who might try to harm her. Mother needed to work but she would not tolerate abuse from anyone—White or Black. We were poor, but poverty didn't rob us of our pride and dignity.

Slowly, Mother was teaching me the lessons about race in America and at the same time instilling pride and self-esteem, teaching me how I needed to conduct myself if I wanted to succeed. The concept of race began to seep into my consciousness.

On the day that my mother first took me with her to Mrs. Camon's house, we were returning in a taxicab from a visit to my great-grandfather who lived with Uncle Robert and Aunt Laureen in a Black neighborhood of Indianapolis. As we crossed a set of railroad tracks that marked the separation of Blacks from the White neighborhoods, I spotted a group of children playing in a schoolyard and asked my mother what kind of children they were.

"They're just children," she said. "Little children."

"But what kind are they?" I persisted. "They look different."

"Well, they're White children."

I looked at them and then at my own arms and hands and asked, "Then what am I?"

"You're a little colored child, Janet," she said quietly.

"Colored?" I asked, a bit bewildered. "What color?"

My mother said nothing in response. I thought about it some more as we rode on.

"Oh," I said, drawing on my experience with my crayons and coloring books. "I'm colored and they're White. But who colored me?"

My mother smiled. Before she had a chance to answer, I poked the cabdriver in the back of the neck and said, "He's White too!"

Mother apologized to the driver.

"That's okay," the driver said. "She's just learning. They get it eventually."

Indeed. We all get it eventually. It may take a little longer for some, but eventually, like the man said, we get it. There are different roles and different rules for those who are Black in America.

I started to get it at five years old when my mother gave up her domestic work for a job selling tickets at the Lido movie theater in Indianapolis. Consequently, we had moved back into a neighborhood where almost everyone was Black. The iceman, the junk man, the ragman, and the watermelon man . . . There were exceptions, of course: the policemen, the postmen, and those who owned the grocery stores, or sold insurance. Then, too, there was the milkman who was always dressed in his snow-white uniform and cap as he delivered the milk door-to-door on a horse-drawn wagon. He was the most popular person of all.

Polk's Milk was the name of the dairy. We lived across the street from the plant that was shaped like two milk bottles. The neighborhood kids were always happy to see the milkman, not only to pet his horse, but also to collect the bottle tops that came with the milk that he dispensed to his customers. If you collected enough milk tops, you received a free ticket to Riverside Park, the Indianapolis amusement park, on "colored people's day." This was the one day a year that we were allowed to enter the amusement park.

I set out on a mission to collect more tops than anyone else. I drank milk with every meal. I pestered my mother and the neighbors too. I even traded sweets for milk tops.

As the time approached for colored people's day, the excitement in the neighborhood grew. All of us were counting our milk tops in anticipation of the fun we would have on all of the amusement park rides.

When the day finally arrived, kids were running around getting ready. "We're going. It's our day to go!"

My mother saw that I expected to go with all the others. She looked at me with great sadness and disappointment and said, "We're not going."

"Mother," I protested, "I've got all of these tops. It won't cost anything. Why can't I go?"

"If we can't go any time we want," she answered, "they can keep their amusement park. They're not going to keep us out the whole year long and then expect us to show up all grateful for the one day that has been set aside for us."

I didn't go to the amusement park that day, or any other day. I gave my bottle tops to my friends and put on a brave face when they returned and told me about the rides they had been on and the cotton candy they'd eaten. It would be several years before I began to appreciate my mother's determination to teach me about the need to remain proud; to never accept second best or bow or bend to those who considered themselves superior. I was never to allow anyone to set limits for me or keep me in "my place." Slowly, I began to understand that a great injustice existed in the world and that I needed to be strong if I were going to challenge it head-on.

In Indianapolis, the racism was not the obvious, "niggers not allowed" brand that you would see in the South. It was as deep, but a bit more subtle. We were allowed to shop downtown, but in many stores we could not try on any clothes. We could go to big movie theaters, provided we sat in the balcony. We could order take-out food from restaurants, but could not be served inside in the dining area. It was institutional oppression all dressed up as social custom. There were barriers that we were never allowed to cross, barriers not always visible to the eye. We might as well have been wearing electrified collars, the kind that keeps dogs from leaving the unmarked property lines of their owners.

The day that I tried to cross one of those boundaries remains fresh in my mind. Mother and I were downtown shopping. At that time, everything in Indianapolis revolved around Monument Circle, located in the center of the city.

We slowly made our way around the circle called "The Circle," window-shopping and going into various stores. It was a good day. We were dressed up for the special occasion of completing my first piano lesson and were having fun buying things we needed and fantasizing about the many things we wanted.

As we walked closer to a luncheonette, Mother said, "Let's go in and have a milkshake and a sandwich. I'm hungry. And you can have a root beer." That was always my favorite treat.

It was a small, plain, but pleasant-looking place, with a counter and a half dozen tables. We sat down at a table near the door and looked at the lunch menu hanging over the counter.

I was seven and proud of my reading abilities, so I proceeded to read the whole menu out loud. Mother smiled with joy and straightened out the place settings, taking paper napkins out of the aluminum dispenser on the table, placing them under our forks on the left, and moving the knives to the right.

The counterman and the waitress bustled about the place serving soups, sandwiches, and blue-plate specials to the lunchtime crowd. There was lively, friendly chatter all around. It was a relief to be sitting down after all of the walking we had done.

The strange thing was that the waitress would not come over and take our order. We sat there and watched people who had come in long after us receive their food. My stomach was growling, and I could see that Mother was getting upset.

Finally, Mother stood and, without saying a word, reached for my hand. In the process, she knocked over the napkin dispenser, which fell to the tabletop with a loud bang. Everything went silent for a second. Then the conversations started up again as Mother righted the dispenser, took my hand, and pulled me out into the street.

I thought she was mad at me; that I had done something wrong. Sometimes when we were out shopping, she would get annoyed at me for asking to go to the bathroom. "I told you to go before we left home," she'd say. "And now we've got to find a place for you to go." But this time, I had not asked to go. I couldn't understand why she seemed upset, just standing there on the pavement.

"What's the matter, Mother?" I said, looking up at her. "Are you mad at me?"

"No, no, no," she replied, shaking her head. "I am not mad at you, honey."

"Well what's the matter, then?" I persisted.

"Let's just go home," she said. "I'll tell you on the way."

Once we got on the bus and sat down, Mother remained silent for a long time. Finally, she turned to me and began to explain: "We would still be sitting there. They were never going to serve us."

"But how do you know that?" I asked. "Because nobody came over? Mother, it was like they didn't even see us."

"That's right," she said, sounding hurt and angry. "Nobody came over because we are colored."

"Because we are colored?" I echoed, not understanding.

"Look, dear," Mother said, "you are a little colored girl, and there are people in this world who won't like you simply because you are colored."

"What did I do at the diner that they didn't like me?" I asked, puzzled.

In a kind voice Mother said, "You didn't do anything, child. Just being colored is enough for some people not to like you."

We rode home in silence. For a while, we were trying in our own way to absorb the experience we'd just had. Then, as if she had suddenly found the words she had been searching for, Mother said, "Janet, it's wrong to dislike people simply because of their color. What you look like isn't important. It's how you behave and treat people that matters. You must be aware of the hateful people, but you must not hate or judge people on color or any differences. In God's eyes, we're all equal. You've got to promise me that you'll never do that. Never dislike people because of their color or for something they can't help."

Colored and *White* took on a new meaning at that moment. Even though I promised to obey my mother, I felt for the first time the anger of being judged by people who didn't even know me. That anger would remain locked inside and like a person afflicted with chronic pain, I would try to manage it through distraction and repression, but never denial.

The nascent indignation I experienced that afternoon foreshadowed the pain and anger that would come with a fuller understanding of racism. That understanding began to develop in earnest a few months after the incident at the luncheonette.

It was early in the fall of 1948. My father, who had shipped out on active duty shortly after I was conceived and who had just recently received his honorable discharge, was coming for a visit on the way to see his family in Kentucky. He had become something of a mythological figure for me. I had seen so many handsome men dressed in their army and navy uniforms on posters and the movie newsreels, the very thought that my father might have been among them filled me with pride. The sight of older people on buses giving up their seats for those in uniform was evidence of the pride and gratitude that America felt about those who had gone off to war.

"You look just like your father," Mother would always tell me. And when I asked what he looked like, she would point to men on the street, saying, "He is handsome like that man." Or, "He is about that height." Or, "He has a mustache just like that."

I had fantasized so often about meeting him, the idea of his actually coming to see me was almost overwhelming. I was up with the sun the day he was scheduled to arrive. Right after I had breakfast, I took a position on the front porch of Miss Maggie's boardinghouse where we rented a room, so I could see him coming up the street. I kept watching for him for what felt like a very long time. Every man who appeared on the horizon looked like he was wearing an army uniform. But when I finally spotted my father, I knew it was him.

He was wearing his uniform, walking tall and erect and carrying a large duffle bag. In the front of our house, he slowed his step and turned up the walk toward the front porch. And when he saw me running to him, he stopped, put down the bag, opened his arms, and waited for me.

"You must be my little Janet. Give your daddy a big kiss," he said, scooping me up.

He hugged me to his chest, pressing my face against the rough army wool. I did not mind, though, because he was so loving. He smelled wonderful, too, like spearmint. I guessed he had been chewing spearmint gum.

He carried me up to the porch, where my mother was waiting, gave me another kiss and set me down. They greeted each other, and we all went into the house together. Inside, the family, other boarders and Miss Maggie gathered in the living room. This was a special occasion, a man returning from the army. I remember my mother asking me to play a few bars on the old secondhand piano she had managed to buy by working odd jobs whenever she could. I heard her tell my father that her dream was for me to one day become a concert pianist. My father smiled and said that he would be in the front row of my first recital.

Then, I joined the other kids and sat on the floor but listened intently to the adults' conversation. They talked about the war and about President Truman integrating the military earlier that spring.

"Well," my father said, "we whipped the Nazis. None of us were afraid to fight those who gassed those poor people in Europe. But, the real battle begins now, here at home for us; after this war, after the Nazis. Truman might've given the order that if you serve you deserve to be treated equally, but colored boys are still getting beat up and killed down South for wearing their uniforms in public. Down there they say, 'What are you niggers doing in those uniforms? Uniforms are for our heroes, not for you niggers.' "

"The real struggle," he went on, taking a sip of lemonade, "is when I go back to see my mother in Kentucky. It burns me up, but I don't know if I want to attract attention to myself on that long bus ride to Kentucky. I think I might just pack this uniform away and ride quietly in the back. I figure that way I am more likely to get there in one piece. White folks is a bitch."

Aunt Leola signaled her agreement with my father. Once when I picked up a small blue-eyed baby that she had been hired to care for, to stop her from crying, Aunt Leola told me to put "that thing" down. "Don't start to feel anything for that thing," she cautioned me, "because as soon as she grows up from looking like your little baby dolls, she's going to call you a nigger. They call us names and say that we're lazy. But they hire us to do all the work that they're too lazy to do. They claim to be superior, but they know that they're not. There's just more of them and they're more ruthless. What else would you call a race of people who would go all the way to Africa, snatch people from their homes and families, bring them here, rape them, lynch them, and treat them like animals? No, don't you ever get close to them or let them get close to you . . ."

I saw Mother scowl at my father and Aunt Leola.

"None of that talk in this house," she said, looking at me, "White people need some humanity, but we can't start acting or thinking like them."

This was not the first time I had heard Mother refuse to let the bias or bigotry of others make her bitter.

There was an older lady in our neighborhood who owned a small convenience store. All of the kids called the woman Jew Bessie. I honestly thought that was her name. One day I was on my way out the door, when Mother asked, "Just where are you going, young lady?"

"Down to Jew Bessie's," I said innocently.

"Her name is not Jew Bessie, and I don't ever want to hear that out of you again. Bessie is her name and she's a nice woman. She happens to be Jewish, but I won't have you be disrespectful. From now on, you call her Miss Bessie. Do you hear me?"

I hadn't meant any harm or slight, since I didn't know what Jewish meant, but my mother was determined to instill in me the need to treat others with decency and respect.

Still, while sitting on the floor listening, at that moment, I silently agreed with my father and Aunt Leola. In what I would later call an epiphany, everything seemed to reach a critical mass for me. All of the insults and rejections, the overheard conversations about racial prejudice, came into focus. In the words of the taxicab driver, "I got it."

Black people were good enough to work for them but not with them; good enough to buy their goods but not try them on; good enough to eat their food but not at the same restaurants; good enough to enter their amusement parks but only once a year; good enough to wear our country's uniform but only on the battlefield, not at home.

I felt a spark ignite in me that would turn into a flame. My soul was not on ice. It was on fire. That fire would propel me to heights that I had not dreamed possible. Metaphorically, it would also succeed in the burning of almost every bridge that I would ever hope to cross.

What's in a Name?

It seems that little in my life has been uncomplicated. Beginning with my name. My mother wanted my given name to be "Jeanette," named for the actress, Jeanette McDonald.

Unfortunately, the Navy doctor who delivered me on December 22, 1941, wrote *Janet* on the birth certificate, and I have remained Janet ever since. Not only did he misspell my name, but he managed to get my race wrong as well.

I discovered later that the doctor had also placed a check mark on the box that designated me as being "White." I've been left to surmise what happened. During the war, many children like me were born at home in their mother's beds. The doctor no doubt had more than one baby to deliver during that time, and when later faced with the paperwork in his office, he must have forgotten which documents were associated with which newborns. Not wanting to make the mistake of designating a White child as being Black (woe be unto him), he must have decided to solve his problem by simply listing all he delivered as being White, which I decidedly was not. Correcting his error created an interesting dilemma for me, but that is a story I'll tell later.

And as if going through life with the "wrong" first name and documented with the wrong race was not confusing enough, there was the matter of my family name to sort through. Even my last name was an issue as I didn't carry the last name of my birth father, Bridges, but rather that of my stepfather, Floyd.

My mother was born Louise Gillenwaters. The family name is the anglicized version of the Shawnee Indian name given in school to my great-grandfather James. My great-grandfather's real name was Toad Fish-in-Water.

My mother was raised by her mother's brother, George, and his wife, Leola, after her own emotionally fragile mother was committed to a mental institution.

When Mother was only sixteen and still a ward of the state, she gave birth to my older sister, Myrna. Mother was unable to care for her baby, and the state prepared to place her for adoption. Uncle George, the dearest, kindest man I've ever known, would have none of this. He came to the rescue once again and raised Myrna as if she were his own child.

My natural father, Sewell Bridges, met my mother in church in the spring of 1941. He had been drafted into the army, and during a romantic courtship that involved dining out at restaurants and dancing nights away at the USO canteen at Camp Atterbury, Mother became pregnant. Before they were married, Private Bridges was sent off to fight the Nazis in Europe. Fortunately, Russell Floyd was in love with my mother and proposed to her. She advised him that she was pregnant, but he was unrelenting in his desire to marry her. He insisted on only one condition—that she never tell anyone that I was not his child. He wanted me to be raised as his very own, which is how I became Janet Floyd. The marriage did not last however, and by the time I was three, my mother and I were on our own.

We spent a good deal of time moving. The first boardinghouse we lived in was Mrs. Ellington's on the east side of Indianapolis. In those days, many elderly people took in boarders to help with the bills. Mrs. Ellington, who was an invalid, rented out rooms in her shotgun house—one of the houses that poor Black families owned in those days with rooms all in a row, where you could shoot a bullet in the front door, and it would come out the back door.

In the evenings, we would gather around the potbellied stove in the living room, which doubled as Mrs. Ellington's bedroom. Even though I was no more than three, I remember those nights so clearly. The lights were always off; it was wartime, and we were poor. In the dark, the stove glowed poker-red on one side and was stone cold on the other. To keep myself warm and entertained, I would rock really fast in a rocking chair. Once, I got too carried away and flipped over, much to everyone's amusement. I was embarrassed rather than hurt but could not understand why my mother and Mrs. Ellington were laughing at me.

After Mrs. Ellington's, we lived in Uncle Robert's house for a while. He was another one of my mother's maternal uncles. And like his brother, Uncle George, he went to great lengths to keep the family together. When we lived with Uncle Robert and Aunt Laureen, there were twenty-six people in that house. No one ever needed a key, as there was always somebody home.

My maternal great-grandfather, Toad Fish-in-Water (we called him by various names—Grandpa Toad, Grandpa, even "that Injun" while others in the family and neighborhood called him Uncle Toad) lived there at that time. I remember sitting on his lap and listening to him tell stories of slavery times. His mother was an African slave, and his father was a Shawnee Indian. Word was, they came up from the South on the Underground Railroad in the area of Ohio, Kentucky, and Indiana. He took after his father, it seems, since he was very light-skinned and had Indian features. That characteristic has been passed through all the Gillenwaters offspring.

Grandpa Toad did not only look Native American; he preserved elements of that culture. Every morning, he would go out back, where the outhouse stood, and chant to the rising sun. *Huh-yuh-yuh-yuh*, he sang crouched on the ground facing East. Aunt Laureen would be in the kitchen preparing a breakfast of country ham and eggs, grits, and Grandpa's favorite "mush," a mixture of cornbread, buttermilk and molasses. She'd peer out the window at him and say, "There's Old Man Toad out there doing all that Injun stuff." To me, at the age of five, he seemed like something out of one of those cowboys and Indians pictures I would see at the Lido movie theater. Perhaps because of my association with my great-grandfather, I identified with the Indians and always rooted for them, even when Hollywood cast them as scalping savages.

I saw a lot of movies in those days. Usually, Mother would leave me with someone while she went to work. But often, she brought me down to the theater with her and had me watch the shows while she worked out in the ticket booth. Mother always had me sit in the same seat in the back row on the aisle, so she could find me easily in the dark when she was on break. It was in that movie theater at age five that I was exposed to other examples of very strong women, such as Bette Davis, Barbara Stanwyck, Susan Haywood, and Joan Crawford. It's ironic that it was also in that same movie house that I would show the first signs of my own strengths, and where I first felt the impulse to protect my mother and to take care of her.

I was sitting in my usual seat, watching the show. An older man whom I had seen at the Lido several times before came walking down the aisle. He stopped at the row where I sat and looked at me in a way that made me uncomfortable. It just seemed there was something evil about him. When he moved into the row and sat down a few seats away, I became even more nervous. I just slid a few seats away at first, then crept several more rows forward. The man kept his eye on me, moving nearer every time I put distance between us. Finally, he sat next to me and started to rub my knee. I slapped him and moved to another row. He watched me but didn't try to follow me again. It was scary, but somehow I felt that I should not go outside and tell Mother about what was going on. I had this instinctive feeling that I had to protect her from knowing about the man lurking in the dark.

I feared that he might either attack her or somehow manage to get her fired by complaining to the manager of the theater. Even when she found me during her lunch hour and berated me for leaving my assigned seat, I still refused to tell her why I had moved.

In retrospect, it was a transforming experience for me—the beginning of a role reversal that has lasted to the day she passed away. In a way, I became a mother to my mother. Despite her ironing board fiasco with Gertrude Bauer, I saw so often her profound sadness and vulnerability. A young girl who longed for the mother who had been taken away from her and locked away in a Kentucky mental institution and her firstborn taken from her just eleven days after birth and raised by her uncle as his own daughter in a better neighborhood in the same town, just out of reach. I heard the depth of that grief late in the night when she awakened me with cries of, "I want my Myrna back."

I tried to console her in our little cold room. I'd ask, "Who's Myrna?"

And she sobbed, "Myrna's my other baby. I want all my children together. I want my baby."

I would snuggle close to her and stroke her beautiful black hair and say, "Don't cry. You've got me, Mother. It's okay. It's okay."

But, of course, things were not okay. Mother worked hard to pay the rent and food bills. She did not have a husband, and I did not have a father. Uncle George helped whenever he could, but he had his own families for which to care.

It was if we were two orphans tossed out onto the streets of a cold and indifferent world. While Mother had lived with Aunts and uncles, she had told me that the happiest days of her youth were in an orphanage where she lived for two years. Even so, she had once tried to escape from the orphanage and managed to break her leg in the process. I feared that any more blows to her body or mind might prompt her to run away again, this time from me. I was determined not to jeopardize our lives together.

And so, we clung to each other as we moved from boardinghouse to boardinghouse. Our embrace was as much self-preservational as it was loving.

After the *Brown v. Board of Education* decision in 1954, Indianapolis began to officially integrate its public schools. For the first time in my life we had the experience of mixing with Whites. My sister, who was a year ahead of me, resided in a district that allowed her to attend Shortridge, the affluent all-White high school on the north side of the city rather than Crispus Attucks, the all-Black high school on the city's west side. The school was named after the first American to die during the American Revolutionary War at the Boston massacre, who just happened to be Black.

My sister found the students there respectful and some even nice while in the classroom. But mostly, each race remained separate and apart on a social level.

While I was curious about the prospect of integrating into the White educational system, I feared that the first time anyone called me a "nigger" I would physically attack them and be ejected from school.

Whatever indecision I felt about the choice of schools, however, was wiped away in the summer of 1955, when Emmett Till was murdered in Mississippi. He was my contemporary, like me, only fourteen years old.

I looked at the pictures of his broken and bloated body in *Jet* magazine and thought, *My God! This is what they did to him for supposedly flirting with a White woman? What kind of people are they?*

Emmett Till's horrible murder only served to reinforce the danger I saw all around me for Black people.

Families fractured; abandoned by unemployed fathers. Single mothers struggled in vain to protect their daughters from yielding to sexual temptations and inevitable teen pregnancies. Fatherless sons deprived of hope and opportunity sought pride and security offered by rival gangs. Ghetto streets were rampant with heroin. Many of my contemporaries sought their rainbow at the end of a needle.

As the Black community turned on itself as a result of oppression and deprivation, the White society's racist policies only served to remind all that there were separate rules, separate facilities, separate sympathies, and separate treatment for us. Two Americas: one for the protected; one for the neglected.

I was angry. Curiously, I also was beginning to feel morally superior; I wanted to be with my own people. At this point, I was no longer plagued with indecision over where to attend high school. I was going to Crispus Attucks! I needed to be in an environment of my own people without distractions, where I could concentrate on my studies. Mother had already told me that she would not be able to pay for college, so I had better do well enough in school to get a scholarship. My grades were good, but improvement was in order. And I knew that if I had to contend with any racist antagonisms, my rage would overwhelm any appeal to reason.

I knew that eventually I would have to enter the White world because that's where success lay, so I wanted to make sure that I was strong and had roots that were deep enough to sustain me in the hurricane winds that were certain to come. I wanted to fight, but more than fight, I wanted nothing to threaten the pride of who I was, or my Blackness.

At Crispus Attucks, I learned that pride from some of the most dedicated, best-educated people I have ever known. These were professional academics who were qualified to teach at the college level but were barred from doing so by the unwritten race rules that governed. They devoted their lives to making sure that the next generation of Blacks was prepared to take advantage of every opportunity that might come our way. They prepared us for success, knowing that the race to the top belonged not just to the swiftest or the strongest, but to the smartest as well.

Twice as Hard for Half as Much

Success became a major goal for me when I was in high school. I had little notion of exactly what form or shape I wanted it to take, only that I was determined to soar above the privations all around me.

Mother, on the other hand, had a very clear picture of my success. "I have visions of you sitting on a concert stage," she would say, "in a beautiful gown and your hair piled up. Just you and the grand piano, with the orchestra beneath you. And you're playing beautiful music."

That was her dream for me, that I was going to walk out onto a concert stage, fluff my dress behind me on the stool, gracefully sit down, prop my hands up, arch my wrists, wait for the conductor's cue, then commence to play Chopin, Schubert, Rachmaninoff, or Tchaikovsky. Over and over, she painted this picture for me. And every time she did, both of us were carried away by her dream.

"Reach for the stars," Mother always said, "even if you have to fall to the treetops. At least reach and dream ... always have a dream.

"I want you to have what I didn't have," she said. "What I wanted for me, I want you to have. You're going to have to work twice as hard to get half as much because you're colored, but you can have anything you want. I don't care how many 'Whites only' signs are up, you can do it. Times will change. By the time you are a woman, you'll be able to do things we can't do now. You've just got to be prepared. Get your education, cultivate your talents, keep your dress down, make yourself special, and you will find that the very best will come to you."

Mother did not only dream. She made sure I had the things I needed to get ahead. She scrimped and saved to buy that secondhand piano and to pay for my lessons. Ultimately, I had neither the discipline nor the talent to pursue a musical career, but I promised myself that I would not disappoint Mother's expectations of me, that I would reach for the stars. *My* vision of success was being able to give her some of the things of which she had been deprived.

I was always very aware of the price she had paid for having children early and the sacrifices she made for us. Mother was a great teacher, and she taught me by example. The night I discovered I was a woman, she sat me down and said: "Janet, coming into womanhood is wonderful, but it's serious."

She proceeded to explain to me about the female anatomy, the cycles, and pregnancy. Then she said: "I've always told you that the girls who don't have sex are the most popular, the nicest, the most respected. You have sex, and there goes your reputation. You're smart and very ambitious and if you have sex early, you can't be the Homecoming Queen, you can't be in beauty contests. The time to have a young man is when you are fully educated, when you have a job and can pay your own bills, and you know how to take care of any mistakes. But now is not the time. And if you ever forget this, just look at my life."

It was a harsh lesson to know that Mother felt that she did not get to have a life because she had begun having children at the young age of sixteen. But it was the truth. I saw how hard she worked just to get by all on her own; how much of a struggle it was to improve her family's lot, however modest.

Mother's deepest desire was to stop moving from one rooming house to another and to have a home of her own, where I could play and make as much noise as I wanted. It hurt her that I was constantly told to "be quiet and sit down" by the landladies. She longed to say: "Now you can make as much noise as you want to."

She literally had a dream in which she climbed up a ladder to get into this one-bedroom apartment in the government project—Lockefield Gardens. Lockefield was a wonderful place to live. It had been built as an experiment back in the 1930s to house Black families.

Families of Black men who had served in the Armed Forces received first priority. So I remember Mother searching for my father's social security number to prove that he had served. That was the key in 1949, the same year that my brother, James, was born, that unlocked the door to our new house. It was beautiful there. There were nicely kept gardens and grass—things you do not always see in ghettos.

The buildings were really solid, made out of brick and concrete.

Most of the places we had lived in before then were wooden houses with wallpaper over the plaster. I have hated wallpaper until very recently, because I have always had these memories of wallpaper covering holes in the wall or peeling away in big layers.

In Lockefield we were always warm. We had steam heat. The radiators would clang, and you knew the heat was on its way. No stoves to tend. No shivering through the night. It was a dream come true.

Mother had always wanted a garden, and when we moved to Lockefield, she finally had one. Every spring, we won prizes for having the best garden. If it was spring, it was clean-up, fix-up, paint-up time.

The nightmare of boardinghouse living was over. There were, for example, no rats in the projects. For me, this alone was significant enough to transform Lockefield's cement buildings into the category of luxury homes. Once while staying in a boardinghouse, I had a rather nasty experience that remains memorable to this day.

Due to the size of the families living in the house and the limitations of space, the children had to sleep three to a single mattress on the floor. Because I was asthmatic and experienced anxiety at the prospect of sleeping in the middle, I was always allowed to sleep on the outside position.

One particular night I felt a sting on one of my fingers that was sharp enough to cause me to awake with a cry. The bedroom was almost completely dark, the moonlight casting a faint shaft of illumination across the bedroom floor. As I looked around I caught a glimpse of a long whipping tail and the backside of a large, spiked-haired rat scampering off into the darkness.

Apparently I had startled it when I cried out. Although my hand hurt, the pain was not severe enough to prevent me from drifting off to sleep.

The next morning, I awoke to my mother's screaming, "Janet, Janet honey, are you alright?"

I looked at my mother as she pulled me into an embrace. Then I saw that blood was spattered on my arms and all over the other kids. The rat had been chewing on one of my fingers, opening a gash that had continued to bleed throughout the night.

Strangely, I did not live in fear of rats. In fact, to the contrary, I wore the scar on my right index finger as something of a badge of honor. I considered it a unifying bond with those who had to contend with the indignities of poverty and deprivation.

As good as Lockefield was by comparison, we could not escape the vermin that continued to permeate our lives. Roaches—some thin and brown, some very antlike, and others the size of beetles— were everywhere. However neat and clean Mother would maintain the apartment, her constant mantra was, "Cleanliness is next to Godliness."

The roaches continued to constitute an invading force. They were in our cupboards, our bureaus, our beds, and we had to shake our washcloths out before washing our faces and wrap our toothbrushes in toilet paper. Whenever I would ask friends over, I would hope and hold my breath that our pesky roommates wouldn't crawl across the ceiling or up the wall.

To this day I always rinse out crystal-clean glasses and dishes that I remove from my kitchen cabinets before serving in them. Old habits, especially good habits, refuse to die.

I remember that the roaches would leave their eggs to hatch in our dishes and our cups. I was so repulsed by these invaders that I would squash the eggs, which made a little popping sound, reminding me of Rice Krispies—even in their size, shape and color. The eggs had to be destroyed since each egg would soon hatch lots more.

In the ghetto there were lots of sounds. In addition to the sound of popping roach eggs, there was another sound that seemed ever present. It was that of a basketball being bounced endlessly on the cement playground, night after night into the midnight hours by a young boy who lived nearby.

Whenever our neighbors complained about the noise, Mother would tell them, "Leave that boy alone. He's special and he's going to do big things someday." Big things indeed. His name was Oscar Robertson, the "Big O," NBA Hall of Famer.

But before the NBA, Oscar was responsible for Crispus Attucks High School winning four consecutive state championships. I remember one year during the finals at Butler Field House, all of the White players on the Evansville, Indiana, team had fouled out. Suddenly our side of the stadium stood, stomped and yelled. The sound was deafening.

I said to my date, "What happened? Nobody scored."

He replied, "Oh, yes we did. Look."

I looked toward the scoreboard and said, "What? What are you talking about?"

He said, "All the White guys on the other team have fouled out. Janet, for the first time in Indiana basketball history, all of the players on the floor are Black!"

I looked over to the other side of the stadium and the Whites were sitting there stunned. However, the Black fans of the opposing team had been just as spontaneous and on their feet as the Crispus Attucks side. We witnessed history.

While it was just the finals, it was the beginning. We had cracked the color barrier and it has endured to this day. Just look at the NBA.

Mother tried to give me as much as she could afford. From the time I was eight years old until I was about ten, Mother was on welfare. What she received from the government was not enough for her to meet her goals for me and my brother, James: to celebrate a joyous Christmas, to give me piano lessons, or to make sure we had nice clothes and good books that were not all ripped up and scribbled in, like the ones we got in school after the White students were finished with them. She wanted us to have things better than she had had them. So she would slip off and work part-time to supplement the welfare checks.

Of course, if you received welfare, you were not allowed to work or have a man around. It was the system's modern version of divide and conquer, limiting the prospects of any male becoming head of the household. The choice was stark—it was work or welfare. The concept of "workfare" would not become part of the law for another forty years. As a practical matter, opportunities for decent-paying full-time employment for a young Black mother with a ninth-grade education were not abundant. Welfare provided a means of survival, a "leg up" so to speak. But its restrictions perversely served as leg irons, confining her to a limited radius of hope.

One day the social worker came by and asked to see the house. Mother always talked to her on the porch, but this time the lady wanted to come in. She saw that I had a piano and said, "How could you afford that?" It was just a secondhand spinet, but even that was more than we were supposed to have.

That was the last straw for Mother. "I've got to get a job, a good-paying job," she said after the social worker left. "I can't take any more of these insults. I'm here raising my children, doing my very best, and she comes in here telling me I don't have a right to have a piano for my daughter?"

Mother managed to find work at Indiana University Medical Center as a nurse's aide, cleaning bedpans, washing patients, and helping to move them from beds to wheelchairs (a fate that would await her during her final four years of her life). She would come home depressed about the sick people suffering on the wards. She cried over the people in pain, the ones dying. She always carried the pain home with her.

And always there was the pain of racism. For years after, she told a story about a man whom she cared for at Robert Long Hospital, which was part of IU Medical Center. They did not have air conditioning in those days, and it was a hot Indiana summer. "Louise," Mr. Clyde called, "it's so hot in here. Can you turn on a fan or something?"

Mother came to his bedside and asked how he was doing.

"I'm fine," he said, "but I'm sweating like a nigger."

"Sweating like a what?" Mother sternly asked.

"Oh," he said, "I-I-I'm sweating like a colored person."

Eventually, Mother moved on and up. With a ninth-grade education, she became ward secretary, taking care of the doctors' and nurses' schedules and booking patients in clinics. She was always amused by the fact that here she was, a Black woman without a high school diploma, running an entire ward and training White college graduates to do the same job she had mastered, and saddened that they were making twice as much.

Mother worked really hard. She would come home after putting in long hours and tell me about the rude behavior that she had to take from her bosses. "Well, why don't you just quit?" I asked her.

"Who is going to feed you if I quit?" she replied. "Who's going to put a roof over your head? I have to take it. I'm just sharing it with you."

I was not prepared to leave it at that, however. At one point, when Mother was particularly stressed out, I went down to her office to see the head nurse, Miss Haulk. I must have been about seventeen years old at the time. Miss Haulk was a big, imposing woman of German descent, with the temperament of a drill sergeant.

"Can I speak to you?" I asked. "You know, my mother works really hard. There's just me, my brother, and Mother. I don't have a father. You probably can't understand this, but it's real hard for us. I know she does a good job, so can you ease up a little bit on her?"

Miss Haulk was very sweet to me and thanked me for coming. "Well, I'm sorry," she said. "You know, we're very busy here. We're helping sick people, and we don't always have time to be the most sensitive to each other."

That night, I told my mother what I had done. "Yes, Miss Haulk told me you came to see her," she said.

"Well, what did she say?" I asked.

"She thought you were a take-charge young woman. And she was pretty nice to me the whole day."

Mother stayed at that job for the next sixteen years until I made it possible for her to retire when she was fifty. That was in 1974, when I had just turned thirty-three and was doing very well in my television career. It was my way of repaying her for all of the sacrifices she had made for me. It was also a tremendously satisfying measure of my success.

During my years at Crispus Attucks High School, the definition of success remained vague and elusive for me. *Inn of the Sixth Happiness* had just come out (the movie based on Pearl Buck's book, *The Good Earth*), rekindling my fantasy of becoming a missionary. I imagined myself strong and passionate, just like the character Gladys Aylward played by Ingrid Bergman in the movie, overcoming hatred and rejection to bring peace and salvation to a faraway place. I pictured myself in Africa, helping to reclaim the independence and freedom of my ancestors.

I studied my African ancestry and American Negro history. Unlike now, where we have an entire month (even if it is the shortest month of the year, February) to focus on Black history, back then it was just a week. Negro History Week.

I did not fully realize it back then, but that was the first time I became aware of the whispers of my ancestors that I hear in my heart to this day. Over the years, this ancestral voice has taken on a shape, a persona: She is a very dark, chiseled Black woman. She is strong, and she is deep, and she has carried her pain through the ages with force and conviction. I have come to believe that as I began the search for myself at the age of seventeen it was she who was my guide, my soul talker. I even named her "Unity." Her whispers were "prevail, prevail."

At a recent reunion with a group of my high school girlfriends, we shared our memories of what it was like growing up in Indianapolis.

For me, I remember hating the summers in Indianapolis. The humidity was so terrible; it was a waste of time for Mother to even try to straighten my hair. I hated the heat so much that I would often sleep late and stay inside to avoid the sweltering days.

We all remembered watching the kids in the neighborhood cool off by opening the fire hydrants for a gush of water. Some of the braver ones would attempt to swim in Fall Creek or White River. Unfortunately, every summer took its toll in drowning victims.

Bodyguards supervised the swimming pools at Douglas Park and at the Y's but nothing could guard us against the dreadful, crippling polio. We recalled many young people either dying or becoming handicapped by polio, spending time in a grotesque tube, the iron lung.

Our discussion led to another fear that lingered over the poor in the swampy Indiana climate: tuberculosis. "Never drink anything after anyone," my mother would always admonish. "Put your hand over your mouth when coughing. Always use a handkerchief to avoid spreading the germs."

Several of my relatives spent years in sanatoriums with what was called consumption, coughing up blood in the more serious cases. I told my girlfriends how I remembered being about five years old going to visit my mother's cousin, Ella Mae. We'd stand outside her window to talk. She'd tell stories like how TB began in our family.

"A young slave girl would hide her bony, frail body in the hollow of a log and stay there until the drunken master had slept off his beastly prowl for sex."

She continued with the young slave girl developing this persistent dry, bloody cough, passing it on to the other slaves, who passed it down through the family. My maternal grandmother was also infected.

I always feared polio and TB, thinking erroneously that with each attack of asthma, I'd either end up in an iron lung or sanatorium. Thankfully those fears were never realized, yet the smothering, drowning feelings of asthma are a hell all its own where there is no cure, only treatments, and if you are fortunate, a life in Arizona, a more arid clime.

Because of my asthma and my lack of athletic ability, I was never a jock in high school. I wanted to be a majorette but, as my girlfriends so kindly recalled, my awkwardness kept me off the team. I had to be content marching with my flute in the band at football games, while watching my more limber classmates, April, Faye, Joyce, and Gloria, star at halftime. I envied their high-stepping, baton-twirling routines.

We discussed how, in later years, I would find *my* niche, gliding and pivoting as a model on glamorous runways. I was to learn we all have our gifts. As Loretta Young would say: "The you you are is better by far than the you you are trying to be."

Of course, in reminiscing with girlfriends you've grown up with, one topic always comes up, and that is your first experience with puppy love. One of the first guys I had a crush on in school was a new arrival at Crispus Attucks, Detroit Spencer. He was the fastest kid in school, the state track champion. When he wasn't sprinting he was marching with the ROTC. On top of that, he was an A student.

We were both fifteen years old. He was one of the most popular boys, and I was one of the most popular girls. He invited me to stand beside him when he got pinned with medals for ROTC, and handed ribbons for track. He was as fast as lightning. In fact, his teammates nicknamed him "Detroit Lightning." I so admired him but couldn't help wish that I could be an athlete, part of a team.

Later as an adult, I would come to have that experience after clearing a four-and-a-half-foot fence on the back of my horse, Delta. Oddly, all of my other many pets had either sat in my lap or perched on my shoulder. This time, I was mounted on the back of my horse rearing into a leap, resulting in a perfect jump. Clearing almost five feet, we landed safely together on the other side. I expressed a sigh of relief. It was exhilarating. With a love pat to her long, muscular neck, I finally felt like an athlete, part of a team.

The memory of the jump with Delta made me appreciate how far I had come since high school. Throughout our discussion, my girlfriends reminded me of the determination I had to rise up above my circumstances. As we all caught up on where our lives have taken us, they all said almost in unison, "Oh, Janet, we knew there was not going to be anything that would hold you back. You always said, 'I'm getting out of here. I'm going to be somebody. I'm going to go places.' "

Going *where* was not exactly clear to me at the time. Two events occurred during my senior year that helped energize my journey into the unknown.

Floyd Patterson, the reigning heavyweight champion, came to speak at our school. I felt a special affinity with him because his first name was the same as my last name, and because he was so famous and admired by Black people.

"I am Floyd too," I said excitedly when it was my turn to shake his hand. "Janet Floyd."

He laughed, tilting his head back a little, and said, "Glad to meet someone who shares the name Floyd."

It was not just the name I identified with, though. In 1958, on the heels of Little Rock and all the racial turbulence that had engulfed the country in the wake of *Brown v. Board of Education* and the Montgomery bus boycott, Floyd Patterson was one of the heroes who gave "the Negro" a sense of power, a conviction that in spite of prejudice and hatred we could compete and triumph. I, too, wanted to inspire my people to greatness. And deep in my heart, I believed that it was my destiny to transcend the limitations of a racist society and reach a pinnacle of success.

During the latter part of the same year, a representative from the Patricia Stevens Modeling Agency and Charm School paid a visit to the school. It was Career Day, something of an oxymoron since, other than my teachers, only White people seemed to have careers in those days. Nonetheless, we had nurses, lawyers, doctors, firefighters, soldiers, and models come to talk about the opportunities that lay before us. Times were, in fact, changing. Blacks in Montgomery, Alabama, no longer rode in the back of the bus, following the bus boycott sparked by Rosa Parks in December 1955. In Little Rock, Arkansas, Black children were attending an all-White high school, albeit after the intervention of federal troops. If things were getting better for our people in the South, then surely, in Indianapolis, we could start thinking about careers in fields other than nursing or teaching.

I had fantasized about being a model and was very excited to learn that a representative of the Patricia Stevens Modeling Agency and Charm School would be speaking at Career Day. I remember taking a little extra time and care getting ready for school that morning, making sure that my clothes were all ironed and my hair just so. When the time came, there were several of us girls in the classroom where the presentation was to take place. An elegant White woman walked in and said, "Good morning, ladies."

"Good morning," we answered in unison, the way we had been taught. I liked the way she carried herself, with an easy grace and an upright, proud bearing.

"I am with the Patricia Stevens Modeling and Charm School," she said. "We teach girls how to be proper young ladies and how to prepare for a career in modeling. We offer courses on makeup, hair, grooming, and fashion, as well as manners and comportment. You will learn not only everything you need to know to be a successful photographer's, runway, or industrial model, but also the finer points of hostess etiquette, such as how to set a table, use the right utensils, and write thank-you notes."

She explained to us at some length the differences between the various types of modeling and what qualities made one suitable and continued to stress the advantages of her agency. She then graciously answered the few questions that we raised and distributed pamphlets about the charm school.

I was starstruck. Here was a school that would teach me how to be refined and then help me start a career in modeling. I could literally see my future begin to take shape. I read and re-read the pamphlet several times over the next few days and by Sunday had made up my mind to enroll in the charm school.

That Monday, I took the bus downtown after school and found the address on Monument Circle that was printed on the back of the pamphlet. A little nervous, but excited, I went up to the office and explained to the receptionist that I wanted to speak to the lady who had made a presentation at Crispus Attucks High School the previous week. I felt a little self-conscious because I had not written down the woman's name and could not remember it. The receptionist politely told me to wait, and that someone would be out to help me.

I sat in the reception area and flipped through the fashion magazines tastefully arranged on the coffee table. When I had gone through all the magazines and even had read several of the articles, I began to fret that I might have committed a faux pas by coming in without making an appointment. But it was too late to worry about that, so I continued to wait.

I was there for more than an hour before the lady who had spoken to us came out and asked me to follow her into a small side office. She did not seem as graceful and elegant as she had been during her presentation at the school. And she was not nearly as kind.

"What is it that you're interested in?" she asked me abruptly as we entered the office. She did not say that she was sorry to have kept me waiting nor did she even offer me a seat.

"My name is Janet Floyd. You made a presentation at Crispus Attucks . . ." I began, but she interrupted me.

"Yes, yes. I remember you."

"Well, ma'am," I said, trying to be extra polite, even though I was starting to feel distinctly unwelcome. "I was very impressed with your presentation. I read your pamphlet, and I would like to go to your charm school. I would like to learn how to do my hair properly, how to write thank-you notes appropriately, how to do the laying of the knives and forks."

"Doesn't your mother know how to do those things?" she asked, sounding annoyed. "Can't she teach you?"

"My mother has taught me how to keep a good house, but she can't teach me to be a model," I replied, starting to lose what composure I had left. "I want to be in an environment with other girls, learning comportment, proper posture, how to walk with a book on my head, things like that."

"I'll tell you what," she said, softening her manner. "I can give you some additional materials to take home to help with some of the things you want to learn."

"But I want to learn how to do my hair and my makeup, so I can model," I said, my words betraying the mixture of anger, confusion, and hurt that I was feeling.

"To be honest with you, Janet," she said, straightening and looking me directly in the eye, "we don't have the facilities to do your *kind* of hair. And I don't think you're going to be doing things or be in settings where you will need the benefit of our full course. It would just be a waste of your time and money."

The only helping hand she offered me was the one that escorted me to the front door. There was no point in my pursuing a dream or pot of gold at the end of a rainbow because there was no rainbow for people like me.

Once again, I felt anger well up inside. A deep flush burned my face and neck during the entire bus ride home that day in 1958. I was not going to allow this woman or anyone else to impose limitations on what I could do or who I could become.

I had earned a scholarship to Butler University, a private Christian school, one of Indiana's finest educational institutions. I was going to overcome any barriers that society could throw in front of me. I was not fully prepared, however, for just how high or insidious those obstacles would prove in the years to come.

2

A Degree in Humanity

College was a critical learning experience for me. At seventeen, I arrived at Butler University in Indianapolis with a scholarship, fantasies of becoming a missionary, and repressing my dream of being a model.

My best friend, April Brown, whose mother was Black and whose father was White, had enrolled in Butler at the same time I did. During registration, we had to fill out forms that asked about our race—Negro, White, or Other (if Other, please explain). I checked off Negro, and so did April.

"Why'd you do that?" I challenged.

"Because my mother is Black," she said.

"Yes, but your father is White, so you are denying him."

"Well, Mother told me to always choose Negro."

"I hate that," I said. "If I were half-and-half, I'd choose Other and make *them* explain."

Butler was my first experience of being in an integrated environment, and I brought all of my anger, defiance, and sense of moral superiority to it. Moreover, I believed that I was smarter than the White kids since I had earned a scholarship and many of their parents had to pay. *They've had all the opportunities handed to them,* I thought, *and I'm the one who had to work hard for mine.*

I remembered my mother's mother always said, "Learn the White man's ways, but don't become like him."

It took a humbling experience to open my eyes to how close I was coming to think just like those who felt superior to Blacks. I was in a freshman English course. It was a large class, and we sat alphabetically. The girl to my left was Judy Flanders. She was whiter than all the other kids in school, and she constantly asked me for help. "Can you help me read this? Can you find that chapter for me?"

I didn't really mind helping her keep up in class, but my superiority complex was acting up in a big way. *My God,* I thought, feeling pretty smug, *here is the whitest kid in class, and she's asking me—the so-called inferior race—to help her.*

That evening at home, I mentioned Judy to my mother. I described her pale skin, white-blond hair, and reddish eyes. I even commented that she reminded me of a rabbit that I had had.

"I think Judy may be an albino," Mother said. "Why don't you look it up?

"If she is asking you to help her read things," Mother continued, "it's because her vision isn't very good. It's a side effect of being albino. It doesn't mean she isn't intelligent. She feels comfortable enough to ask for your help, and you've got no call to think you are better than she is. You should be more compassionate, Janet. This is something she's got to live with the rest of her life."

"Yes, and I've got to live with being Black for the rest of my life," I said.

Mother responded, always having the wiser last word, "There are more crippling things in life than being Black."

It was the beginning of my education about the dangers of the word *all.* I thought that all White people had it better than Blacks. In fact, I would see White people begging in the street and have little sympathy for them because I thought, at least they were White. Why can't they succeed? The world is designed and set up for their success. They could go places and do things I could not do. To me, any White girl—especially a very, very White girl—was automatically more privileged than I was. To learn firsthand that this was not so was very humbling.

Overcoming deprivation and discrimination may have inflated my own sense of self-worth, but it did not justify my notion that I had been elevated to a superior status. Not one of us is handed a deck of cards that contains only aces. Society may choose its favorites, but life does not. It can be very democratic when it inflicts hardship or pain.

Philosophers have suggested that the recognition of one's ignorance marks the beginning of wisdom. Thanks to my mother, I discovered that it was humility, not my sense of moral superiority, that would guide me on the journey to enlightenment. But before I was to commence that journey, I had one more score to settle. I used my contempt and my smarts in that same freshman English class.

The assignment was to give an oral report on a topic of interest. We were told to "do what you know." I decided to give my speech on the census bureau, particularly, the accuracy of population statistics in America.

During my oral presentation, I noted the number of White people born in America in 1938, compared to the number of Blacks born that same year. However, in tracking the numbers to the present year, there were some discrepancies.

While the census bureau could account for all White people being born and having died, a significant number of Black people were unaccounted for.

In researching these discrepancies, I discovered that many Blacks who could pass for being White, were taking the opportunity when they came of age—never to return to being counted as Black again.

I remember making the statement to the class that, "I may not be the only Black person in this classroom. Many Black people may currently be passing for White, but genes will prevail. The Black gene is the dominant gene and will reveal itself sooner or later, maybe when your children are born."

The class was stunned; my professor looked outraged. Being the oldest person present, he knew there was great truth to my report, yet he seemed less than happy with my audacity in reporting that truth.

I had wanted to show my contempt, and I was successful in doing so. I had really stirred things up. Looking back, it was amazing to me that society had produced such anger in a mere seventeen-year-old.

I had been coached by one of the greatest thinkers on race, comedian and satirist Dick Gregory, whom I had met at the age of fifteen while employed at my first job, the Dairy Queen. It was 1956, the year after the death of Emmett Till, and Dick had invited my friend April and me to hear his remarks at a local church. The title of his speech was, "It's Open Season on Negroes in America."

What stirred me were his comments that even deer and rabbits had more rights than Negroes in America. That The Man had set aside a certain time to kill deer. It was called deer season and had specific regulations. You had to use a special kind of gun, and you could only kill so many. And if you dared to violate any one of those rules, you could be fined and/or jailed.

But in America, you could kill as many Negroes as you wanted, any way you wanted, any time you wanted, without penalty, without justice. After hearing that, I was never going to be the same. Dick has remained my friend and mentor.

In college, I readied myself to follow my dream of being a missionary by majoring in religion and education. Although I would not have admitted it to Mother, my father, who I knew had become a minister after he returned from the service, also played a part in my fantasy of being a missionary. I imagined him uplifting downtrodden Black people with his sermons, and I wanted to be like him.

At Butler, I discovered a new way to relate to faith. I had this wonderful Old Testament professor, Dr. Singer, who was also a rabbi. In his class, I learned that you could approach theology from a rational, historical, or academic point of view—that you could ask questions. Suddenly, I felt a connection to the spiritual world that had never been there before.

I had been raised in the Southern Baptist tradition, which leaves little room for individual exploration of faith. You are discouraged from asking questions that can't be answered. To press for the answers was interpreted as questioning God, which was blasphemy. You submit to the mystery, and that's that. Somehow this just did not make sense to me, even when I was a young girl. *This is my immortal soul we are talking about,* I would think, *and I can't ask questions of the God who created me? How can that be? I should be able to ask God anything.*

And here was Dr. Singer, this handsome man who looked like an older Cary Grant with shocking white hair, who said, "Ask." It felt as if he had given me permission to breathe. Faith no longer had to be blind obedience; it could be a dialogue. I did not have to submit; I could participate.

The other discovery I made in college was that I would most likely not be satisfied with the life of a teacher and my chances of going to Africa as a missionary had to remain a dream. I had spoken with a few working teachers and was very disappointed to learn how modest their salaries were. How could I take care of my mother? I wondered. I was sure that I could do much better. My ambition was larger. The dream my mother had had for me of a glamorous life as a concert pianist called to me. Although I had given up the piano by this point, I did fantasize about being in front of large audiences, of being admired and celebrated.

College had another surprise in store for me. Intoxicated by all the attention I was suddenly getting from the boys, I pursued my social life much more diligently than my studies. My grades slipped, and I lost the scholarship. The following year, I went to Indiana University at Indianapolis, intent on getting good enough grades to regain my scholarship and return to Butler. But by this point, I had lost interest in school.

Cordie King, a beautiful Black model who had been engaged to Sammy Davis, Jr. at one point, returned to Indianapolis around this time to marry a man from a prominent local family. She had seen that there was a growing demand for Black models and decided to start a modeling agency and charm school. It was called Cordie King's Castle, and it was very successful.

I left IU and enrolled in Cordie's Castle. Cordie had the grace and poise of a queen. When she walked, she seemed to glide effortlessly and had a modulated voice with a soft, Southern belle accent. She was another one of the strong women I admired and looked up to. Cordie took me under her wing. She said she saw herself in me and, like my mother, wanted me to have the chances she couldn't have. Cordie's Castle gave me the opportunity to reconcile my contradictory dreams of being a missionary and a model when I auditioned for and won a spot with the Ebony Fashion Fair in 1962. Inspired by Mrs. Jessie Covington Dent, the wife of Dr. Albert W. Dent, former president emeritus of Dillard University, the Fair was conceived in 1956 by John H. Johnson, publisher, chairman, and CEO of Johnson Publishing Company, and his wife, Eunice W. Johnson, as a way to help raise money for Black charitable causes around the country. The first Fashion Fair had toured ten cities in 1958, benefiting leading social and civic groups, as well as sororities and fraternities. While Mr. Johnson owned the company, it was run with an iron hand by the legendary Freda DeNight.

The Ebony Fashion Fair did much more than raise funds for Black organizations; it raised the spirits of the African-American community. At a time when the majority of us could not vote, pursue most careers, or even try on clothes in department stores, the Fashion Fair gave Black people a chance to see other Blacks in the glamorous outfits of the best designer houses in the world. "We are beautiful. We are chic. We are proud," the show boldly proclaimed. It was a very different kind of mission, but a mission nonetheless—one that inspired Black people all over this country to claim their own beauty and significance.

To me, at twenty, the invitation to travel with the Fashion Fair on a sixty-two-city tour on a Greyhound bus felt as if my destiny was beginning to unfold. I had followed its models in the pages of *Ebony* and *Jet* magazines with awed fascination, and now I was going to be one of them. It was a heady mixture of emotions: Wide-eyed excitement and pride, the glee of vindication tinged with bitterness, and a growing sense of responsibility. I saw the Ebony Fashion Fair as an immediate opportunity to inspire and an opening to a career that I hoped would give me the visibility to make a difference for my people.

There was a personal price to pay for following this dream. Lockefield Gardens, being a government project, had a regulation that you could only have one bedroom per gender of a child, so my mother and brother had to move from the two-bedroom apartment where we had made our home for more than twelve years into a one-bedroom.

My brother, James, was fourteen, just coming of age. Mother ended up having to sleep in the living room. She took it hard.

"Here I am almost forty years old, and I'm going backward in my life," she said. "Now that you're old enough to help out, you're leaving. Things are supposed to get easier not harder."

That was difficult to hear. She had worked so hard to move us forward, and now it seemed that my succeeding meant her falling behind again. I felt sorry, but not guilty. I did not feel responsible, because I knew it was not my fault. She had run into the mathematical cruelty of an inflexible system. But I left, vowing to myself that I would become successful enough to free my mother from further dependence on governmental largesse and benign indifference.

Big Country

The farthest I had ever been outside of Indianapolis was on a trip to Detroit that I took with my mother when I was twelve years old, when we ventured across the border to Windsor, Canada. That was the time I discovered that racism was not a geographic phenomenon. I was twelve and believed that the farther north you went the freer Black people were. I was shocked when a White girl who was working a hot-dog stand on the Canadian side served every White person who approached and simply ignored me, even though I was standing right in front of her for what felt like a good ten minutes.

Mother finally called to me, "Come on, Janet. What are you doing? We're going to miss the bus back to Detroit."

"I am trying to buy a hot dog," I yelled back at the top of my lungs, "but I guess they don't serve colored people here either."

I thought about that incident in 1962, as I boarded the specially chartered Greyhound bus with the other Fashion Fair models to set off on our countrywide tour. I also conjured pictures of the Freedom Rides of the previous summer—the bombed-out buses, the savaged but brave Freedom Riders, the hatred and contempt stamped on the faces of White policemen and jeerers. Our trip would take us south, through many of the same places. *What will it be like?* I wondered. *What will I be like in the face of that kind of hatred?*

The daily routine of travel and the excitement of our public appearances quickly took my mind off the darker aspects of our journey. In the Black communities we came to, we were stars. And the tour was run like a traveling finishing school. We were all treated like Miss America, with our own trunks of clothes, dressers, and a chaperone who made sure that we behaved and were treated like the young ladies our audiences expected us to be.

There were about twelve of us models. To me, all the others seemed so worldly and sophisticated. Terri Springer, who was considered the star of the show, had been with the fair since 1959 and had traveled all over the country. We had girls from Brazil and Haiti, and a guy from Colombia. At twenty, I was the youngest and felt the least experienced. As I later found out, the others shared this opinion and called me "Big Country" behind my back. Although I would have been hurt by the nickname, it was not inaccurate for a "colored girl" who hardly knew anything of the world outside of the Indianapolis ghetto.

The Ebony Fashion Fair was often sponsored by local fraternities and sororities, such as the Alphas and the Deltas, as well as organizations such as the Shriners and the Masons. Most of our sponsors were upper-middle-class groups who underwrote the shows to raise funds.

One of the first big surprises for me on the tour was the wealth in some of the Black communities we visited in the South. We got to see this side of Black life even more closely. We could not stay in hotels unless they were "for colored only" and they were usually pretty seedy. So we stayed in the homes of the Black doctors, the lawyers and the businesspeople who belonged to the organizations that sponsored us. I had never seen such beautiful homes or that kind of wealth, Black or White. These homes were even more luxurious than the White homes my mother had worked in. It was a real culture shock that filled me with pride.

I particularly remember the bathrooms with their luxurious towels. We models wore gobs of makeup, and I cringed to see a lot of the girls just take the lovely guest towels these people put out for us and soil them with mascara, powder, lipstick, and oil. It seemed so unkind, so undignified. My mother had taught me to leave a place better than I had found it, and I was mortified to leave dirty towels in other people's homes. Instead, when traveling outside the South, I developed the habit of borrowing hotel hand towels to use for removing my makeup when I knew I was going to the South.

One of the things that stuck me like a cold knife was seeing the signs "Colored Only" and "White Only" as we drove through Mississippi. It wasn't humiliating enough that these people had us drink from different water fountains, but it was downright inhumane to see the physical discrepancy. White drinking fountains were modern, clean, and well-kept. The ones with the "Colored Only" signs were often too low to reach and more like a hose with a faucet handle and dirty, rusty water basin. I can only imagine what the toilet inside looked like. While there was a comfort station on the bus, it was filled with our clothing trunks and always an effort to access. Out of defiance, I decided I would rather hold it in than be assigned to such inferior conditions because of my race. I got back on the bus and held it in for the two hours it took before we arrived at the home of one of our hosts. It was a painful act of defiance but I was determined to see it through.

While traveling in Texas, the Brazilian and Haitian models decided that they were not going to stay in hotels that were for "colored only." They remarked that they wouldn't tolerate that sort of discrimination. The Haitian girl said, "We're not Americans, we don't have to take this insult. In our countries, we're not considered Black." They walked into the White hotels and insisted that they were from foreign countries and were not to be treated as American

Negroes. Because they had lighter skin and spoke with foreign accents, the hotel clerks, suffering no doubt from the cognitive dissonance that anyone who spoke with a foreign accent couldn't possibly be Black, yielded. I admired their brazenness, but disliked their air of smug superiority. When one of the girls suggested that I could pass for being Brazilian and join them in their hotels, I would have none of it. I was not about to reject my nationality to enjoy the comforts offered to Whites or "foreign Blacks." I disliked them for using their foreign status. I hated the circumstances too, but I felt they should have hung with us and stayed in the seedy hotels as an act of unity, even if they could get a pass. Many years later, I learned of the poor conditions they lived in as free people in their countries of Brazil and Haiti, and I realized that what I thought was arrogance may have been pride.

Hotel life offered other revelations. I quickly realized that the Ebony Fashion Fair traveled a similar circuit to those of many other Black entertainers and celebrities. We often stayed in the same places as the Harlem Globetrotters, the Temptations, the Coasters, and many others.

In Las Vegas, I met Joe Louis, the casino's greeter. The funny thing is I met him because of Jerry Lewis. We walked into our hotel—I think it was the Sands—and there was Jerry. I was so surprised to see him in person, I put my hands up to my face and blurted out, "Ah, Jerry Lewis."

He looked over, put his hands up to his face, and went, "Ah."

It was such a good imitation, that I burst out laughing and ran over to introduce myself. Just as I was telling Jerry what a big fan of his I was, I saw Joe Louis come lumbering across the lobby. Before I even knew what I was saying, I asked Jerry if he could introduce me to Joe.

When Jerry took me over to the aging fighter, all I could manage was, "Mr. Louis, this is such an honor. I've heard folks talk about you all my life."

Joe said a dignified "thank you" and moved on, with everyone bowing and scraping to him as he went.

As wowed as I was by the people I met and the things I saw during the tour, it was my time on the runway that was the most spectacular. We modeled the finest clothes by the best designers the world over. I wore Givenchy, Balenciaga, Oscar de la Renta, Bill Blass, Rudi Gernreich—all the famous fashion names of the era.

My favorite was a Russian sable coat. It was gold lamé on the outside and rich, luxurious fur on the inside. I loved walking out on stage to the *oohs* and *aahs* of the audience, swirling the shimmering fabric as I walked and then pausing to fling the coat open to reveal the sable. The only problem was that the coat was better traveled than I was at this point and came with a passport of its own—a set of customs tags for its return trip to Russia that had to remain attached to the inside no matter what. It was always a struggle to spring the surprise of the fur lining on the audience without having the tags come swinging into view.

I kept a diary all through that first tour. As I read it now, I am struck by how much fun I was having and how much I was growing. We were stars. Mr. Johnson made sure of that by running pictures of us in his weekly and monthly magazines. Our faces were familiar to Black people all over the country. Usually by the time we got to a particular community, people knew us by name. I would walk down the street, and people would say, "Look, that's Janet Floyd." That kind of attention would turn any girl's head. But my ego was not the only part of me that was nourished by such remarks. My missionary soul was also pleased by the thought that I had begun to achieve some of the visibility I believed would give me the power to promote Black pride and self-esteem, and to help me inspire my people to overcome racism.

Above all, the tour was hard work, and it gave me a sense of my own discipline and professionalism. I took my responsibility to our audience very seriously. People expected us to be fabulous, and I felt I owed it to them to be fabulous, not only up on stage but also getting on and off the bus, walking in to dinner, strolling downtown. I was always on, and it started to wear me down. I began to discover that deep inside I am an introvert who needs time for silence and solitude.

I was also homesick. After months on the road, I badly wanted to return to my home in Indianapolis. I never dreamed that I would miss it so much, but when the tour ended in Los Angeles, I wasted no time and hopped on a United Airlines flight to Indy. It was my first time on an airplane, and I felt like a big shot stepping off the ladder and waving to my mother and brother.

I had gotten a taste of the big country out there, but I was not yet ready to break away from my family and my community. I secured a job as a telephone operator at Indiana Bell to give myself time to think through the next steps. I'll never forget the hundreds of tearful conversations I overheard as I connected long-distance calls on the day President Kennedy was killed. Earlier that year, William Moore, Medgar Evers, and four little Birmingham girls were killed amid an increasingly violent backlash against the progress being made by the Civil Rights Movement. I felt too far removed from the struggle for freedom. My world felt very small and sheltered, and I wanted something bigger. I wanted to play my part.

The Face in the Mirror

The opportunity to get back out into the world came in the fall of 1964 with an invitation to again join the Ebony Fashion Fair tour that was already in progress. One of the models had to drop out, and Mr. Johnson asked me if I would take her place. I agreed gladly, gave notice at Indiana Bell, and packed my things.

Within a few days, I was back on the runway, bringing excitement, glamour, and pride to Black audiences. I knew in my heart that I would not return to Indianapolis, that my destiny lay elsewhere. Change was all around me, and I felt myself carried along by its force. It seemed as if my country and I were coming of age at the same time. Before I entered adulthood fully, however, I needed to meet again the man who, with my mother, had brought me into the world.

I had not seen my father or corresponded with him since the time he visited us when I was seven. At twenty-three, I wanted to get a sense of who the man was and why he had abandoned me. I had learned through Cordie King, who was very close to Mahalia Jackson, that my father was an associate pastor at a Baptist church in Los Angeles where Mahalia sang occasionally. When I came to L.A. with the Fashion Fair of 1962, I was tempted to call him, but decided against it. I knew my mother did not want me to have anything to do with him. In 1964, I was determined to see my father. The tour would end in Los Angeles again, and I would take the opportunity to meet him.

Trouble was that I did not know how to get in touch with my father. I did not want to just show up at his church. Somehow I needed to let him know that I wanted to see him, needed to know if he would want to see me. Finally, I just called directory assistance for Los Angeles and requested information on Sewell Bridges. Fortunately, his name is unusual enough that there was only one listing, at 1827 Middleton Place. That address is still indelible in my mind.

The first time I called him, I fell back on my experience as a telephone operator and said, "Hello, I have a long-distance call for Sewell Bridges."

"This is he," said the man who answered. And I promptly hung up. I just did not know what to say next.

I called again a few days later. Even though there was little chance my father would have recognized me as "the long-distance operator," I disguised my voice.

"Mr. Bridges," I said, "I am a cousin of Louise Gillenwaters back in Indianapolis. I am heading out your way and would certainly love to see you. I don't have any other kin out West."

"You must have gotten the wrong number, ma'am," he said calmly.

"Oh, I am sorry," I said. "You are not Sewell Bridges?"

"Yes, I am," he replied, "but I am no relation of Miss Gillenwaters."

"I should apologize, then. I thought you were related," I was taken aback by his denial of my mother. At a loss for words, I just blurted out, "Do you have a daughter?"

"No, I don't have any children," my father said flatly. With that, I apologized again for disturbing him and hung up.

I was disappointed and angry. How could he just pretend that I did not exist? In a way, that made me even more determined to see him. I wanted to show him that there was nothing I needed from him, that Mother and I had succeeded in spite of his abandonment.

After I'd had time to think over the conversation, I decided to write my father a letter to tell him that I wanted to meet him. I was very careful to let him know that that was all I wanted.

My name is Janet Floyd, I wrote. *I am the daughter of Louise Gillenwaters. She tells me that you are my father. We met when I was seven years old. I remember your coming home from the war in uniform, but I don't remember what you look like.*

I am coming to Los Angeles with the Ebony Fashion Fair, and I would like to meet you. I am not making any claims on you. I am twenty-three, so there is no law that requires you to support me. I just want an opportunity to get acquainted.

Within a couple of weeks, I received a reply through *Ebony*. It was a sweet letter. My father wrote about meeting Mom at the USO club in Indy, going off to war, and then coming to visit us after his discharge. He asked me how I was doing with my piano lessons. His writing was direct and thoughtful.

We continued to correspond for the remainder of the tour. As the Fashion Fair itinerary took me closer to Los Angeles, I again asked my father to meet me, telling him the dates I would be in town. He replied that he would be happy to, and I set about arranging the meeting. I did not want to see him in a public place like a restaurant. I wanted something more private, where we could talk freely. Mr. Johnson had an office in L.A., and I asked him if I could use it to meet my father. After I told him the whole story, he was glad to oblige.

When we got to Los Angeles, I called my father and arranged for us to meet that next Friday at Mr. Johnson's office. The morning of the day we were to meet, I felt like I was getting ready for the first day of school. I wanted him to see how successful I had become, how well I had turned out, even though he had not been around to help Mother and me. In those days, I always dressed up to go out in public, but for this occasion I went all the way. I wore a beautiful gray suit with a little fox stole, and a turban matching the suit.

In Mr. Johnson's beautiful office overlooking all of L.A., dressed to the nines as I was, I imagined myself a character out of a Joan Crawford movie, about to meet my long-lost father. I waited and thought about the sixteen years that had passed since I had last seen him. I rehearsed all the things that I wanted to say to him. I tried to picture what he might look like.

Meanwhile, the appointed time had come and gone. I began to worry that I had given my father the wrong address, since I did not know Los Angeles. My fantasies turned to fretting: What if he decided not to show up at all? After half an hour of this, I called him.

I was surprised and disappointed to hear him answer the phone. "Aren't you coming?" I asked.

"Janet, I am so glad you called," my father said. "I completely forgot that today is my bowling night. I am the president of my team, so I really have to be there. Could you meet me at the alley?"

My heart just froze. All the warmth I let myself begin to feel over the months of corresponding with him drained out of me.

You son of a gun," I thought. *I come all this way to see you, and you are telling me that your bowling team is more important than I am.*

"All right," I said, trying not to sound too angry. "What time?"

"Well, it's actually two nights, so maybe it'd be better if we do it tomorrow."

Now I was really angry. It felt like he was trying to ditch me again, just as he had when I was a little girl. This rage welled up in me—an indignation at being hurt carelessly, unnecessarily.

I said, "No, I cannot do it tomorrow. I will see you tonight, as we agreed."

My father gave me the address of the bowling alley, which was all the way across town, and we agreed to meet at six. I had a couple of hours to kill and no particular place to go. To pass the time, I stopped at Bullock's department store. I was so upset, I could not even be bothered to look at anything. I just wandered through the store, seething.

"Janet?" I heard a familiar voice call.

I turned and saw Marilyn McCoo, whom I had met on the road with singer Lamonte McLemore. This was at the very beginning of her career, long before she found stardom with the 5th Dimension. When we first met, she was with the Hi-Fis, a singing group that toured with Ray Charles in 1963. But as I learned in the course of our conversation, there was trouble in the group, and Marilyn was back in Los Angeles finishing her degree at UCLA. She was working at Bullock's part-time to help support herself.

"You look fantastic, Janet," Marilyn said, smiling. "Big plans?"

"Oh, Marilyn," I said, my eyes welling up, "it's been such an awful day."

The whole story rushed out of me. It was such a relief to tell someone about my disappointment. I would have wanted to tell Mother, but I did not want to admit that I went against her wishes and got in touch with my father.

Marilyn listened with great sympathy and said, "Look, L.A. is really spread out. I will get off a little early and drive you over to the bowling alley."

I tried to protest, but she insisted. "You don't know this city. Besides, it'll be nice to have some more time to catch up."

It was slow going in traffic, so we had a good, long conversation. I am generally fairly reserved with my emotions, but that day I was too hurt to hold anything back. I talked and talked. All of my feelings of abandonment, all the resentment, all the years of growing up without a father came spilling out.

When we finally got to the bowling alley, Marilyn offered to wait for me. "This guy may not even show up," she said.

"Thanks so much," I answered, touched by her kindness. "Don't wait, though. I don't know how long I am going to be, and even if he doesn't show, I have enough money for a cab back to the hotel."

"In this town, it'll take you forever to get a cab," she insisted.

I thanked her again and assured her that I would be alright. Although as I watched her drive off, I suddenly felt very alone. It had been such a wonderful gift to have a friend show up at my side so unexpectedly, and now it was hard to see her go.

I pulled myself together, checked my makeup in a hand mirror, and walked into the bowling alley. The wall clock read five till six, but there was not a single Black face in sight. I slowly walked down the long row of lanes, getting a few quizzical looks as I went. I did look like I had walked onto the wrong movie set. Especially since I was the only Black person in the whole place.

Finally, at about a quarter past six, I went up to the woman dispensing the shoes and running the cash register and said, "Excuse me, is there a Sewell Bridges here?"

"Not that I know of," she said curtly.

"Well, he is here with his team. Are there teams here tonight?"

"All of these are teams. It's team night," she said, looking over my head at the customers lining up behind me. "Do you know the name of the team?"

"No. No, I don't," I said and started toward the door. By this point, I was perfectly prepared to believe that my father, thinking that I wanted something from him, had sent me on a wild-goose chase.

"Wait a minute," the woman behind the counter called after me. "We have another set of lanes downstairs."

I caught my breath, said "thank you," and walked down. As soon as I stepped off the last step, everything became much clearer. Here, everybody was Black. *Of course,* I thought. *God forbid that we should even bowl together.*

Sam Cooke's smooth voice was coming from the jukebox. He had been shot to death in south central Los Angeles just a few days earlier, on December 11, 1964. The reminder of this latest loss for the Black community mingled with my own sadness, leaving me feeling bereft and hopeless as I walked down the alley looking into the faces of the bowlers to see if I could recognize my father. At this point, I did not even want to meet him anymore. I just wanted to see what he looked like, because Mother always said that I looked just like him.

As I approached the end of the alley, I noticed one man who kept peering toward the door and up at the clock. There was nothing in his appearance that suggested he was my father—just another light-skinned Black man in a group of light-skinned men—but his expectant face told me that it might be him. I stopped before he noticed me and watched him for a long time. I studied his face and thought about how hard my mother had had to work, raising me all on her own. I thought about his saying on the telephone that he did not have any children. I thought about waiting for him in Mr. Johnson's empty office. It felt as if I was trying to find my footing in a complex landscape of longing and loathing.

After what seemed like twenty minutes of standing there, I was about ready to leave. That was when he noticed me. I was not exactly hard to spot, wearing a fox stole and a turban in a bowling alley. My father looked over in a flirty kind of way. He is only about eighteen years older than I am, so it did not surprise me that he might give me the eye.

He said something to his buddies and walked over to me. As he got closer, I could see the family resemblance. "Excuse me," he said. "You look like somebody I used to know."

"Oh, really," I said, still thinking he was flirting.

"You wouldn't be my Janet, would you?"

"Yes," I replied, trying to harden my heart by remembering that I was in a bowling alley, that he never took care of me, never helped with my education, or even sent me a Christmas gift. "Yes, I am Janet."

"Oh, you are my baby," my father said tenderly and pulled me to him for a hug.

Just then, someone from his team called out, "Hey, Sewell, you're up." And he practically dropped me to the floor to take his turn.

I was getting angry with myself now, thinking, *How many times are you going to let this guy reject you?*

To make things worse, my father's buddies started asking him who I was, wanting him to introduce me.

"Oh, this is my friend Janet," he said. He could not even bring himself to say that I was his daughter.

I had come such a long way to see him, however, I was going to see it through. So I sat there while they finished bowling, drinking beer, and kibitzing with one another. When they were all done, my father excused himself and went to change. I was really surprised when he returned wearing his minister's collar.

We went out to eat at a Black restaurant, and he was suddenly the epitome of fatherly warmth. He kept hugging me and kissing me, asking me about my life, but mostly talking about himself. I asked him if he had any children with his wife, and he said he did not. Then I asked whether he had ever told her about me. Again he said no.

Finally, there had been too much rejection, and I blew up. "You are a man of the cloth," I said sharply. "How do you reconcile abandoning me with your faith? Jesus said, 'Suffer the little children to come unto me.' I am your flesh and blood, and you just left me."

"Well, it's complicated, Janet," he said, shifting uncomfortably in his seat. "Your mother had other children, and I didn't feel that I should be supporting them."

"But you sacrificed me," I replied, all the hurt now coming to the surface. "Couldn't you just send money for me? Or at least write me a letter? Did you ever think about what would have become of me if something had happened to my mother? I understand things don't work out between people. But I was innocent. You had a responsibility to me. How can you stand up there in the pulpit and preach about values and faith when you turned your back on your child?"

"It's hard to explain," he said in a quiet voice. "I had gone through so much in the war; I just couldn't shake it. I spent almost a year at the VA hospital, getting over the trauma. I didn't feel like myself for years after."

"Well, that didn't stop you from going into the ministry," I shot back at him.

"That's different," he said. "Preaching the Word of God saved my life."

I said what I had wanted to say, so I let it drop. My father drove me to the Olympic Towers, the hotel where we were staying, and we said our good nights. He kissed me and asked whether I would stay for Christmas.

"We could celebrate your birthday together," he said, "and then Christmas."

"No thanks. It's a tradition that I, Mother, and my brother spend the holidays together."

"You've spent all those Christmases with your mother," he said, suddenly eager for my company. "Spend this one with me."

"My brother and I are all Mother has," I said firmly. "I want to be with her. Thank you. Why don't you come to the show tomorrow," I added as a peace offering. "You can see me work."

"That would be nice," he said, "but at least let me give you a little something for your birthday. It's coming up in a few days."

He reached into his pocket and pulled out some money. Even in the dark, I could feel that it was a single bill. As I slipped it into my pocketbook, I saw that it was a one-dollar bill. I wasn't asking or expecting anything from him, but I couldn't imagine he would give a woman of twenty-three, a daughter he hadn't seen for sixteen years, a one-dollar bill! I thought, how strange. However, I thanked my father, kissed him good-bye, and got out of the car. I was certain that I would never see him again.

I was shaking when I walked into the hotel lobby. All I could think was, *I hope I don't run into any of the Globetrotters.* They were staying at the same hotel, and I would usually bump into one or more of them in the lobby and stop to chat. Tonight though, I just wanted to get to my room and cry. I was counting on my roommate's being out; she was always out having a good time.

My prayers were answered. I did not run into anybody I knew, and the room was empty. I went straight into the bathroom, took off my turban, and cried until I had cried off all my makeup. I just stood over the sink and bawled harder than I had ever done in my life. When I finally calmed down a bit, I wiped my face and looked in the mirror. And there was my father's face looking back at me.

My God, I thought, *Mother is right. I look exactly like him.* That struck me as very sad, but I had no more tears left. I just collapsed onto the bed and went to sleep.

At the show the following evening, I looked for my father in the audience, in spite of myself. I kept telling myself that he would not be there, but still I looked. Then, as I went out after one of the many changes, I heard loud clapping and cheering in one section of the audience, but I could not see who it was. At intermission, though, the stage manager told me to go back to my dressing room. And there was the most beautiful bouquet of roses with a card that read, FROM YOUR FATHER. YOU LOOK BEAUTIFUL TONIGHT.

This guy's something else, I thought. *He's got me on a roller coaster.*

After the show, he wanted to take me out, but I said I had to go off with the other girls. I had gotten to meet him, and that was enough for me. We took a picture in front of the Christmas tree at the Palladium. I still look at it every once in a while, and I am always amazed by how much we do look alike.

That was the last time I saw my father. He would write occasionally to tell me that he had seen my picture in a newspaper or a magazine. He would send me clippings and tell me how proud he was of me. But we never met again.

About four years ago, I woke up with a strange feeling that my father was gone. I called Los Angeles information, just as I had done more than thirty years ago, and asked for his number. There was no listing. And I left it at that.

Winds of Change

By the time I returned home at the end of the 1964 Ebony Fashion Fair tour, I had made up my mind that I was going to move to Chicago. I had traveled there several times with Cordie King to audition for various modeling jobs and had fallen in love with the city. It was also the headquarters of Johnson Publishing, and being close to Mr. Johnson and his widely read publications seemed like a good career move.

I had a little money put away but could not afford to just pick up and move. Over the course of the next few months, I commuted, auditioning for modeling work and looking for a job that would give me the security to strike out on my own. Finally, I found a part-time clerical position at the Cooke County School of Nursing and prepared to say good-bye to my childhood home.

Mother did not want me to leave. Chicago is a gangster city, she would say. And I would joke and tell her to stop watching *The Untouchables*. I knew she was fretting about not having me around to lean on, but I also knew that my life was calling me away.

When it came time for me to go, though, Mother gave me a wonderful gift. She sat me down in her kitchen in Lockefield Gardens and said, "I want you to know it's really been fun raising you. You're very, very smart. Too smart, sometimes."

"Yes," I said, laughing, "you always told me I was a little hellion, a bit too sassy, too much mouth."

She laughed, too, and then got serious again, "You're a live wire, alright, and some people won't like that. But don't you ever lose that spirit. Don't bow to anybody."

Even at twenty-four, I knew that Mother was giving me a blessing that would sustain me on my path through life. I walked around the table, hugged her, and said, "Thank you."

Both of us tried not to cry, but we did anyway. And then we said good-bye. Earlier that year, Sam Cooke's wistful "A Change Is Gonna Come," which was discovered after his death, had been released. As I left my mother's house and headed out of Indianapolis, the song's refrain kept sounding in my mind: "It's been a long, long time coming, but I know a change is gonna come."

I could not have prepared myself for what a change it would be. In those heady days of the Civil Rights Movement, many of the activists gravitated to Mahalia Jackson's home in Chicago—Martin Luther King, Jr., Andy Young, and Jesse Jackson among others. Cordie King was close to the "Queen of Gospel Song," and arranged for me to stay at Mahalia's until I could get an apartment of my own. Cordie's friendship was unconditional and unbounded. She was my mentor and guide. I was reluctant to impose, but Cordie would have none of that. "You don't know Chicago," she countered my objections. "You don't have money, yet. You are going to stay with Mahalia." So for the first few weeks in Chicago, I stayed with Mahalia Jackson.

I was absolutely in awe of Mahalia. In Chicago, she was a *grand dame*. While I stayed with her for only a few weeks, it was more than enough time to gauge the greatness and magnetic force of the woman. One word that described her beyond her magnificent contralto voice, was *character*. She had achieved popularity by singing gospel during the dark days of the Great Depression. She resisted the pressure to shift from gospel to the more popular and lucrative "blues" of the fifties and sixties. She felt that gospel could touch and lift the soul, whereas when the last note of blues ended, well, it just ended.

From all that I had read and heard about Mahalia, it wasn't that she didn't like jazz, ragtime, or blues. She enjoyed the works of many artists, such as Bessie Smith, Ma Rainey, and Ida Cox. Perhaps because she had achieved fame and success, she simply couldn't be tempted to explore regions that were alien to her heart. To me, however, her refusal was the mark of character, of being true to herself.

She was so gracious and made me feel very much at home in her house. I still had to pinch myself every once in a while. *Oh my goodness,* I would think, *I am staying with Mahalia Jackson.*

From that vantage point, Chicago seemed like the center of the African-American community in the United States. There were more Black people in Chicago than there were people in Indianapolis. There was a thriving Black press. It was a major hub on the entertainment and culture circuits. Every prominent Black person in the country, it seemed, either lived in Chicago or visited frequently. It was an amazing place for a wide-eyed, ambitious twenty-four-year-old.

I was immediately swept up in the life of the city. Bob Johnson, the managing editor of *Jet* magazine (no relation to Mr. John H. Johnson, the owner and publisher of Johnson Publications) took me under his wing and introduced me to a wide circle of people. He and I had met back in 1962, when he came to Florida for a photo shoot of the Ebony Fashion Fair for *Jet*. We had hit it off right away and had talked for hours about racism and what we should do about it. He liked that I was so spunky.

"I thought you were really bright and political," he told me when we met again in Chicago. "Here you are a girl who doesn't have to deal with race, just go on your looks, but you are interested in the issues. You may be a little naive, but you've got passion."

I was really flattered. Bob was older than I, and a whole lot smarter. And he knew everybody. *Jet* was the place where Black people got all their news (still is in many places). So all doors were open to Bob.

The two of us would spend time talking about the outrageous conduct of White America. Not only did Blacks in the South have to ride in the back of buses, we had to enter the front door to pay for the fare, then step off and enter the door at the rear. Rosa Parks helped put a stop to this when, with steely resolve, she refused to give up her seat for a White man, preferring a jail cell to the indignity of yielding to a member of the alleged "superior race."

There was no shortage of experiences that Bob and I could and did share. I told Bob about the time I was asked to audition for a Hot Point stove commercial. All of the apartments in the Lockefield Gardens housing project had Hot Point stoves, courtesy of the federal government, so I assumed that the company was anxious to display Blacks enjoying the pleasure of cooking with their product.

Apparently, I had impressed one of the company's field representatives, but when he told me that a decision to allow a "colored" woman in one of their advertisements would require authority from the corporate headquarters, I suggested where he might find an appropriate place for his ads.

Schlitz beer company offered another wonderful display of enlightenment. I had been hired to do a commercial for the company that ran on White Sox baseball television. The company's goal was to entice those in the Black community to consume more Schlitz beer. Blacks could see that I was one of them. But the company precluded me from doing the very same ad for radio. The producer of the commercial came out of the control room and into the recording booth after forcing me to repeat the script several times.

"What am I doing wrong? I asked, confused about the need to keep repeating what I had performed flawlessly.

"Can you talk a little more Black?"

"I am Black. You can see that. Just exactly what is it that you think sounds Black?"

"You . . . You know. You just don't sound Black. So try it again."

I knew exactly what he was trying to force me to do. I was not going to accommodate him, not for one second, and not for any amount of money. They could keep their damn ad, which is what they did.

Bob shared with me how *Jet* publisher, Mr. John H. Johnson, had his own encounters with major companies and their ad agencies. Despite the fact that Blacks were a major target audience for General Motors, their representatives had to be persuaded to place advertisements in *Ebony* and *Jet*. He told me usually the ads would include a photograph of a beautiful Cadillac, the car being the most expensive object of desire. Interestingly enough, Blacks were never allowed to appear in the ads. Dogs were more in vogue than people of color, however. Bob showed me one picture of a large, fair-haired, regal-looking Afghan sitting at attention in the passenger seat of a new red Cadillac convertible. "Damn," I joked, "even the dogs have to be blonde to succeed in this world." We both broke into laughter, easing for the moment the pain inflicted by the racist society in which we had to live.

This was early 1966, and the Southern Christian Leadership Conference (SCLC), under the guidance of Martin Luther King, Jr., was in the process of launching a "war on slums" in Chicago. Along with every other Black person in the country, I had closely watched the confrontation in Selma that previous year.

My heart was divided. I held Dr. King in awe as the spirit and the conscience of the movement that had won so much change for our people. Yet, I identified with the anger, frustration, and impatience of the young militants in the Student Nonviolent Coordinating Committee (SNCC) who were questioning the efficacy of Dr. King's philosophy and strategy. In fact, it was Malcolm X with whom I resonated the most. His 1964 assertion that "now we have the type of Black man on the scene in America . . . who just doesn't intend to turn the other cheek any longer"[1] gave perfect voice to my attitude toward racism. I was ready to fight, and I hoped that with an SCLC direct-action campaign in Chicago I would have the opportunity.

Well, as they say, when the student is ready the teacher will come. As I settled into my life in Chicago, I avidly followed the news reports of the SCLC's assault on the ghetto and its growing challenge to the city's establishment to dismantle this "domestic colony." And when Bob Johnson asked if I wanted to go to the Chicago Freedom Movement rally on March 12, I jumped at the chance.

The event was an entertainment festival to raise funds for the Chicago campaign. It was wildly successful, with more than twelve thousand people gathered at the old stockyards.

Chicagoans and the movement's supporters from around the country turned out in force. The place was packed, and there was a vibrant energy in the air.

Bob squired me around, stopping frequently to say hello to the innumerable people he knew. As we were making our way across the floor, I noticed Sidney Poitier standing with a large group.

"Bob," I said, stopping, "I've got to meet Sidney Poitier." I had grown up watching Sidney making history in film after film. After he became the first Black man to win an Oscar for best actor in 1963 for his role in *Lilies in the Field*, he was even more of a hero to the Black community. I just had to shake his hand.

Bob laughed and said "Come on," as we started to push our way through the crowd toward the cluster of people with whom Sidney was talking. I was totally starstruck. So much so that when we got

[1]From a speech by Malcolm X at Cory Methodist Church in Cleveland, Ohio, April 3, 1964, excerpted in *1001 Things Everyone Should Know About African American History*, Jeffrey C. Stewart, Main Street Books, New York, 1998, p. 161.

near I did not notice that there was someone standing in my path. My eyes were fixed on Sidney's handsome face, and I ran straight into the smaller man who seemed to be at the center of the group, spilling my Coke all over his suit.

There was a sudden commotion, with several of the men standing around me stepping forward with a slightly menacing urgency. The man whom I had bumped into held up his hand and said, "It's all right. It's all right."

The voice. I had heard it a hundred times on the radio and on TV. Its Southern preacher's timbre was unmistakable. I did not want to believe it, but I knew that I had just spilled Coca-Cola on Martin Luther King, Jr. I felt myself begin to blush as I fumbled to think what to do next.

At this point, Bob Johnson came to my aid, saying in a teasing tone, "Martin, meet Janet Floyd." Everyone laughed, and the momentary tension broke.

"Oh, Dr. King," I said, reaching into my clutch for a handkerchief, "I am so sorry."

"That's all right, child," he replied, dabbing at his beautiful black mohair suit. "I am pleased to meet you." He had the warmest eyes. And his manner was so sweet, my embarrassment evaporated.

Just then, one of his entourage leaned in and said something in Dr. King's ear. He nodded, told us that he had to attend to something, shook hands, and moved off with the rest of the group.

As I watched them walk away, I realized that I had not gotten to meet Sidney Poitier. I was disappointed, but also completely mesmerized by having been face-to-face with Dr. King. He was so much larger than life in my imagination—the icon of our struggle for freedom and equality—that it was hard to reconcile his mythical stature with the reality of the gentle, slightly haggard-looking man with whom I had just shaken hands.

Little did I know that Dr. King would become one of the key mentors in my life. It seemed that destiny was conspiring to have me learn at his feet. I met Dr. King again at Mahalia Jackson's, with whom he and Coretta were close. He remembered me and had everyone in stitches telling the story of our first meeting. I could not get over how funny he was. Here was this Nobel Peace Prize laureate who had the timing and delivery of a stand-up comic. He had us all howling and crying with laughter. As I learned with time, there was rarely an instance when you would be around him and not get a belly laugh. Dr. King was profound, but he was also a lot of fun to be with.

If there was one thing that was clear to all of us at Mahalia's, it was just how much she loved Dr. King. She was totally committed to him and treated him like her son. She had openly supported the bus boycott he had led in Montgomery, Alabama, in 1955 and prior to his "I Have a Dream" speech that he delivered on the steps of the Lincoln Memorial in 1963, she sang, "I've Been Buked and I've Been Scorned."

She would pad around in her housecoat and slippers, fixing him traditional "soul food" dinners. She was also quick to chide him if she thought he was being foolhardy. Dr. King, in turn, would look for ways to toy with her.

Knowing that Mahalia was well within earshot, he told a group of us gathered in the living room, how during one of his marches, a young lady emerged from the crowd and began calling him a "dirty nigger" and other choice epithets.

Dr. King approached her and asked, "How can someone as beautiful as you be filled with so much hate?"

When he reached the end of the march, inexplicably, the young woman was waiting for him. She waved to him, repeating, "Dr. King, Dr. King, do you remember me?" He had won her over, not through an exchange of angry insults, but through his kindness— and using his famous Southern charm.

Knowing that it would provoke Mahalia, he added in a stage whisper, "She sure was a fine-looking woman."

Mahalia, not missing a beat, came padding out of the kitchen and said, "Now, Martin, you take care. White women will give you nothing but trouble. You hear?"

Dr. King, breaking into a broad smile, said, "I hear you, Mahalia. But she sure was a fine-looking woman."

Everyone erupted into laughter, including Mahalia, who realized that Dr. King was having a little fun at her expense.

That night at Mahalia's, his joking and teasing got me going, and I told the story of my birth certificate. When I moved to Chicago, I figured I might continue to travel, as I had done with the Ebony Fashion Fair—maybe even go overseas. Cordie King, in giving me career advice, had said that it was important to be prepared to go where the work was and to be ready to leave at a moment's notice. With that, I figured I best get a passport, in case I did get an opportunity to work abroad.

I went on to tell how I had written to the Indianapolis Bureau of Vital Statistics requesting my birth certificate. When the copy arrived, I looked it over out of curiosity. You can imagine my surprise when I noticed that my race was listed as "White." The same harried doctor who had misspelled my given name had also gotten my color wrong.

I called the Vital Statistics office in Indiana to rectify the situation. "There is a mistake on my birth certificate," I explained to the clerk who answered the phone. "I am colored, and the certificate says I am White. Can you please send me a corrected version? I need it to get my passport."

"I can't just change it," the clerk said incredulously. "You have to come down here and get it notarized, and so forth."

"I've got to go all the way to Indianapolis from Chicago just to get an obvious error corrected?"

"These are legal documents, miss," she replied. "You can't simply call up on the telephone to have them changed."

I was starting to get annoyed, and I lost my composure. "Look," I said, "how many White people do you know who want to change their birth certificate to read Negro?"

To her credit, the clerk stuck to the regulations. I was not willing to go to the trouble of traveling to Indy, so my birth certificate remained unchanged.

As I told the story, everybody laughed heartily, and I was suddenly at ease. There was a lighter side to everything in life, even race. I laughed, too, and told the group about my maternal grandmother. I met her for the first time when I was about eighteen, when Mother brought her up from Kentucky for a visit. The first day she was visiting, I remember her going all through our cupboards and closets.

"What are you looking for?" Mother asked.

"I'm just looking at how neat you are," Grandmother replied. "You have the shelves lined. Everything ordered by color and shape and size. My word, Louise, you've got things just like White folks."

We all laughed to think she considered that a compliment, as if only White people could be neat and have things all pretty.

I was trying to match my funny stories with those of Dr. King's and the others. I told them of my grandmother's beauty habits. Because her skin was so fair, she would always pinch her cheeks in lieu of rouge. When she was out of face powder, she was accustomed to using baking flour instead. One time, she put a little too much on. Outside in the light, you could see how white her face was. My mother shrieked, "Mom, you've got too much flour on," And Grandmother would reply, in her self-assured, haughty manner, "That's alright, Louise, it'll blow off."

Dr. King's wisdom, humor, and humanity reminded me of my grandmother. One of the most important lessons I learned from him was to keep laughing, even in the face of danger and uncertainty. I saw more and more of that side of Dr. King as I spent time with him and his many friends. I remember a group of us coming out of the Palmer House hotel in Chicago after dinner at Trader Vic's. They had these beautiful martini glasses, with a black stem shaped like a female figure, that you could keep as a souvenir. One of the men in the group took his glass with him, in his coat pocket. I was in a playful mood and got into the revolving door with him. Well, as we tried to get through, the glass broke in his pocket, with a great big popping sound.

Everybody ducked, except Dr. King, who just stood still looking at us. When we stood back up and discovered what the noise had been, he started laughing.

"All of you," he said in his teasing tone, "you're always trying to protect me. You all hear a little popping sound, and you hit the deck.

"Let me just assure you, you all are safe," he continued with a little more edge, "When that bullet comes, it's coming for me." None of us realized at that moment just how prophetic his comment would prove. On April 4, 1968, James Earl Ray lined up only one person in the gun sight of his high-powered rifle.

For Dr. King, the danger was palpable in those days. He had already been "a sneeze away" from death, when Izola Curry stabbed him with a letter opener in Blumestein's department store in New York City in September 1958. He had been attacked, threatened, and imprisoned repeatedly in the course of his struggle to fight racism through nonviolence.

By 1966, the FBI had Dr. King under constant surveillance. Wherever he went, the G-men and the police were always around.

"Who are these people, Dr. King?" I asked the first time I noticed this strange entourage.

"Well, you see those guys over there, the funny-looking ones?" he said with a smile. "They're the FBI. And see the beefy-looking ones over here? They're the City of Chicago police."

"That's nice of Mayor Daley," I said, surprised. "Really nice."

"He ain't being nice," Dr. King replied, putting on a really thick Southern accent. "He just don't want this Negro killed in Chicago on his watch. He doesn't want his city to burn."

Sometimes I could not understand how he could laugh about such things. I was so enraged. I felt White people—racist White people—were evil. They enslaved us, deprived us, and humiliated us. I watched my mother be humiliated on welfare. And now I watched a man who was recognized the world over as a champion of peace live under the constant threat of death in his own land.

"How can you even joke about this, Dr. King?" I once asked him.

He thought about it for a while and said, "Because I know a better day is coming. A different world is coming. I won't see it. You may not see it. But it will come. And that's all that matters." He always had that belief, along with a sense of humor.

Reason to Rage

When James Meredith was shot outside of Memphis on the second day of his one-man "walk against fear," on June 6, 1966, the attention of the country again focused on the civil rights struggle down South. Although the various groups that comprised the movement came together to continue the Meredith march, it was clear from the beginning that a new militancy in the air was dividing the Black community. At a June 16 rally in Greenwood, Mississippi, SNCC's Stokely Carmichael proclaimed, "We want black power."[2] This was as much a rejection of Dr. King's philosophy of nonviolence as it was a challenge to the White establishment. Stokely, as Malcolm X had done before him, was saying that Black people were not going to take it anymore.

Dr. King, it seemed, was under constant criticism and assault. He was accused of being a "Communist" and a "troublemaker." He was also labeled a "womanizer." I traveled in Dr. King's circle for the last

[2]*Bearing the Cross: Martin Luther King, Jr. and the Southern Christian Leadership Conference*, David J. Garrow, Quill/William Morrow, New York, 1999, p. 481.

two years of his life and never saw him in the company of other women. Moreover, he had always behaved appropriately with me. At the time, I simply attributed all of the rumors and labels to hate-mongering by the White establishment. But not all of his critics were White.

Some Blacks thought he was simply too passive. In addition, Congressman Adam Clayton Powell, Jr., the chairman of the powerful House Education and Labor Committee, had insinuated that Dr. King and civil rights leader Bayard Rustin were more than platonic friends. It was a patent lie that was circulated in an attempt to discredit Dr. King in the eyes of other Blacks. Dr. King had enough White enemies, I thought. He surely was not in need of Black ones to attack his character.

Aside from what I considered a mean-spirited and spiteful tactic by Powell, I was still awed by his legislative accomplishments. He drove the desegregation of public schools, housing, employment, transportation, and the military. He even broke down the long-standing barriers in the United States Capitol that forbid Black congressmen and their staffs from using Capitol Hill facilities that were reserved for members only.

Yes, he was arrogant and disdainful, with an in-your-face-attitude toward the segregationists who dominated the politics of the times. And just as I identified with Malcolm X and Stokely, I identified with Powell's take-no-prisoners philosophy of fighting back instead of turning the other cheek.

As much as I admired Dr. King, I thought his philosophy of nonviolence was naive and that it would never succeed in tearing at the conscience of the White world. That view, however, would change later that summer.

For several days, starting on July 29, 1966, the Chicago Freedom Movement held marches and vigils in the all-White neighborhoods of Gage Park, Marquette Park, and Cicero to protest discrimination in housing. Although the police were on hand, they did little to protect the marchers from the angry White crowds who threw stones, bottles, and trash at the protesters.

One of those evenings while staying with Mahalia, we were watching television together. She was resting in bed to ease her heart condition, when suddenly, the news flashed terrible footage of thousands of angry Whites attacking the demonstrators. One shot showed Dr. King being struck in the head with a brick.

"Look at what they are doing to my boy," Mahalia said while lying in bed in her pink signature dressing gown with matching robe, getting more and more agitated.

I was sitting at the foot of her bed and was stunned when she suddenly leaped up, put on her matching slippers, and hollered downstairs to someone, "Get me my car. Bring my car around. I'm going out there. I'm going to get Martin."

Everyone in the house tried to calm her down, remind her of her health, but with tears streaming down her cheeks, she was determined. "If none of you have the courage to drive me, I'll drive myself."

She got into the car and as she was driving out of the driveway, one of her aides opened the door, jumped into the passenger side, and went off with her.

Later that evening, she returned with Dr. King and the others. As they came in, Dr. King was supporting her as she made her way through the door. She was clearly exhausted, saying, "This movement is going to be the death of me."

The aide who had gone with her later told us what happened. When Mahalia pulled up in her robe and slippers and drove up to the barricade in her big gold Cadillac, a White police officer came over to her and, before recognizing her, shouted, "Go back, go back!"

Realizing the driver of the Cadillac was Mahalia Jackson, he softened his tone. "Ms. Jackson," he said, with surprise and respect, "what are you doing out here in this mob?"

"I've come to get my boy," she replied. "You allowed these crazy people to stone him. I saw it on television. Where is Martin? Let me through. I want to know how he is."

The police officer knelt by her door and, like everyone else in Chicago, he knew she had been ill. He spoke softly, "Now Ms. Jackson, you know it's not good for you to be out here—especially in this heat. Just go on back home. Dr. King is alright, I assure you."

Several hours later, after the march ended, Dr. King, Andy Young, Bernard Lee, the Reverend John Thurston, and a few others came over to Mahalia's. She had dinner ready for them—greens, chitlins, corn bread, and macaroni and cheese.

"Y'all are going to be the death of me," Mahalia said when everybody had something to eat. "You going to kill me. Stay away from those White folks. They're never going to let us have anything. Never. Why do you have to be out there dealing with those people?"

Then she went on upstairs to rest. And I picked up where Mahalia left off.

"Dr. King," I said, "I'm just so outraged. You see how upset Ms. Jackson is. Why do you let them do that to you? How can you get down and pray when they stone you?"

He smiled in a tired sort of way and said, "Well, it's a nonviolent movement."

"Yes," I countered, getting more and more riled up, "but they're spitting on you. They're calling you nigger. Next time you march, I'd like to go with you. I'll show them a thing or two."

Dr. King got serious. He asked, "What would you do if they spat on you?"

I said, "Spit back."

"You know, they were dropping bags of urine out of the trees," he said. "What would you do about that?"

"I'd show them how fast I could climb a tree. I'd be up there after them."

"And what would you do if they called you nigger?"

"I'd punch them and teach them a few words they don't know. Low-down dirty peckerwoods, White trash . . ."

"You can't march, child," Dr. King said sternly. "You can't march with us."

"But why not, Dr. King?" I asked, my feelings a little hurt.

"As I said, this is a nonviolent movement. Nonviolence is our strategy. It is the right thing to do, and it is the smart thing to do."

"How's that?" I pressed him.

"One, we stand out because we are Black," Dr. King began to explain in a gentler tone. "We are a minority. There are more of them. And you know what else? They have all the guns. All they want is for us to do just what you want to do. So they could have a reason to crack our heads. If one of us does what you want, it will get us all killed.

"This is a moral and an intellectual march," he continued. "We have an agenda here. We will get what we want. And in the end, they'll be happy to give it to us, because we will make them ashamed of themselves. We've got the moral high ground, they will come to see that through nonviolence."

Suddenly, I felt completely deflated and very naive. I thought I should have gotten a badge of honor for my rage, and here was Dr. King telling me that I could not march with him because of it. It took me a long time to understand what he had tried to explain that evening—that outrage is not the same as rage, and that strategy is as important as passion in getting what you want in life.

I never did march with Dr. King, but in the two years that I knew him, Dr. King taught me much about integrity, faith, humanity, determination and above all, he taught me about courage. The most profound lesson he offered me, however, was the need to think strategically about the role of nonviolence in the Civil Rights Movement; to employ logic and to appeal to justice in forcing America to live up to the noble declarations of the Founding Fathers. White Americans worshipped their ancestors who had declared that we were all entitled to equal rights and equal treatment under the law (even though few of them had ever matched their words with deeds). In essence, he was saying, we are demanding that you practice what you preach. You brought us here and we are not going away. You built America's prosperity on our backs and payment in full is long overdue. We are here to collect.

3

Stormy Weather

I had always greatly admired Bess Myerson. She was the first Jewish woman to become Miss America, at a time when the pageant's rules read: "Contestants must be of good health and of the White race." In 1945, Jews were considered a little too ethnic to satisfy the race requirement, so it was a major breakthrough that Bess Myerson won the crown. More importantly, she refused to change her name, as the contest's organizers pressured her to do. I thought that her courage made her that much more beautiful.

When I learned that Dr. King had had a meeting with Miss Myerson in New York, I was really excited to hear about what she was like in person. "How tall is she?" I asked. "Is she as beautiful in person as she appears on *The Big Payoff* television game show?"

"She's no more beautiful than you," Dr. King answered.

"But she's Miss America," I said, embarrassed by the compliment.

He looked at me in a thoughtful kind of way for a few seconds and then said, "Well, she may be Miss America, but you, Janet, are a queen."

"But I could never be Miss America, because I'm Black," I said, glossing over his comment. I could not conceivably have foreseen that while I would never be allowed to compete in the Miss America contest, I would be asked to serve as a judge for an unprecedented four times.

"No," Dr. King persisted, "maybe you can't be Miss America, but just remember where you come from. Remember the people you come from.

"There is a throne waiting for you," he continued. "It may have cobwebs on it and dust because it hasn't been sat on for a long time, but it is waiting for you. Nobody else can sit on your throne.

"You come from royalty. The fact that your spirit has survived intact through everything that's been done to us, that's the true test of royalty. That's the true test of a queen. And one day it will be yours. Go claim it."

I was stunned. To have Dr. King praise me in this way—to see in me something I, myself, had not yet glimpsed or could imagine—was an awesome tribute. I knew he was not speaking of royalty that comes with the trappings of ermine and jewels, or the kind that rules or reigns. He was challenging me to see beyond the false nobility and power bestowed by titles and to seek in myself the true royalty of character, principle, and leadership.

In that moment, I heard again the whisper of that ancient blood in my veins. I remembered my grandmother looking at me and saying how much I reminded her of the strength of her own mother in a different time. I remembered everything my mother had taught me about working twice as hard for half as much.

I am so blessed, I thought, filled with pride and purpose. Dr. King had encouraged me to reach above any limitations that society imposed on me, to achieve a spiritual grace that would allow me, not to reign over others, but lift and lead them to a more enlightened awareness of our common humanity.

Runway Bride

While growing up I had little in the way of material possessions, but I did possess an abundant supply of ambition and self-confidence—two indispensable qualities for anyone eager to compete in beauty contests. Over the years I entered scores of them, not for the accolades or admiration they brought, but for the monetary rewards they offered. I saw them solely in material terms, as a means to gaining financial independence and helping to further my education.

I won every contest that I entered, more on sheer chutzpah than beauty. I knew how to turn on an attitude. There was a brass ring out there for me if I were bold enough to grab it. There are times when I reflect on those moments and laugh at my naiveté. I did not know fear, and I never thought about failure. I just knew that I was starting out at the bottom and nothing was going to stop me from reaching the top.

In Chicago, where I was working with and competing against Black and White girls, race, once again, was a factor that only strengthened my resolve. Like all African-Americans of my generation, I was raised to believe that I not only had to conduct myself in a fashion that brought credit to myself and my family, but that I had a responsibility to hold up my entire race as well.

"They are only going to let a few of us in," the argument went, "so if you set a bad example, if you don't do well, if you let us down, then that makes it harder for Blacks coming up behind you." It was an awesome responsibility to have to carry my entire race on my back just so some anonymous strangers whom I did not hold in any high regard would not hold us in less.

I wanted to be Lena Horne, not Charles Atlas. But the need to carry the additional burden of constantly exceeding society's low expectations of our race only added fuel to my drive and determination. Whites would often say to me, "You're different. You're not like the others. You are a credit to your race."

I remember one time a Black man was on the front page of the newspaper for having done something criminal. One of the White women that I worked with had the paper sitting on my desk when I arrived and said, "Janet, how do you feel about this? He's a discredit to your race."

I shot back, "How do you feel about Hitler? Was he a discredit to *your* race?"

In Chicago, during the sixties, most of the models were White and had the luxury of specializing in their fields. Print models, for example, posed for photographs in advertisements and catalogs, runway models swiveled their hips in the fashion shows, and industrial models worked conventions and auto shows.

There were different requirements for each of these specialties. Sponsors liked you on the voluptuous side for the industrial shows. For the runway, you had to be really thin and graceful. And for print, the camera had to love you.

There was a growing demand for Black models, and at the time, I was something of a rarity in that I was able to perform all three types of modeling. I was thin and fairly tall and thanks to the Ebony

Fashion Fair, I had runway experience. My personality seemed to come through on camera, and I did add a bit of zest to conventions.

I had to gain weight for the industrial shows and then lose it for the runway performances. It was a heady time for me. I was building a career while "holding up my race." While I found the experience demanding, it was personally gratifying to know that I was paving the way for other Black models to pursue similar careers.

I achieved a number of "firsts." Perhaps the most memorable at the time was modeling for Marshall Field & Company. In Chicago, the Marshall Field family enjoyed the prominence of New York's Morgans and Rockefellers. The family was immensely wealthy and powerful. Their company is still considered the crème de la crème of retail department stores.

I was very excited when Marshall Field & Company asked me to be one of their fashion models. They had already employed a Black model but wanted to move beyond mere tokenism. I did a few shows for them, which were quite successful. Then several months into the job, a surprise came.

I went in for a fitting and was told to try on a bridal gown. I got dressed and suddenly the room was abuzz. All of the models and seamstresses were crowding around me, *oohing* and *aahing* as women tend to do.

I simply thought that they were admiring the dress. I did notice, however, that Dori, the store's first Black model, was the only one who didn't seem particularly excited. It occurred to me at the time that she might not only be feeling a bit jealous because of the attention that I had drawn, but a sense of entitlement to wear the dress because she was the *first*.

What I did not realize at that moment was that no Black woman had ever been asked—or permitted—to wear a bridal gown. In those days, every fashion show ended with the bridal gown, and it was the fresh-faced White ingenue, the girl of the moment who was selected to be the "bride."

When I learned this, I understood why Dori was upset. She had worked for the store longer and, no doubt, was disappointed that she had been bypassed for this honor.

By the time the show took place in Oakbrook, Illinois, there was a buzz in the audience about the fact that this was the first time Marshall Field's would have a Black "bride." While I was thrilled with the opportunity to model the gown, I thought it silly that these so-called sophisticates were focused, not on the beauty of the dress, but on the fact that a Black woman was wearing it.

I was a little nervous walking out onto the runway, pulling that long white train behind me, careful not to stumble or trip, mindful, once again, that I was carrying the expectations of my entire race with me.

The audience responded with enthusiastic applause and a few cheers. Cameras clicked and flashes popped. This was a moment, and everyone in that room seemed to know it. I walked toward the end of the runway, between the "bridesmaids" lining the sides, and took in the crowd. For a second, I thought about all those times I had fantasized about my own wedding, as most young girls do. I even thought that I was, in a way, fulfilling my mother's dream of having me perform as a concert pianist before a large audience in a gigantic hall . . . I did have on a beautiful gown, had my hair piled up, and was performing in front of a large audience. With that thought, I then turned to start my walk back toward the curtain.

Dori, who was one of the "bridesmaids," turned in behind me and stepped on the gown's train, almost ripping the dress.

Oh, my God, I thought. *In another second, I am going to be like Katharine Hepburn in the movie* Bringing Up Baby, *trying to cover up my behind.*

At the time, I did not think it was anything other than an accident, although I found it strange that Dori did not say "sorry" when we came off. I gave her the benefit of the doubt, though, thinking that she simply had not noticed what she had done.

We did a second show that day, and the exact same thing happened. We turned, and she stepped on the train. This time, I knew that she was doing it on purpose.

Dori's conduct was an example of what a friend in Boston, Miss Alma Lewis, would later tell me about "plantation thinking" after I complained to her that Black people in the city did not seem to be supportive or be there for me when I came under verbal attack.

"Well, you have it a little bit better than most people," she said. "You've gotten a few opportunities that others did not get, and it is human nature to be jealous.

"But," she added, "we Blacks do suffer from something called plantation thinking." She went on, "Imagine Miss Ann, the wife of the master of the plantation, decides to clean out her closet. She is a size eight. Most of the slaves are size twelve or fourteen or twenty, except for one, puny little slave who is an eight, like Miss Ann. So she gets to wear all of Miss Ann's dresses. And what do the other slaves do? Rather than complaining to Miss Ann to get dresses that fit everybody, they rip the dresses off the one who can wear them."

There was another aspect of preferential treatment involved among the slaves, called color coding. Dori was beautiful, dark brown in color, possessing a rich, deep tone that enhanced the gleam in her eyes and the brightness of her smile. But she fell victim to the familiar expression:

If you're White,
you're alright;
If you're Black,
get back;
If you're yellow
You're mellow;
If you're brown,
stick around.

These sentiments, of course, were but another insidious manifestation of the legacy of slavery and its evil racism. Those who had lighter skin (many, not all, being the descendants of rapist slave owners) were deemed by Whites, and some Blacks, to be more attractive and socially acceptable. It was understandable that those who were darker would either envy or resent those who seemed to enjoy greater opportunities offered by the White power structure.

For me, the very notion that skin tone should define my acceptability to anyone—White or Black—was absurd and only served to fuel my rage. I had little patience or tolerance for anyone—including Dori—who bought into this contemporary caste system and experienced either envy or resentment.

I was disappointed with her, and I was not going to let it go.

When we had changed, I went up to Dori, pulled her to the side, and said, "I don't want to have this conversation in front of these White girls, but we're going to have us a 'little bandana talk' here.

"Dori, I want you to understand something. As long as I'm wearing this dress, it's *my* dress. You step on it while I am wearing it, I'll consider that you're stepping on me. If you want to take the dress when it's hanging on the hanger and rip it to shreds, that's between you and Marshall Field. But when it's on me, don't touch it. . . . Watch your step!"

She was taken aback because I had always made it a point to be friendly and polite. I could wear velvet gloves and play the ingenue on the runway, but if anyone either disrespected me or tried to undermine my career, I could just as easily wear brass knuckles. Unfortunately, in my early career, I had had to don the brass knuckles—more so with those in the Black community than those in the White. Years later, at a party my friend Millicent had for me to reunite with my old friends in Chicago, I was surprised and happy to see that Dori was there. She was warm and welcoming.

My experience with Dori was played out, again and again. Even within the Civil Rights Movement, we were not immune from plantation thinking and its color-conscious divisions. I once attended a SNCC meeting with *Jet* magazine editor Bob Johnson. He knew I was drawn by the organization's Black power rhetoric and invited me to attend one of their gatherings. We walked into a darkened room, full of young people sitting on the floor. Stokely Carmichael, also known as Kwame Ture, sat at the center. He was black as coal, with chiseled features, and big, beautiful, penetrating round eyes. Handsome and wearing African dress, he looked like a Somalian prince.

He was definitely holding court. When Bob and I walked in, he interrupted his conversation and motioned Bob over. In a whisper loud enough for me to hear where I was standing near the door, Stokely snapped, "You get that yellow pinup girl out of here."

There was a commotion of voices and movement behind us as Bob quickly escorted me out of the room. I could not believe what had just happened. I felt such affinity with these people. They were speaking my truth, and I wanted to stand up to the system as much as they did. But apparently I was not welcome. My color and my profession disqualified me.

"Don't take it personally," Bob said. "There are so many informants, so much surveillance, they have a right to be paranoid."

"Yes, but they don't have a right to judge me, just because I'm in beauty contests, and I model, and I have lighter skin," I said bitterly. "He has no idea how angry I am at the bigots. And he just did to me what he is fighting White people for doing to us."

Again I was bumping into the limitations of generalizations. It was simpler to think in terms of Black and White, in the absolutes of the word *all*: "All White people are this; all Black people are that. All light-skinned Blacks have it better; all darker Blacks are more righteous and true. . . ." But the world kept showing me that things are more complex. All Black people did not accept and welcome me, no matter what my success was doing to uphold our people, while many White people went out of their way to advance my career. And yet in those very moments of greatest stress, I forced myself to remember the writings of W.E.B. DuBois, Dr. King, and so many others that it was the struggles and sacrifices of Black people who made it possible for me to realize my dreams.

The question of color, however, along with other people's assumptions about it, continued to keep me on an emotional Yo-Yo string.

Once when I was working as the secretary to the head of housekeeping in the Pick-Congress Hotel in Chicago, a young man burst through the laundry room door and said something to me in Spanish. I had no idea what he said as he moved on and headed toward the kitchen. Several minutes later, two White men dressed in business suits and wearing Jack Webb *Dragnet* hats entered and asked me what direction the young man was headed. Innocently, I pointed in the direction of the kitchen. Later in the day, the chef came into my office and began to chastise me.

"I know we Puerto Ricans have our differences with the Mexicans, but when it comes to dealing with Whites, with the government, we're all Hispanics."

I was stunned by his assumption of who or what I was. Once again, I had encountered jealousies among ethnic groups who found themselves united by a common enemy: the White man.

"First of all," I responded, "I'm not Hispanic. I don't speak or understand a word of Spanish. Second, I'm not Puerto Rican, I'm Black and an American. And third, I don't have any problems or differences with Mexicans."

The chef apologized for his error, but I took no solace in my defense. I understood exactly what he was saying about the need for minorities to unite against a common enemy, and later learned that the young man was in the country illegally, but had been working two jobs to support his family. The men from the immigration department found him hiding in the kitchen refrigerator. He was later deported back to Mexico.

I felt enormously guilty over what I had done. For years, the White power structure prevented Blacks from learning how to read and write for fear that the fiction about their superiority would be destroyed. The Hispanic workers were banned from speaking their native language to one another in the presence of Whites at the risk of losing their jobs. Bilingual education in the classroom was either discouraged or prohibited (unless the second language happened to be French, which was viewed by some as a gateway to sophistication for the elite). I was told that schoolchildren in Texas were even whipped by nuns in some of the parochial schools if they were caught speaking Spanish. I believed that it was right to insist that English be the first language of America, but not its only one.

On that day I vowed that I would become bilingual. I knew that if I was to become fluent, I had to immerse myself in the language. I couldn't go to Mexico, and I knew classroom Spanish would never be good enough. So for the next full year I associated with people who only spoke Spanish. I didn't become fluent, but I am easily understood and appreciated for trying.

Miss Chicagoland

By the late fall of 1966, I had become the toast of the town in Chicago. I competed in the Miss Chicagoland beauty pageant and won. The pageant was a very big deal in the city. It was the local version of Miss America, with Black and White women from the entire metropolitan area—Chicago, Calumet City, Evanston, Oakbrook, Wilmette—competing for the crown. For me, it was an especially important contest to win. To have a Black Miss Chicagoland in 1966, when we were still fighting for fair housing and schooling in that city, made a real statement. And I was proud to be the one to make it.

I was crowned by the great jazz man, Louis Armstrong and popular singer, Tony Bennett. I remember coming on stage at McCormick Place, the big convention center in Chicago, with the two of them standing side by side, smiling. Since I was wearing a crown, I thought I would get to stand in the center, flanked by these two entertainment giants. Tony, however, had another idea. He was such a big fan of Louis, he said, "With all due respect, Miss Chicagoland, I want to stand next to Louis Armstrong." So there we were: Louis in the middle, with Tony and me on each arm. It was such an honor to be crowned by Louis Armstrong, I did not even mind being a little up-staged.

That December, *Jet* ran a picture of me on the cover. It was a bit sexy, with me in a Santa hat and showing a little cleavage. Suddenly, I was a celebrity. People on the street would call out, "Miss Chicagoland" or "Janet." It was exhilarating but, just as before, also somewhat unnerving to realize what it meant to live in the public eye.

For the most part, though, it was just great fun. I got to meet more and more wonderful people. One of my favorites was Duke Ellington. It was enough of a treat to see him in concert, with his fantastic orchestra and Ella Fitzgerald singing. But then Bob Johnson leaned over and said, "You want to meet him?"

We went backstage and stood in the wings, watching Duke conduct the orchestra. A vocal number was next, and while Ella sang, Duke came off for a brief rest. Bob introduced us, saying "Duke, I want you to meet Miss Chicagoland."

"So pleased to meet you," Duke Ellington said. He was a real charmer. "I wrote a song for you," he said.

"You did?" I exclaimed.

"Yeah," Duke said. "You stay right here. When I go back on stage, I'll play it for you."

Of course, the song was "Satin Doll," but I had never heard it before. So when he came off again, I thanked him and told him how touched I was. He laughed, scooped me up, and danced me around in the wings. He was in his late sixties, but he was smooth, light on his feet, and charming as he could be. He just wooed me. Even though he was old enough to be my grandfather, I found him wonderfully captivating. When dancing with Duke, age didn't matter. He had a special kind of charisma that transcended age. It was a thrill to be around him.

I was still gushing about Duke at dinner later that evening. "Wasn't that song wonderful?" I said to Bob Johnson. "And Duke said he had me in mind when he wrote it."

Bob laughed and said, "That song is probably older than you are. It's 'Satin Doll.' And if you were a little older, he would have played 'Sophisticated Lady' for you."

We both laughed.

I still love Duke, even though he had conned me a little. Whenever

I hear "Satin Doll," I think of dancing with him and of his dazzling, sly smile.

It was a magical time for me. I was getting to meet all of the heroes of the Black community—Jackie Robinson, Joe Louis, Floyd Patterson—and all of the people I had read about in *Jet* and *Ebony* magazines and had seen on TV and in the movies. Each of these encounters was a revelation, where an icon took on human form. Each had something special to teach me.

When I met Jackie Robinson, for instance, he was already a legend. He had been inducted into the Baseball Hall of Fame in 1962—the first African-American to achieve that honor. Every Black kid knew Jackie Robinson and his historic status as the first Black player in Major League Baseball. We had all watched *The Jackie Robinson Story* and knew about the abuse he took from the fans and fellow players.

I saw Jackie in a Chicago club. The place was crowded and he was standing off by himself, leaning against the wall. He was very handsome, dark, with beautiful brown, soulful eyes. He was middle-aged, and wore his years heavily. There was a sadness that seemed to hang over him.

I looked at him and saw one of the trailblazers who had made it possible for me to model, to be Miss Chicagoland. All the style and grace and aplomb with which he had played baseball were still evident, but there was also a perceptible weariness in his shoulders. I recently read something that Jackie's teammate Pee Wee Reese once said about Jackie, and it made me think of that sadness I had seen in him.

"I don't know anyone who could have stood all the abuse Jackie had to take in breaking into baseball and stuck it out to become the great player he was. When you know the true nature of Jackie . . . what a fighter he was and how he had to keep it inside of him . . . it's just unbelievable."[1]

That evening in Chicago, I went over to Jackie and introduced myself. "Thank you for everything you've done," I said.

"You're welcome," he said simply. There was no false modesty, but also no sign of an overinflated ego. He was just a quiet man, aware of his accomplishments.

---

[1]Pee Wee Reese, as quoted in *1001 Things Everyone Should Know About African American History*, Jeffrey C. Stewart, Main Street Books, New York, 1998, p. 368.

Jesse Owens had a similar air of quiet confidence and gentleness about him. I met him when I was modeling for Kaiser Jeep at an automobile show in Detroit in 1967. Jesse was a spokesman for Chrysler. He had become a national hero when he won four gold medals in track and field at the 1936 Berlin Olympics to the great displeasure of Adolph Hitler and his "master race." In 1950, the Associated Press named him Athlete of the Half-Century. I remember that once following one of the auto shows a group of car dealers had all gathered together with the models at a cocktail party at the Hotel Pontchartrain. In some fruitless effort to demonstrate their manliness, they kept indulging in loud, foul language. Jesse looked over at the models and then said, "Excuse me, gentlemen, I think you should remember that there are ladies present." Then he came over to me and said, "I'm sorry."

For the Black community, Jesse Owens was an indispensable figure in our struggle for pride and equality. To me he was also the perfect gentleman. Despite of the racism in this country, he represented the strength and resolve of America in the face of Nazism. Hitler was so incensed to have his racial theories publicly debunked by the accomplishments of a "Negro" (Jesse Owens alone won as many medals in track and field in the 1936 Games as the athletes of any country combined), Hitler refused to congratulate Jesse on his victories and instead stormed from the stadium.

I always loved Jesse's response when people asked him how he felt when Hitler would not shake his hand. "I'm still here," he would say, "and he is gone." To me, it sounded like a reminder that the determination and dignity of Black people would outlive whatever racism could throw at us.

That was a lesson I also learned from Muhammad Ali, with whom I became friends during this time and who offered me profound inspiration.

Learning from "The Greatest"

I met Muhammad Ali through our mutual lawyer, Chauncey Eskridge. A kind and generous man, Chauncey was the lawyer for many of the prominent African-Americans in Chicago, including Dr. King.

After my picture ran on the cover of *Jet*, I received a call from Chauncey. "Muhammad Ali saw you in the magazine," he said. "He thinks you are beautiful, and he wants to meet you. He's going to call you."

"Cassius Clay wants to meet me?" I replied in amazement.

"Yeah," Chauncey said, "but whatever you do, don't call him Cassius Clay. He abhors that name."

Muhammad had changed his name in 1964 after he had joined the Nation of Islam. First, he wanted to be known as Cassius X, as a sign of rejecting his "slave name." Then he settled on Muhammad Ali. Even two years later, when we met, his name remained controversial. Many Whites refused to use it, and many Blacks were confused by it. For the most part, Elijah Muhammad's Muslims were seen and treated by the White community as a radical fringe group and many Blacks feared any association with them.

I waited expectantly for Muhammad's call. When the phone finally rang, I picked it up and immediately recognized his distinctive voice and cadence on the line as he said, "Hello. Is Janet Floyd there?"

"This is Janet," I said, goose bumps all up and down my arms.

"I bet you don't know who this is, do you?" Muhammad said playfully, in that lilting tone of his. "You probably won't believe me when I tell you."

"You're Cassius Clay," I blurted out, too excited to remember Chancey's admonition.

"If we're going to be friends," Muhammad said, "that's the last time you get to call me by that slave name. Okay?"

"I'm sorry," I said. "I'm sorry. Chauncey said I should call you Muhammad."

"That's right. My name is Muhammad Ali. And you know I'm pretty, don't you."

We both laughed.

"And you're pretty too," he continued. "I saw you in *Jet,* and I'd like to meet you."

"Well, Cassius, that'd be lovely," I said, flattered and impressed that he was such a gentleman.

"I told you now, my name ain't no Cassius," he said in a mock gruff voice.

We both laughed again. It took me a while to get used to calling him Muhammad. But in that first phone conversation, we had set the tone for our relationship. We were like brother and sister, always laughing and teasing.

For all intents and purposes, we could have been siblings. We were the same age, born within a couple of weeks of each other. Our folks came from the same part of the country, down in Kentucky. We often joked that our parents probably dated each other. "You know," we'd say, "all Black folk in Kentucky are kin. We even might be related."

Muhammad and I flirted with each other, but I could never tell when to take him seriously. He would kid me, "You wear them short skirts and makeup. You eat ham. You won't be no good Muslim wife. You won't wear a scarf on your head or sit separate from me in the mosques."

"You got that right," I'd retort, laughing.

"I could never marry you." he said.

"What makes you think I'd want to marry you?" I asked.

Muhammed replied, "Cuz I'm pretty. I'm the greatest."

I found him exciting, fun, and, yes, pretty. But it was an affection and bond that was spiritual rather than physical. He treated me as part of his family. We just enjoyed being around each other.

When he was in town, he would come to my house, and we would talk about race, the war, our dreams, and from where we came. I remember one time he stopped by when I was expecting Dr. King, Dick Gregory, Bernard Lee, and Andy Young for dinner. Dr. King was fond of Southern food, and I liked cooking for him and the men in his inner circle. I had seen how much they enjoyed Mahalia Jackson's soul food, and I tried to emulate her.

On this particular occasion, I was cooking up chitlins, greens, macaroni and cheese, and crackling corn bread. I was in the kitchen cooking and thinking about Mrs. Cox, the home economics teacher at Crispus Attucks High School, who had taught me how to make spoon biscuits. The doorbell rang. I wiped my hands, took off the apron, and went to answer.

When I opened the door, Muhammad was in the hallway. He did not come in, but sniffed the air wafting out of the apartment. Now, you have to know that chitlins have a unique smell.

"You're cooking ol' nasty pork, ain't you?" Muhammad said, making a face and wrinkling his nose.

"Well, yes," I said. "Dr. King, Andy, and the others are coming by. I am just making some soul food for them."

"We don't eat pork," Muhammad said, sounding offended. "I can't come into a house where there's pork. I am leaving."

"Why don't you at least stay to meet Dr. King?" I pleaded.

Muhammad relented, but unfortunately Dr. King was running late that evening. He was often late. Finally, Muhammad left, so I never did have the privilege of having both of them at my house at the same time.

I've often thought how incredible and special it was that both of these giants were in my life. I remember one special occasion when Muhammad invited me to Houston to see his fight with Ernie Terrell. We had met just a few weeks before, and he thought it proper for me to be chaperoned, so he flew me down to Texas with his parents to see the big match. I expected to spend time with him, but managed to see him only once aside from the fight itself.

Terrell had refused to refer to him by his chosen name, and all through the fifteen rounds Muhammad kept yelling, "What's my name? What's my name?" Terrell paid for his disrespect that night in the ring.

The following morning, before we left for the airport, I was having breakfast with Muhammad's parents. His father ordered ham and eggs. Just as he started eating Muhammad whipped into the hotel's restaurant with his large entourage in tow. When he saw what his father was eating, he put on one of his patented displays of discontent. "You know I'm a Muslim. How many times do I have to tell you not to eat that nasty, filthy pig?"

Then in a grand, dramatic gesture he left the restaurant with his bodyguards and hangers-on caught up in his swirl. Howard Bingham, his confidant who remains next to him even today, was right at his side. Muhammad's father, losing not a beat, simply shrugged, smiled, and continued to eat.

Later that morning Muhammad took me to the airport in his chauffeured limousine. As it happened, I saw Dr. King later that day at a meeting in Chicago. And it suddenly occurred to me how awesome it was that I got to spend time with Muhammad Ali and Martin Luther King, Jr., on the same day.

Sadly, the storm clouds were gathering over all of us. Muhammad had requested an exemption from military service on the basis of his religious beliefs. (The Nation of Islam subscribed to a strict philosophy, which had political dimensions as well as its spiritual values. Elijah Muhammad, acting on his beliefs, had been imprisoned in 1942 for his refusal to join the Army.) Muhammad did not want to fight in Vietnam. "I'm a Black man oppressed by a White man who stole land from a red man," he often repeated, as if it were a mantra. "I'm not going to go kill a yellow man for that White man who's oppressing me. That yellow man ain't done nothing to me. He ain't burned no crosses on my lawn. I don't have all my rights here. Hell no, I won't go."

Muhammad's request for an exemption was denied, however, amid an outpouring of public condemnation and ridicule. In March 1967, his A-1 draft classification was upheld, and he faced federal charges if he continued to refuse induction into the military.

On one occasion during this time, I was traveling first class to San Francisco to hear Dr. King deliver a major speech. Muhammad and his driver, Hassan, took me to the airport. Muhammad, who was always the gentleman, walked me to the gate and stayed until I boarded the plane.

During the course of the flight, an airline attendant approached me and said that there was a reporter who was sitting in the coach class section of the aircraft and had something important to discuss with me. Since he was not allowed up front, he asked if I could visit with him for a few minutes in the coach section. I thought it a strange request and my initial reaction was to ignore it. But on reflection, I started to worry that it just might be important.

When I walked back to meet him, I could see that he was a neatly dressed, clean-cut–looking White man. He looked relatively young even though he had salt-and-pepper colored hair. He said that he was a reporter for the Associated Press. I had no reason to question his credentials and didn't ask for any identification. "You said that you had something important to discuss with me, so?"

He pulled a thin, silver Minolta tape recorder from his coat pocket. It was the smallest recorder that I had ever seen. While I knew that tape recorders were the working tools of journalists and reporters, his looked as if it was a piece of spy equipment.

He asked if I might answer a few questions, and proceeded to turn the recorder on without waiting for my consent.

While his manner was pleasant, his questions were too aggressive and more than a little personal.

"I saw you were with Muhammad Ali at the airport gate."

"Yes?"

"I'm doing a profile on Muhammad. What's he like? How did you first meet him? How long have you known him?"

My antennae went up immediately. "If you're doing a profile on Muhammad, and you saw us at the gate, why didn't you approach him? He's always been open to the press. Why are you asking me about him now?"

I was angry at being interrupted by this man and abruptly returned to my seat.

When I met with Dr. King in San Francisco, I described my encounter on the airplane.

"He was no reporter," Dr. King said. "In all probability, he was an FBI agent and he was following you on your trip out here. In fact, you should assume that your phones are all wiretapped. They're trying to dig up anything they can on Muhammad and me."

I was stunned. The notion that the FBI would be recording my conversations and following me was chilling. This was *my* government, using *my* taxes to put *me* under surveillance. If true it was an outrage. But how else would they have known that I was on that flight to meet with Dr. King? It may have been Dr. King's or Muhammad's phones that were being wiretapped rather than mine, but it didn't matter. If they were under surveillance, then I was caught up in J. Edgar Hoover's net of suspicion. Their phones or mine, it was shameful and un-American. But I was damned if I was going to let them intimidate me.

In the meantime, Dr. King began to speak out publicly against the war in Vietnam. He had long struggled with his sense of moral responsibility to call for peace. His advisers feared that an antiwar stand would alienate the Civil Rights Movement from the American mainstream. By early 1967, however, he could no longer remain silent and on February 25 gave a speech in Los Angeles that was entirely focused on Vietnam.

Dr. King articulated his opposition to the war on ethical and political grounds. It was leading, he said, to America's "declining moral status in the world" and eroding the gains made by the domestic programs of the Great Society.

Dr. King met with Muhammad Ali in Louisville, Kentucky, in late March 1967 to express his support for the fighter's stand against the war. He also focused more and more of his personal energy on putting an end to America's involvement in Vietnam. In his now famous "Beyond Vietnam" speech, which he delivered on April 4, 1967, at Riverside Church in New York City, Dr. King eloquently articulated a sentiment strikingly similar to Muhammad's. Harry Belafonte was there as one of the leaders of the antiwar movement.

The war, Dr. King said, was sending poor men to fight and to die in disproportionately high numbers compared to the rich in our society. It was "taking the Black young men who had been crippled by our society and sending them eight thousand miles away to guarantee liberties in Southeast Asia which they had not found in southwest Georgia and East Harlem."[2]

Dr. King went on to say that in counseling "young men about military service, we must clarify to them our nation's role in Vietnam and challenge them with the alternative of conscientious objection . . . Every man of humane convictions must decide on the protest that best suits his convictions, but we must all protest."[3]

The response to Dr. King's speech was immediate and virulent. The press accused him of everything from betraying his cause to treason; they even labeled him a Communist. Even within the movement, reaction was extremely negative. The NAACP board, for instance, issued a public resolution declaring that Dr. King's stand against the war was a "serious tactical mistake."

Courageously, Dr. King continued to speak his heart's counsel. Muhammad Ali, for his part, also stood by his principles. On April 28, 1967, Muhammad refused to be inducted into the Army. New York State, as well as many others, immediately revoked his license to box.

On April 30, in the sermon to his congregation at Ebenezer Baptist Church in Atlanta, Dr. King praised Muhammad for his courage. He explained his own antiwar sentiments and told his parishioners that "the calling to speak is often a vocation of agony." Dr. King went on to say that "it is a dark day in our nation when high level authorities will seek to use every method to silence dissent."[4]

---

[2]Martin Luther King, Jr., "Beyond Vietnam," delivered at Riverside Church, New York, New York, April 4, 1967, *A Call to Conscience: The Landmark Speeches of Dr. Martin Luther King, Jr.,* Clayborne Carson and Kris Shepard, eds., Warner Books, New York, pp. 142–143.

[3]Ibid, pp. 155–156.

[4]*Bearing the Cross: Martin Luther King, Jr. and the Southern Christian Leadership Conference,* David J. Garrow, Quill/William Morrow, New York, 1999, p. 560.

Muhammad Ali did indeed pay a heavy price for his dissent. He was indicted on charges of draft evasion by a federal grand jury on May 8, 1967, and on June 20 was found guilty of violating the Universal Military Training and Service Act by a jury in U.S. District Court in Houston, Texas. He was sentenced to five years in prison and a fine of $10,000. Although he was released on bond pending appeal, Muhammad was stripped of his title and barred from boxing. He was prevented from making a living at what he did best.

I will never forget the next time I saw him. I was taking part in the Bud Billiken Day Parade as Miss Chicagoland. I was sitting in the back of a convertible, in my crown and sash, waving at the people lining the main street on the South Side of Chicago. Suddenly, I saw Muhammad standing alone amid the crowd.

Tears came to my eyes. There was nobody with him. No bodyguards. No entourage. No limousine. He was just an ordinary guy facing life's troubles and standing up to them.

I lost my queenly composure and called out, "Muhammad, what are you doing here? Where's Hassan, your driver? Where is everybody?"

He waved and said, "I'll meet you at the end of the parade, when you get out of the car."

At the end of the parade route, I rushed over to meet him. We got in his car and drove along Lake Shore Drive. The lake and the trees looked so beautiful.

I had seen him drive a car only once before, when he was mobbed by a group of adoring Black kids. I found myself suddenly taken back to that time. We had pulled up to a filling station and, while the car was being serviced, Muhammad spotted a group of Black youths and called over to them, "Hey, come over here, y'all."

They looked over and saw it was "The Champ" and were all over him. Muhammad did the handshake, and mocked them with some punches, like he was sparring with them. They were in awe and sparred back with delight. After a few jabs, he handed each of them five to ten dollars, whatever was on him. He said to them, "You can say you met the heavyweight champion of the world, and he was Black like you. Now go on and make something of yourselves. Get some education."

I remember that night on the drive home, I told him how special that was. He said, "I loved and admired Joe Louis, but I never saw him when I was a little boy. Whenever I saw him in the newspapers, he was always surrounded by White folks. I wanted those kids to see me in their neighborhood, in the flesh."

So on that drive following the parade, I looked out the window and thought how beautiful the lake and the trees were and how ugly and unfair life could be, which jarred me to say, "Muhammad, what have they done to you? It must be awful for you. How do you feel?"

"I'm fine," he said calmly.

I could not believe how cool he was. "But they've stripped you of your title," I said incredulously. "You fought and won in the Golden Gloves and the Olympics and brought the gold home for America. You're the heavyweight champion of the world. This is all you've ever wanted to do. And now they've taken everything."

"No they didn't," Muhammad said forcefully. "They didn't take everything from me. They didn't strip *me* from me. I got me. I got my dignity. As long as I got that, they can't take anything. And let me tell you, these White folks will never take my dignity from me.

"If that poor old White boy Elvis wants to go into the military, he's got something to fight for and die for. He's got something to kill for. We don't. Plus, it ain't right.

"I represented this country in the Olympics, just like Jesse Owens, and they burned a cross on my mother's lawn. I fought for America in the ring; I come home and they're burning a cross down there in Kentucky in front of my folks' house, harassing my parents. I am not going to kill for them. I ain't got no quarrel with the Vietcong."

I started crying. "Muhammad," I said, "but they took your title. That's how you make your living."

"Let me tell you something, Janet," he said. "I've got my dignity, and that's all you ever need to make it in life. I know you want to be somebody. You're always in beauty pageants and sitting on back of floats in parades and stuff, but don't ever want something that only *they* can give you.

"You're a poor Black girl; you want a lot of things you don't have. And there are a lot of things out there in the world to take, but don't want those things more than you love and want yourself. Never want anything that badly, because that's when they can take *you* from you."

I have never forgotten that lesson Muhammad shared with me. It reminded me of what my grandmother had taught me: "Never sell more of yourself than you know you can buy back later."

It was a real inspiration to watch Muhammad hold on to his beliefs and his dignity. He remained true to his principles. He did not fight again until 1970. In 1971, the U.S. Supreme Court overturned his conviction. He did not regain his title as world heavyweight champion, however, until 1974. The rest, of course, is history. He remains an icon today as the greatest boxer of all time. But for me, he's a giant not only for his victories in the ring, but also for his uncommon courage in holding on to his principles in the face of a country and a system that inflicted a terrible wrong.

The Ultimate Sacrifice

The summer of 1967, which came to be known as the Long Hot Summer, saw some of the worst race riots in history in the ghettos of Atlanta, Boston, Buffalo, Milwaukee, Newark, New Haven, and New York. Dr. King, although deeply troubled by the growing violence and the calls for militancy among African-Americans, held true to his commitment to nonviolence.

"I don't believe in the death and killing on any side, no matter who's heading it up—whether it be America or any other country, or whether it be for Black folks. . . ." Dr. King explained to his longtime friend Howard Baugh, "Nonviolence is my stand, and I'll die for that stand."[5]

He worked tirelessly through the summer and the fall to launch the Poor People's Campaign, which was intended to address the racial and economic injustice that he saw as the root causes of the violence. But Dr. King spoke more and more frequently of his own death in private conversations, as he had joked when the glass exploded that night as we were passing through the hotel's revolving door. For him, as he articulated in his final speech on the eve of his murder, the die had been cast: "It is no longer a choice between violence and nonviolence in this world; it's nonviolence or nonexistence."[6]

"Well, I don't know what will happen now," Dr. King concluded

---

[5]Ibid, p. 573.
[6]Martin Luther King Jr., "I've Been to the Mountaintop," delivered at Bishop Charles Mason Temple, Memphis, Tennessee, April 3, 1968, *A Call to Conscience: The Landmark Speeches of Dr. Martin Luther King, Jr.*, Clayborne Carson and Kris Shepard, eds., Warner Books, New York, p. 209.

that evening in Memphis. "We've got some difficult days ahead. But it really doesn't matter with me now, because I've been to the mountaintop. And I don't mind. Like anybody, I would like to live a long life—longevity has its place. But I am not concerned about that now. I just want to do God's will. And He's allowed me to go up to the mountain. And I've looked over, and I've seen the Promised Land. I may not get there with you. But I want you to know tonight, that we, as a people, will get to the Promised Land."[7] It was like he knew what was coming.

I was in New York on April 4, 1968, working for Kaiser Jeep at the New York automobile show held at the Columbus Circle Coliseum. That evening, I went to see the all-Black version of *Hello, Dolly!* with John Chamberlain, a man I had dated on and off in Chicago. The show starred Pearl Bailey and Cab Calloway, who came out of retirement to play Horace Vanderbilt. I had really wanted to see the production because I was a big fan of Cab Calloway's, having met him in my travels with the Ebony Fashion Fair. He was always so lively and engaging—a born entertainer.

But that night, Cab Calloway just did not seem to be himself. From where I sat, I could see into the wings, and every time he came off stage, Cab would go and sit on something that looked like a milk crate and hold his head in his hands. I thought it was really sad that he was getting so old. How in the world could he continue to perform for an audience when he seemed so tired?

At the end of the performance, however, Pearl Bailey came out onstage and, rather than simply taking a bow, talked to the audience for what was an unusually long time. "I could feel your love come over these footlights all during the performance," she said. "I love you back. We love you back, and now more than ever we need love in this country."

This is odd, I thought. *Actors don't come out after a performance and talk about philosophy.* But I had seen Pearl Bailey on *Ed Sullivan* and knew of her reputation for ad-libbing. I figured she was just being Pearl Bailey.

I did not think much more about it. The show had been fun. I felt really up. We were having a good time. On the way back to the hotel, John and I stopped into a Walgreens drugstore to pick up a couple of items I needed. I was walking through the aisles when John came to-

[7]Ibid, pp. 222–223.

ward me with a newspaper in his hand. He looked like he had just seen a ghost.

John gestured for me to come closer. "What is it?" I asked. He could not answer but held out the paper for me to see. DR. KING KILLED, the headline read.

I went numb all over and fell back hard against a display case. Then I just stormed out and ran into the hotel, trying to get up to my room as quickly as I could. I did not want to cry outside in public, and I needed to cry. On my way, I kept thinking, *Please don't let me encounter any White people. I don't want to see a single White face.* Fortunately it was nearly midnight; the streets and the hotel lobby were deserted. The elevator did take a while, and I kept hitting the button as if it was to blame for what had happened.

Once in my room, I shut the door, put the key down, fell to my knees with my head on the bed, and simply lost it. I wailed—wailed harder than I ever have in my entire life. I wailed at God. I wailed at White people. I wailed at the evil and duplicity of this country. I wailed at whoever the shooter was, even though his identity did not matter—I believed the whole nation had pulled the trigger either by its agitation or its silence.

After a while, I could hear John knocking on the door. "Just go away, John," I screamed. "I have to be alone. Just go away."

To his credit, John persisted. He kept knocking until I calmed down a little and let him in. We sat up talking practically through the night. But words could neither contain nor express the grief, anger, and rage that I felt at this loss.

Somehow Dr. King had known all along that he would lay down his life in the cause of our people. At his funeral on April 9, which was nationally televised, a recording was played of his sermon at Ebenezer a month before he was killed. In that sobering oration, Dr. King spoke to an imaginary eulogist and asked to be remembered as a man who tried to "give his life serving others" and attempted to "love and serve humanity."

Dr. King did, in fact, serve a higher purpose. As I listened to the scratchy recording of his familiar voice, I saw him sitting on a throne much like the one he had described for me. He had recognized his destiny and had the courage to live up to it. I bid farewell to him praying that I would have the wisdom and spirit to follow his example and serve my higher purpose.

*   *   *

I had planned to fly to Memphis, Tennessee, follow the large entourage of mourners to Atlanta, Georgia, and pay my final respects
to Dr. King. A call from my mother intervened and altered those
plans.

"Janet, you need to come home," Mother said gravely.

I assumed that she felt it was important during this time of
mourning that I be home with my family and friends in Indianapolis.

"No, Mother. I'm okay. It's important for me to be in Memphis
right now."

"Are you sitting down, Janet?" she asked.

"Yes," I said, with a shadow of apprehension starting to gather in
my thoughts.

We had always promised each other that when we had to convey
bad news to each other, we would caution one to sit down.

"What is it?"

"Little Myrna is dead."

Little Myrna was like a niece to me. She was the daughter of
Paula, a neighbor who had been one of my closest childhood friends.

"What happened?" I couldn't believe that another tragedy had
occurred.

"She was shot," my mother responded.

When Paula was pregnant with Myrna, she had moved in with us.
I shared my small twin bed with her and toward the end of her pregnancy, I could feel her baby kicking me in the back. It was a won-
drous sensation. Now her daughter was dead, shot by a crazed man
who had entered the church where she was singing in the choir and
started shooting wildly. One bullet blew away a large portion of her
head.

I changed travel plans immediately and flew to Indianapolis to
lend my support to Paula and our family. Two people I loved had
been cut down violently in a matter of just three days. It was not the
first time, however, that my family had to contend with violent
death. Years earlier, my cousin Jimmy had been lynched in Georgia.
He was just sixteen at the time. One of the thousands of what singer,
Billie Holiday, called *Strange Fruit,* found swinging from the trees of
the courtly, civilized South.

As I moved through the local funeral director's warehouse, helping to select an appropriate casket for little Myrna, I could hear a
television set playing in the background. Among the tributes praising
Dr. King's life, I could hear poignant songs emanating from a famil-

iar voice. It was the voice of Mahalia Jackson. She had lost "her boy." And the sadness in her voice was profound as the depths of the hole in our hearts and hopes.

Firemen

I was flooded with all these memories in the fall of 2002, as I followed the controversy sparked by critical remarks made by Harry Belafonte about Secretary of State Colin Powell. Harry compared Colin's toeing the line on the Bush administration's policy toward Iraq to the servile acquiescence of a "house slave."

Pressed by Phil Donahue on the October 17, 2002, edition of the host's MSNBC show to explain his position, Harry recounted an exchange he had with Martin Luther King, Jr., shortly before Dr. King was killed:

> The last conversation I ever had with Dr. King, face-to-face before he was murdered, just about a week before he died, he looked quite . . . he was quite sober. And I asked him why he looked like he was troubled. I said, "What's the matter, Martin?"
>
> And he said, "You know, Harry, we fought long and hard for integration. But I'm coming to believe that we're integrating into a burning house."
>
> And I kind of took aback. "What do you mean by that?"
>
> He said, "America's lost its moral soul. It's lost its sense of democracy and purpose. And I think that we're integrating into this condition with a society that is still quite resistant to our being part of the total fabric."
>
> I said, "What do you think we should do in that case?"
>
> He said, "I think we're going to have to become firemen. We're going to have to become firemen."
>
> I said, "But we're just a part of a population."
>
> He said, "Yes, but we're the essential part of the population. We have a close proximity to slavery, to racism, to all of those things. We bring a moral history to the table."[8]

[8]Transcript, *Donahue* for October 17, 2002, MSNBC News, FDCH e-Media (f/k/a/ Federal Document Clearing House, Inc.), 2002, p. 3.

Listening to Harry speak, I remembered the day in New York in the spring of 1967 when I went with Dr. King, Andy Young, and Chauncey Eskridge for a meeting at Harry's apartment on Riverside Drive to discuss the movement's response to the government's action against Muhammad Ali. What had struck me particularly on that day was the love and admiration the two men had for each other. Harry was all fire and passion, and Dr. King was the voice of reason, the strategist. The two of them, though, added up to a single whole— an unquenchable desire to see Black people free of the bonds of oppression.

I was truly conflicted over the controversy. I admired Colin for the very reasons that his critics derided him. He was, they claimed, a "reluctant warrior." First and foremost, he *was* a warrior, which contrasts sharply with some of today's most strident political conservatives. Many either had avoided or evaded the draft, claiming a higher set of priorities than fighting in a war in Vietnam. And for any of them to now express regret that they missed the camaraderie and fraternity that can only come from sharing a foxhole strikes me as shameful hypocrisy.

Colin fought in the very war that Harry, Martin, and Muhammad opposed. But he held on to his convictions with the same strength as they did theirs. He rose through the ranks to become the Chairman of the Joint Chiefs of Staff, a National Security Advisor, and Secretary of State. That he was reluctant to send our young men and women into battle except as a very last resort was not a measure of weakness in my mind, but one of strength and courage.

During the four years that I had the privilege of serving as "First Lady of the Pentagon," I came to love our military with unbounded passion. I see them still as my sons and daughters. I've seen their sacrifice, bravery, and patriotism up close. I want them to defend us against threats that are real. I don't want them to kill or be killed because some ideologues want to use them to carry out agendas that ultimately undermine our national security and values rather than reinforcing them.

I applauded Colin's behind-the-scenes efforts to convince President Bush to seek the support of both Congress and the United Nation's Security Council. By all accounts, he waged a lonely battle against substantial odds and prevailed at least in securing a vote.

I held Harry in equally high esteem. He, too, had worn his nation's uniform. He, too, was a man of conscience and principle. He had lent his support to Muhammad in 1961 when Muhammad refused the court's order that he report for military duty and be prepared to fight in Vietnam. Over the years, he had demonstrated to millions the world over that his was not simply the voice of Caribbean Calypso, but one of profound moral conviction. He had been on the front lines of the battlefield in the war against racism in America and apartheid in South Africa. He had placed his life and livelihood in harm's way. Celebrities—especially Black celebrities—were to be seen and not heard. Just amuse or entertain us. Protest at your peril.

For Harry to speak out in such a frank and unvarnished fashion took great courage. Colin is viewed as an icon in contemporary America. Harry had little to gain in accusing Colin of serving the "plantation master," and much to lose. He was likely to be dismissed and ridiculed as a pacifist and appeaser.

But he never flinched, backtracked, or apologized for his comments. He was there for Muhammad, for Martin, and for Mandela. And he no doubt felt duty-bound to uphold Dr. King's call for those of our race to remain faithful to our duty as firemen and women, and to do no one's bidding in order to secure or maintain access to the corridors of power.

Harry's criticism and Colin's riposte that he was indeed serving a higher goal through quiet but determined diplomacy, may have amounted to little more than a footnote in the turbulent riptide of daily events. But to see two powerful Black personalities speak out on the issue of how to wage war against terrorism, how to promote peace while preserving our security, was a testament to how far America has traveled in the last five decades.

4

Talking to the Stars

After Dr. King was murdered, the country exploded in violence. In the ghettos of Baltimore, Chicago, Denver, Washington, D.C., and one hundred cities across the nation, the grief, anger, and sense of helplessness of our long-suffering people spilled out into the streets. In Chicago alone, twenty West Side blocks were burned and nine people were killed during the "race riots." Tragically, the rage that the Black community vented was primarily self-directed. The inner cities sustained the most devastating damage during those awful days in April 1968. We were so locked in, so "ghettoized," that we could only strike out at the things closest to us—our own neighborhoods.

As I watched the news coverage of the riots, I was surprised to feel myself shrink from the rage that had burned inside me for so long. Dr. King's teaching had become deeply ingrained, and I instinctively understood that the riots were giving the bigots and reactionaries the moral cover they needed to justify repression and violence. Indeed, the Civil Rights Act of 1968, which Lyndon Johnson signed on April 11, 1968, while mandating open housing, included new anti-riot provisions that would later be used to prosecute civil rights and anti-war leaders.

I kept thinking back to what Pearl Bailey had said at the end of the performance of *Hello, Dolly!* on the night Dr. King was killed; love did seem like the thing we all needed most at that time. It was a profoundly personal response to a national loss. For me, Dr. King's death put an end to a kind of innocence. It brought me face-to-face with our inscrutable fate as human beings, as Africans living in America. It reminded me of my mother's early warning: There are people who won't like you because you are colored. If a man like Dr. King could be cut down, then any evil was possible.

I saw that loss of innocence once more in the way many Americans responded to the terrorist attacks of September 11, 2001. "How could this have happened?" Their sense of safety and order was ripped from them. Some became enraged, others depressed, and still others lost faith. Everybody, to one extent or another, lost their bearings for a while and had to examine their life's priorities. Just how, most wondered, could we become the object of so much hate that resulted in this attack?

Black Americans have long been the object of hatred and the victims of terrorism in this country by their fellow countrymen for no reason other than being Black.

Now, for the first time, Americans of every color and race realized that there were people in the world who hated us all, and, collectively, we were likely to face a future filled with terror and fear.

In the spring of 1968, I felt very much adrift in a sea of grief and confusion. I needed a rock to cling to, the safety of someone's arms to soothe me while I mourned the loss of two people I loved: little Myrna and Dr. King, a remarkable friend and teacher. As my rock, I chose Melvin Anthony (Tony) Langhart, a young Chicago police detective I had met just a few months earlier.

Tony Langhart and I met early in 1968 in the Chicago Playboy Club. Right away, I liked him, because he reminded me very much of Jerry Lewis. He was kind and easygoing. But when at the end of the evening he asked me whether he could take me out sometime, I said, "Sorry I don't date White boys."

I assumed that he was White because he has light skin and straight hair. We all have our preconceived notions of who is Black and who is not. I also misheard his name and thought he had said "Rheinhardt." So I thought he was German.

"I'm not White," Tony said, sounding as if he had had to say that often.

"Well, what are you doing with a German last name?" I asked.

"My name is German, but I'm not," he replied.

"Okay," I insisted, "you're still White."

"No, I'm not," Tony said patiently. "Here, I'll show you."

He pulled out his Chicago Police Department identification and showed me where it listed his race as "Negro."

"Oh," I said, surprised and a little embarrassed, "you are Black."

"My family is German and Creole," Tony explained, "from Louisiana."

I laughed and said, "Well, I guess it's okay to date you then."

Tony laughed, too, and I gave him my telephone number. After that, we went out on occasion. He was clearly smitten, but I was not really interested in getting serious. I was twenty-six by this point, practically an old maid in the environment where I grew up. Most girls would get married and have babies at eighteen, nineteen, or twenty. But I had learned my lesson well from my mother, who always said, "Be somebody. Don't sacrifice your life by having children too early."

By 1968, I had focused so much on my career, I thought I was too old and would probably never marry. Frankly, I was enjoying my independence too much to want to share my life with another person. So when Tony proposed to me shortly after we started dating, I refused even to consider it.

"I hardly know you," I said sensibly. "You may be ready for marriage, but I am definitely not."

All that changed when Dr. King was killed. He had always promised me that when I got married he would perform the ceremony. Although I had had my doubts about marriage, I had often fantasized about Dr. King blessing me on my wedding day, the way many girls fantasize about their fathers walking them down the aisle. I had longed for that day, and after he was gone, my heart ached at the thought that it would never come to pass.

Tony was there through this time, loving and protective, and still eager to get married. Suddenly, it seemed like what I wanted to do also. I knew that my reasons were different.

I wanted to make a symbolic gesture, to affirm life, to show the world that we would press on. I was not alone in this. Chauncey Eskridge also got married at this time, as did four other people in our circle.

To me, it felt important to take this step while Dr. King's spirit was still in the world. Tony and I became engaged in late April and were married on May 24, just six weeks after Dr. King died.

We moved into the apartment Tony had acquired for us and set about trying to build a life together. We got a little kitten, whom we named TJ, for Tony and Janet, furnished the place, had friends over to dinner. But try as we might to create some harmony and stability, the world continued to seem to fall apart all around us.

That May, more than two thousand American soldiers died in Vietnam, while the peace talks that had opened in Paris earlier in the month became deadlocked. On June 5, Bobby Kennedy was shot and killed in Los Angeles, after declaring victory in the California Democratic presidential primary. On August 8, Richard Nixon won the nomination for president at the Republican National Convention in Miami Beach, while a few miles away, the Black neighborhoods of Miami erupted in riots, resulting in four deaths and hundreds of arrests. On August 21, Soviet tanks and troops invaded Czechoslovakia to put down the reforms of the "Prague Spring."

Closer to home, on August 22, four days before the opening of the 1968 Democratic National Convention, which was taking place in Chicago, police killed a seventeen-year-old protester. For the next seven days, I watched in horror, along with the rest of the nation, as television cameras recorded increasingly violent clashes between the police, National Guardsmen, and peace demonstrators. Worse still, my husband was out there with orders to "crack heads." Tony, who had only recently become a detective, had been ordered back into uniform and was on the streets with the units enforcing order.

I watched the brutality on television and got angrier and angrier. *What am I doing married to a man who beats up on Democrats and peace protesters?* I thought, even though I knew in my heart that Tony would not abuse his power. It was a way of expressing the truth about our marriage that was difficult to admit: I had married Tony for the wrong reason. I did not really know him, and I did not love him.

Just as these feelings were crystallizing for me, I discovered that Tony had jilted another woman in marrying me. I had heard rumors of this earlier in the summer but had chosen to ignore them. In August, I was ready to know the truth, so when this "other woman" called me, I wanted to meet her.

Ironically, Patricia McCoo was a cousin of my friend, Marilyn McCoo. She was from a well-respected Chicago family and worked for United Airlines as a flight attendant. She was beautiful, with a sweet, gentle manner.

I asked Patricia to come to our apartment, so we could talk in private. From the moment she started speaking, I could tell that she was really in love with Tony. And in her own soft-spoken way, she was fighting for the man she wanted to marry.

As it turned out, Tony and Patricia had had a long relationship—a somewhat stormy one. He had left her at the altar once before to marry another woman. Amazingly, they were planning their wedding again when he stunned her by marrying me.

I thought that was most unbecoming, that it was indicative of Tony's character. Although I probably would not have said it outright at the time, I was looking for a reason to leave him. This story of betrayal gave me that reason. *If he could do that twice to this woman with whom he has had a long history,* I thought, *how can I trust him? We hardly know each other.*

Our divorce became final in December. I remember Chauncey calling me right before my birthday to tell me that the decree had gone through. So all told, Tony and I had met, dated, become engaged, married, and divorced in less than a year. As they say, that is the danger of making life decisions while in mourning. We certainly were not the only ones who did not make it. Of the four couples who got married in our circle at that time, I think only Chauncey's and one other marriage lasted.

Tony and Patricia did end up together, however. I met them a few years later at a convention in Chicago. We had all matured and had a friendly and gracious conversation.

The funny thing was that, although we did not travel in the same circles, people often thought that Patricia and I were sisters. We looked enough alike and both had the unusual name of Langhart. I had decided to keep the name after the divorce. But that is a story in itself.

Tony's mother, Mrs. Langhart, was never particularly warm toward me. I thought she considered me kind of low class because I was a model, and all models were thought to be hussies by some people in those days. Of course, when I was first married, I did not know about Patricia, for whose suffering I am sure Mrs. Langhart blamed me. In any case, she did not seem to have much use for me.

One day shortly after the divorce became final, Mrs. Langhart called me on the telephone. I was surprised to hear her voice, but thought she might be calling to express her regret that Tony and I did not make it. Instead she said, "Janet, you will go back to your maiden name, won't you?"

"Well, I just got divorced," I replied, stunned. "I don't know what name I'm going to keep. Professionally, everything I have been doing the last few months has been under Langhart. You know, the papers and the magazines. And I kind of like the name Langhart. It's prettier than Floyd. But why do you ask?"

"Oh, it's just your being out there, always in the press," she said. "I don't know what your dreams and ambitions are. Tony tells me you want to be on television. I just want you to be mindful that we are a fine family, and Langhart is a fine name. I wouldn't want you to do anything that disgraces our name."

I was taught always to be respectful to my elders, but it was all I could do not to say a few choice words to her. I took a deep breath, composed myself, and in as polite a voice as I could muster said, "Mrs. Langhart, I just want to make a couple of things clear. Number one, I got the name the same way you did: I married a man named Langhart. So it's as much my name as it is yours. And two, I am the one who's in the papers and press. I am the one who's well known. So you make sure nobody in your family does anything to disgrace me."

"Well, I didn't mean any harm," she said backpedaling, "I just wanted to find out if you were going to use the name."

"You know what?" I said, "I think I will."

Making the Most of Opportunity

Although we as a people had to pay a heavy price, by the late 1960s the Civil Rights Movement was succeeding in bringing the issues of equality and justice for African-Americans to the forefront of the nation's conscience. The National Advisory Committee on Civic Disorders, which had been appointed by President Johnson to investigate the root causes of the growing unrest in the inner cities, concluded in its March 1968 report that America was headed toward splitting into a Black and a White society, "separate and unequal." We needed a commission to come to this startling conclusion, I opined to myself.

"White society is deeply implicated in the ghetto," the commission report maintained. "White institutions created it, White institutions maintain it, and White society condones it."

The media were singled out by the commission as especially culpable in maintaining the racial divide. The absence of a Black point of view in the media perpetuated inequality in representation. "The painful process of readjustment that is required of the American news media must begin now," the commission report concluded. "They must make a reality of integration—in both their product and personnel."

By 1969, this bold recommendation had begun to create employment opportunities for Black people. Although the media were still firmly controlled by White men, the need to demonstrate a willingness to integrate Blacks led to some of us landing in front of the camera and the microphone.

Unfortunately, the spirit of opening up broadcasting to give Blacks an opportunity was not genuine. Because we never held expectations that there would be opportunities open to us in television, we had little experience or training. There was no attempt to help us nurture or develop those skills. The attitude of many in the industry was, "See, we were willing to give them the chance, but they just can't hack it." It was just sink or swim. As a result, many did not survive.

Somehow, I knew instinctively that the important thing was to show up. I used to tell my friends, "Hey look, we've got five minutes. Black folks are in for now. In another five minutes, it's going to be the Hispanics or the Native Americans. But we've got the five minutes here, so we better make the best of it."

I got my shot in the summer of 1969. I was hired first as the Phone Gal on WGN, where I announced the winner on a prize show, then as the weather girl for *A Black View of the News,* which was produced and broadcast by Channel 26, a Chicago UHF station. The show turned out to be a springboard for a couple of us. Don Cornelius, who was the sportscaster, went on to develop *Soul Train.*

Now, I didn't know anything about the weather, or television reporting for that matter. I remembered vaudeville star and stripper Gypsy Rose Lee's advice and thought I had better have a gimmick to take advantage of this opportunity. I knew I had to stand out and somehow get noticed. I needed to make the weather my own.

This was July, and hot as blazes. So I decided to do something playful, a sight gag. I borrowed my friend Millicent Proctor's mink coat and on July 4 went on the air wearing fur. I did the national part of the weather with a straight face, as if there were nothing out of the ordinary. Then, as we were breaking to commercial before I came back to do the local weather, I said, "I know you're all wondering why I'm wearing a fur coat on the Fourth of July, when it's ninety degrees. When you come back, I promise to show you what's underneath."

After the commercial break, I did the local weather without reference to my promise, and then finally said, "A promise is a promise." I opened up my coat, and there I was in a bikini.

Well, people started talking about this Black girl on *A Black View of the News* doing the weather in a bikini and a fur coat, and our ratings started to go up. Not everybody approved, of course. I got a call from a older Black lady from the South Side of Chicago, who said, "I watch you every night, honey. You're a nice little girl, and you don't have to go that far to get attention."

She was right in that I should not have had to go that far to have a shot at success. But I knew that it was my gumption that had always helped me advance, and I needed to make a splash in this new medium.

As it happened, my instinct was right. Apparently word of my weather exploits got around, and I was offered more modeling jobs. Then I was "discovered" by WBBM-TV, Channel 2, the network-owned affiliate of CBS in Chicago.

My agent called one day shortly after I had appeared in a print ad in the newspaper and said, "CBS just saw you in the paper, and they want you to come over and audition. They are trying to integrate their on-air look."

"Audition for what?" I said, excited and surprised.

"They said the weather."

"Oh," I said, "I don't know the first thing about the weather. I pretty much make it up over at Channel 26. I guess they must have seen me in the mink."

"Well, they didn't say anything about that, but they sure liked you in the newspapers. So go on in and do the audition."

I went over to WBBM and interviewed with Mr. Leon Drew, the general manager. We hit it off well, even though he seemed tired out.

"I've interviewed about three hundred and fifty girls this week," he told me as I was getting ready to leave. "You're the last one. I'm tired. You get the job."

He had chosen me to do the weekend weather. I was grateful and elated. This was a real break.

Mr. Drew would always joke that the only reason I got the job was because I was the last one he saw that day. I always laughed, figuring it was his way of making sure my head didn't get too big.

He was a wonderful man, always kind and supportive. I still remember his birthday, September 8, and think of him and the opportunity he gave me every year on that date.

When I met with Mr. Drew and the programming manager, they were very clear: "We don't want any gimmicks. No bikinis. No mink coats."

I knew better than to say, "I don't know what I'm doing. I haven't the foggiest idea about the weather." I figured I would wing it until I learned what I needed to know. And learn I did. Everyone at WBBM was so nice to me. They gave me every opportunity to succeed. I was really flattered to have received congratulatory notes from Frank Stanton and Mr. William S. Paley, the head of CBS, and from a variety of other people within the community.

The one, however, that pleased me the most was from the League of Black Women Voters. They actually sent me a copy of the note addressed to CBS management, which read, *Thank you for hiring Janet Langhart. Our organization has a membership of 1,000 Black women and, as you surely know, each member represents ten times that amount in viewership. We want you to know that we support our sister and will support CBS as long as she's there.*

These were women I didn't even know. But they supported me as an act of unity. I felt that support and unity throughout my time in Chicago.

Once I got comfortable in my own job, I realized that what you needed to succeed was personality and common sense. I had enough of both, and I had ambition, drive, and daring to keep looking for opportunities and to take advantage of those opportunities to move up the line. I would pitch in, sit in, and try new things.

I built a reputation as a go-getter, which led to my next break. At the time, Lee Phillip, who is married to the man who owns and writes for the soap opera *The Bold and the Beautiful,* was doing an interview show in Chicago. In early 1971, when Lee was off on vacation, I was asked to sit in for her.

"I'll give it a try," I said, thinking that I really didn't know how to interview anyone. This was something I wasn't sure I could fake.

"Just ask questions that you're interested in," the show runners said. And that is what I did.

My first interview was with Woody Allen. *Bananas,* his second movie, had come out in April 1971, and we had a grand time looking at clips and laughing at the lovelorn antics of his Fielding Mellish.

Later that year, I interviewed Topol, the Israeli actor, who had won international acclaim as Tevye in *Fiddler on the Roof.* The Norman Jewison film had been released in November 1971, and Topol was nominated for an Academy Award for best actor.

I loved the play and the movie. There was something about its melancholy humor and wisdom that resonated with me on the deepest level. There was one scene in particular that has stayed with me throughout my life. Tevye does not want his daughter to marry a non-Jew.

"But Papa, I love him," she says. "He loves me."

And Tevye replies, "A fish may love a bird, but where do they make their home?"

That line penetrated my soul. *Where is home for me?* I thought. It was the foreshadowing of a very different journey that I would take later in life.

In 1971, however, I decided to take the giant step of signing a lease on my own apartment. Up until then, I had rented rooms in boardinghouses or had the second floor of a duplex owned by a Black family. But that always felt like being back home with Mother. They would want you in by a certain time; you could not turn up the volume on the radio or the TV; you could not have too many people over. I decided I wanted to have a home of my own and moved to a high-rise on Lake Michigan, on Outer Drive East.

It was an integrated apartment building. I had a magnificent view of the lake and the North Side. And I had the best time decorating the apartment—everything was new, modern, and in shades of creme and white. I just loved the way it looked.

It was a big risk. I was able to pay the rent with just my runway modeling earnings, but modeling was not a sure thing. Neither was television. I had a three-year contract with WBBM; yet, I was painfully aware that it was no guarantee of employment. I was thirty years old, and I was used to living very frugally. I had always sent money to my mother, often as much as half my paycheck. The added responsibility of high rent seemed like a big burden to take on, but I wanted to push myself and to give myself more incentive to work harder.

It was a phenomenal time. I just threw myself into my work. I could not wait to get up in the morning and do all the things I loved to do. I was modeling, I did the weather on WBBM, and I continued to sit in for Lee Phillip.

It was on her show in 1972 that I met both Sidney Poitier and Harry Belafonte again. This time in an interview about their movie, *Buck and the Preacher,* a sort of Black version of *Butch Cassidy and the Sundance Kid.* Sidney directed the picture in which he starred with Harry.

I was scheduled to interview them on St. Patrick's Day. Chicago, like Boston, is a very Irish city. Everybody is Irish in Chicago on St. Patrick's Day. In keeping with tradition, we gave green carnations to all our guests, and there was a kind of festive air in the studio.

I remember how the atmosphere changed when Sidney and Harry strode in. They looked like giants. They were both in their forties but had the presence of young studs. They were tall, handsome and lean, and they were bigger than life. I wondered if Harry would remember our first meeting when Dr. King took me and Andy Young with him to Harry's house to discuss Muhammad's refusal to be drafted. If he did, he did not acknowledge the occasion.

I offered each of them a green carnation, but both refused.

"We're not Irish," they said indignantly.

"Well, it's St. Patrick's Day," I countered. "Most of the people here are not Irish. Some of us are Polish. Some of us are Black. But on St. Patrick's Day, everyone claims to be Irish, it's the custom."

I recognized the defiant rage behind their refusal. At the time, however, I didn't identify with it. For even in my all-Black elementary and high school days, we all wore green on St. Patrick's Day. It was all about leprechauns and shamrocks, not about real people who might be racist and represent police brutality. Yet, ironically, a couple of years later, I refused to wear the green myself on Boston television. At the time, because of court-ordered busing, the Irish in South Boston were stoning Black children on their way to school. So there was to be no "Erin Go Bragh" for me on that St. Patrick's Day.

But the hateful days in Boston would have to wait. Shortly after my interview experience with Harry and Sidney on the *Lee Phillip Show* on CBS, I was offered another challenge. Again, it seemed destiny was unfolding. I got an opportunity to do a public affairs show in my hometown of Indianapolis.

Queen of Route 65

Early in 1972, there was a big conference of the regional CBS affiliates in Chicago. Station managers from across the Midwest came to meet with the O&O—owned-and-operated—WBBM-TV, Channel 2. Among them was Dave Smith, the program manager of WISH-TV, Channel 8, in Indianapolis.

Dave saw me doing the Lee Phillip interview show and was apparently impressed. "What does this girl do when she's not sitting in for Lee Phillip?" he asked Mr. Drew.

"Well, she's our weather girl on the weekends," Mr. Drew told him.

Somehow, Dave got my home telephone number and called there rather than getting in touch with my agent.

He introduced himself and said, "Would you be interested in doing a show in Indianapolis?"

Well, a guy with a name like Dave Smith calling me at home to offer me a show in Indianapolis seemed awfully suspicious. I thought he was somebody either pulling a prank or trying to pick me up.

"You're putting me on," I said. "You know that's my hometown, don't you?"

"No," Dave said, sounding pretty convincing. "I didn't know that was your hometown, and I'm not putting you on. I saw you do Lee's show, and I thought you were great. They told me down at WBBM that you did modeling during the week but were only committed to them on weekends, so I thought maybe you might like to do a weekday show here in Indy."

"Oh, you're kidding," I exclaimed. "I would love it. My family could see me on TV, because obviously they can't see me here in Chicago. I'd love to do it. What kind of show is it?"

Dave explained that the name of the show was *Indy Today*. It was designed as a public service show, with a real community focus. As I learned later, many stations were developing stronger community outreach programs to satisfy the Federal Communications Commission (FCC) requirements for public access in order to hang on to their licenses. *Indy Today* would spotlight local politicians, celebrities, and community leaders. It seemed like the perfect vehicle for me.

I made a tentative agreement with WISH-TV, provided I could get an okay from WBBM. I asked Mr. Drew if they had any objections to my taking the Indy show, and he said, "That's great, just as long as you do the ten o'clock weekend news." This was not a problem, but a blessing, made easier since both stations were affiliated with CBS.

That became my life for the next year. I would do the Sunday weather, which took seven minutes, than jump in a cab that I would have waiting, and be on the Greyhound bus to Indianapolis by 11:00 P.M., arriving in Indianapolis by 3:00 A.M. Within a matter of weeks, I knew all the bus drivers by name. They dubbed me the Queen of Route 65, the interstate highway that connects Chicago and Indianapolis.

I had rented a furnished apartment in the building just up the street from the station on North Meridian Street. (My mother and Jane Pauley lived in the same building.) I would be in bed by about three in the morning and then be up by six or seven and be in the studio, ready to go live, at nine from Monday through Friday. After Friday's show, I would take my time getting back to Chicago, so I could be there fresh for the Saturday and Sunday newscasts.

Indy Today was live, from nine to nine-thirty, five days a week. At the time, I think, it was the only live programming on in Indianapolis. We did not have much of a budget. It was just me and my producer, Marti MacPherson. She was a bright woman from someplace in rural Indiana. The two of us just hit it off. We brought two different points of view to the issues that we covered, but we also agreed on our approach. She was very aggressive, very driven, and so was I. We were a great team, really quite a little force.

The show was a perfect fit for my energy, my personality, and my directness. I would always want to take another point of view, to approach a subject from a different angle. And I was willing to take risks and ruffle some feathers.

I did an interview with Richard Lugar, who was then mayor of Indianapolis and is now a senator who chairs the Foreign Relations Committee. I was looking for trouble, and I found it. I had done some research into the Indiana constitution and discovered that it still had many anti-miscegenation laws that prohibited interracial marriage on the books. So, I came loaded for bear.

I kept pressing Mayor Lugar to explain why a state that was not even part of the Confederacy still had so many racist articles in its constitution. He was so polite, gentle, and sweet. But I was out to make a point. Honestly, I still feel a little badly about jumping all over him. As I have learned over the years, Dick Lugar is one of the most progressive people in politics. I later learned that he and his wife, Charlene, as a statement of support for integration, sent their kids to the same all-Black school that I had attended—Crispus Attucks.

I wanted to ask pointed questions. At the time, it seemed as if it were my responsibility. It is also a natural inclination. I am blessed to be reasonably intelligent, curious, and interested in other people. But I was also outraged by the oppression we had had to suffer. The pain and the rage of my childhood and youth were my constant companions, and they shaped much of my outlook. I saw American culture as hypocritical and full of contradictions, a culture of racism. I felt that it was incumbent on me, given the platform I had, to challenge that racism wherever I saw it.

Most of the people I interviewed were White. From my perspective as a Black woman, it seemed essential to challenge them on questions of race. I remember being told more than once that the subjects under discussion had nothing to do with race. Many times that was true, but my race seemed to matter at almost every encounter I had with Whites. I thought turnaround was fair play. It seemed that the larger society felt that they could always bring up race whenever they felt it was convenient for them to do so. And if I questioned that right, then I had an attitude, a chip on my shoulder.

More often than not, however, my questions opened the way to interesting, honest conversation. I remember interviewing Don Nelson, a White basketball player, who went on to be a coach in the NBA. Basketball has always been a major sport in Indianapolis; we are all Hoosiers, after all. We talked about the game, and I asked him what it was like to play with Black teammates. I thought he might be unnerved by the questions, but it was I who was surprised. He was very cool—not at all apologetic or condescending—just very straightforward.

We also did softer stories. For instance, I interviewed Jane Pauley on Halloween, deliberately, as to celebrate her birthday. I was always impressed that Jane, as young as she was then, was so poised, so way ahead of her years in terms of her carriage and understanding of issues. She and I mostly talked about her reporting activities and her having worked on a political campaign. Jane has always been a real lady, just a really special person. It was later that we were to compete to succeed Barbara Walters at *The Today Show*. (Jane won and NBC offered me the weather girl job, which I refused out of defiance. I thought it was a consolation prize.)

I remember at the time Mr. John H. Johnson advised me to take the job, saying, "One has to stoop to conquer," and gave me examples of how he's done that throughout his very successful career.

However, in looking back through all the Black weathercasters, none have succeeded in being full-time host for the morning shows.

The combination of the focus on local issues and celebrities, the uniqueness of having a Black host, and the daring questions I asked—the kinds of questions that were rarely raised on TV in those days, especially in places like Indianapolis, which was the headquarters for the KKK during my youth, added up to major success in the ratings. In our first few months, we beat out well-established competition for the CASPER Award, which the city of Indianapolis gave to broadcasters for outstanding community service.

That year, shuttling between Indianapolis and Chicago, was probably one of the happiest times of my life. Sometimes the more you work, the better you do; and the better you do, the better you feel about yourself. I did not have any distractions. No beaus or hobbies. It was all about my career and my success.

I was doing well financially, making more than $30,000 a year between all the TV and modeling work. In the early 1970s that was a lot of money. I could continue to help support my mother and still live better than I had ever lived.

Plus, I got to be a television celebrity in the hometown where just a few years earlier I had been told by a local modeling school that as a colored girl, I wouldn't have any need for the social amenities, and certainly not any preparation for appearing on television. It felt great to have the opportunity to prove the bigots wrong. Most importantly, though, it was an opportunity to make my mother proud. It was very gratifying to have her see what I did on television. It helped that when your child is a celebrity, the celebrity kind of rubs off on you. Mother became a little bit more important in her bridge and bid whist club, and that helped her appreciate my success.

Boston Bound

My mother was not the only one who was watching what I was up to in Indianapolis. Our ratings were so good, word was that the competition said, "We want her off the air." Apparently, however, the Indianapolis stations had an agreement not to take talent from one another. To switch stations, you would have to agree to stay off the air for a certain period of time. Obviously, if they offered to hire me away from *Indy Today*, that would not have been an attractive option. The best thing was to get me out of town. And that is how I found myself auditioning for a job in Boston in 1972.

The ABC affiliate in Boston, Channel 5, had undergone a very traumatic change in ownership. In a notorious case, WHDH-TV lost its license because of inappropriate contact—or collusion—between the president of the *Herald-Traveler* newspaper, which owned the station, and an FCC commissioner. The story was widely publicized in Sterling "Red" Quinlan's 1974 book *The Hundred Million Dollar Lunch*. The new owners, Boston Broadcasters Inc. (BBI), renamed the station WCVB-TV and relaunched it on March 19, 1972.

In its bid for the license, BBI had promised to deliver, among a host of other community benefits, live local programming and an integrated on-air presence. *Good Morning* was one of the flagship shows that would satisfy not only the promise of live programming but also that of racial integration. It was to the producers of that show that the Indianapolis ABC affiliate sent my tape.

As you can imagine, I was delighted to get the call from Boston, the "Athens of America;" the "Cradle of Liberty."

"We saw your tape," the man said, "and we'd like to bring you out to audition for us."

"Thank you," I said. "Could you tell me how you happened to get my tape?"

"Well, our affiliate in Indianapolis sent it to us."

"Oh," I said, amused, "what a nice compliment." Then we made arrangements for the audition.

I flew to Boston and auditioned with John Willis, the man I would cohost the show with for the next four and a half years. I did very well. I was primed from my success in Indianapolis and in Chicago. I was not afraid of anything. The producers liked me right away. It was the first time I heard myself described as having chutzpah, and I have loved that word ever since. The job was mine. All I had to do was get out of my contract with WISH-TV.

I went back to Indianapolis and talked with Dave Smith. "This is an opportunity for me," I said. "Would you please let me out of my contract?"

"If you find somebody to replace you," he agreed, reluctantly but graciously, "I'll let you out of your contract."

I immediately thought of my childhood girlfriend, April Brown Searcy. She is a beautiful woman and very bright. She worked for Indiana Bell as a sales representative, so I thought she would have good communication skills, at least, even if she had never done television.

"I don't want to give up the security I have with Indiana Bell," she said. "I don't know the first thing about television. If I try this and they fire me, I will have lost all the security I have built up with Indiana Bell. I am going to stay where I am."

It was hard to argue with that logic. You had to have the desire to take the risk. Too many of us were failing in jobs for which we were not prepared. And I cared for April too much to see that happen to her. It had to be something for which you had a passion.

My next choice was Alpha Blackburn, a very prominent Black socialite in Indianapolis, who was married to Walter Blackburn, the award-winning architect. I knew she was bright, attractive, and very gregarious and would like the opportunity to try her hand at television. She was indeed delighted when I approached her about doing the show, and I was free to pursue the opportunity in Boston.

Nothing is that simple, of course. There was one more responsibility to which I had to attend. *Good Morning* was slated to launch on September 24, 1973. That happened to fall two days before the Presbyterian–St. Luke's Fashion Show, a big charity event given by Marshall Field's in Chicago. I had continued to model for them and had a special place in my heart for the store, since they had given me the chance to be the first Black woman to model a wedding dress. At the time I didn't think it was so much of a breakthrough for me as it was for the store. They had entered the human race by recognizing that I was already there. Still, I very much wanted to be there for the charity show, which was a major annual social event in Chicago.

I said to the producers in Boston, "Look, I am going to be there for the launch of the show. But I've worked for these people for years. I made history with them. This is their big show. They're counting on my being there. I'd like to go back."

I had to fight for it, but finally they let me take a day off to fly to Chicago. So I started the new show in Boston on September 24 and then appeared in the Marshall Field's charity show on September 26. I have a gold bangle that was engraved commemorating the event. It is one of the few pieces of jewelry I have held on to over the years. I cherish it because it is a part of my history and the love I have of

Chicago and from a time when my television career was really taking off in Boston.

I remember walking out onto the runway at that last Marshall Field's show in a beautiful Pauline Trigere dress, looking out at the audience, and feeling very much like the queen Dr. King said I was. I felt triumphant. In spite of all the prejudice, all the obstacles, I had prevailed. I was on my way.

The triumph, as with all triumphs, was somewhat fleeting. As I settled in Boston and began to make a name for myself there, I started to encounter new challenges and new opportunities to grow.

5

Good Morning, Boston!

As I looked at the skyline of Chicago from the window of the plane taking me to Boston that day late in September 1973, I cried like a baby leaving her mother's arms. The city had nurtured me over the seven years I had spent there. It had helped to shape my character and had given me opportunities to grow and succeed. I had made a life there, and I wished that I could hang on to that life while pursuing my professional ambitions. I also knew, of course, that this was another lesson about the kinds of compromises we all have to make on our journey.

At thirty-one, I had unshakable confidence in the plan I had laid out for my life. I was building my career, my name recognition, my platform. With enough visibility, I would have the freedom and the power to take on racism and injustice head-on. I was working my way toward a spot on national television, and I knew that the job in Boston was a major step in that direction. It was also a part of a long, personal quest to prove to my mother that her sacrifices had not been made in vain, and to my father, that I had made it in spite of his absence.

I could hardly have imagined how profoundly the move to Boston would affect my life. My professional success created exciting new opportunities and led me to confront intense new challenges. In its own way, Boston became a crucible for growth, as Chicago and Indianapolis had been. *Good Morning,* the show that I cohosted with John Willis, was in many ways a pioneering concept. It was one of the first live morning shows in the country, combining hard-hitting interviews, lively banter, entertainment, and useful information.

John and I were an odd team. He was about twenty years my senior, rather unassuming, but very bright. He was really well versed in politics and history and was a serious, thoughtful interviewer. I, on the other hand, was young, gregarious, and daring. I was not afraid to say anything on the air and liked to surprise the audience. In an interview with the *Boston Globe* in 1989, on the occasion of the show's fifteenth anniversary, Terry Knopf, who had been one of our associate producers, said, "John was a middle-aged, gray conservative. Janet was a Black free spirit."[1] Somehow, though, we added up to a wonderful mix. It was like salt and pepper; we just made each other better. As the years passed, I came to appreciate him more and more, especially his frankness in admonishing me to be less talkative. "Janet, you don't have to say everything today. Remember, there's always tomorrow." Good advice that I rarely accepted!

The early seventies were a time of great unrest and change for this country. The war in Vietnam dragged on. The struggle for civil rights continued around such issues as school desegregation and court-ordered busing. The women's movement was gaining public attention. And of course, Watergate dominated the news. Our first year on the air was the last year of the terrible drama that played out in Washington and eventually led to Nixon's resignation on August 9, 1974.

It seemed as if the very foundation of American society was collapsing. People were angry, fearful, and confused. They wanted information, reassurance, and entertainment. The format of our show allowed us to provide the *Good Morning* audience with all three.

We did the show live every weekday morning for an hour and a half, from nine to ten-thirty. It was then rebroadcast around 2:00 A.M. the next morning (the station was on around the clock, so a lot of programming was rebroadcast to fill the time). Practically from the moment we launched, the show consistently generated news and the highest ratings in the Boston market for the time slot. We were enormously popular and reached a very large audience, which increased dramatically when we went out over the regional New England

---

[1]"Channel 5 Marks an Eon of Good Days," Bruce McCabe, *The Boston Globe,* January 27, 1989, p. 39.

network and then eventually into syndication. At the height of our popularity, seventy-five stations around the country carried the show. Tony Schwartz of the *New York Times* declared that WCVB-TV, an affiliate of ABC network, was the best local station in the nation. It was reported that I was the first Black woman in America to do a nationally syndicated talk show.

Good Morning became such a lucrative property and ABC began to take notice and to study the program. ABC's national morning show in those days was *A.M. America,* which was not doing terribly well. By 1975, ABC had decided that our format would help revive *A.M. America.* In fact, the network went a step further and adopted our name, launching *Good Morning America* with David Hartman and Nancy Dussault. Joan Lunden soon followed. We were politely informed that we would have to change the title of our show to *Good Day* as not to confuse the Boston audience. When I think back, it would've made more sense to keep our name, *Good Morning,* and just add *Boston.*

"I almost had a fistfight with ABC president Fred Silverman," Bob Bennett, the general manager of WCVB-TV at the time and one of the directors of our parent company, Boston Broadcasters Inc., recalled in 1989.[2] He had good reason. Not only did the network take our concept and our name, they also considered hiring me away from Boston. That was where WCVB-TV drew the line. We were so successful in generating revenue for the three-year-old station, Bob, who carried some weight with the network, flatly said, "You are not taking my talent." I was flattered by this loyalty, but also felt like he had squashed my chance to go national. There was an echo of working on a plantation, of being owned, that lingered with me.

For the most part, however, I thoroughly enjoyed my time on *Good Day.* It was professionally and personally satisfying. I was quickly becoming a celebrity in Boston, and I was making a very good living. One of the most awesome things about my first year on the show, in fact, was that I was earning enough to be able to make it possible for my mother to retire.

I was so grateful to her for everything she had given me. My success was also hers, in part, and I wanted to share it with her. I had felt so sorry when she had to move to a smaller apartment at

[2]Ibid

Lockefield Gardens, the government housing project, because I had left home. The very first thing I did with my earnings was to purchase a home for her. It was such a wonderful feeling. Now, I wanted to help her enjoy the kind of life she could not have when she was younger. The image of her being passed around from relative to relative and ultimately sent to an orphanage was always in my mind.

I called her up on the telephone and said, "You know, Mom, you have always worked so hard, why don't you just stop now? Just retire."

"And what will I live on, Janet?" she asked. "I am only fifty. I can't get a pension."

"I meant that I will help you," I rushed to explain. "I can afford it. And if there comes a time when I can't, your pension will have kicked in. So just retire."

Mother agreed, and I felt so blessed that I could do this for her. In those days, there were not that many African-Americans of my socioeconomic background who were successful enough to buy their mother a home or help her retire. The few who did make it were mostly men in professional sports. So for a Black woman of thirty-two to be able to afford this was a real sign of success. It amazes me to this day to think how far I had gotten in those first ten years of my career. Looking back, my country and I both were "overcoming" and coming of age together.

I also discovered during this time the depth of my faith. When I was growing up, Mother always taught me that if you waste not, you want not. While she managed to give us everything we needed and a lot of what we wanted, she was a scrimper and a saver. She also instilled in me a belief in the abundance of the universe. I was convinced that it was endless and infinitely bountiful. I knew that if I worked hard and stayed strong, it would always provide.

To celebrate Mom's retirement, I gave her a fiftieth birthday party at the newly built Stouffer Hotel on North Meridian Street in Indianapolis. Even though there was a beef boycott going on at the time, I went all out and had a surf-and-turf main course of filet mignon and lobster tails. I also invited some of her bosses and colleagues, along with our family and friends.

We had decided to make the announcement about Mother's retirement a surprise. We had cocktails and dinner. Then, over dessert, Mom stood and after greeting her guests and thanking them for coming said, "I have good news. I am pleased to say that thanks to my daughter, Janet, I'm retiring."

"Oh, Louise," several people said, "you've got too much energy. You're too young. You're going to go back to work."

"No, I won't," Mother said, and she never did.

Mother was finally able to do what she could never do while my brother and I were young. She had always wanted to stay home with us, be a homemaker. Now she was able to stay home and be with my brother's kids. She could do things with them that she had missed out on with us, like taking them to ballet lessons and to karate class and attending their school plays.

All my life, I had watched my mother struggle to provide for her family. She had worked as many jobs as she could hold just to give us the things we needed. And now she was taking tremendous pleasure in simply being home, cooking, cleaning her own home, and being a doting grandmother.

I was happy to be a part of Mother realizing her dream of staying home. Knowing that she was finally enjoying life, I was motivated to continue to work hard even on those days when I was not feeling well. "I'm getting up for Mother today," I'd remind myself and slip out of the bed to face the day.

That was what I knew of women and our place in society. In the Black community, women had long worked alongside the men, or alone, to take care of the families. From that perspective, it was difficult for me to relate to what the feminist movement was talking about—it seemed to be contradictory to the very struggle that we had as Black women.

I found it ironic that many White women wanted to leave the kitchen and the children to go out into the work world, Black women, like my mother, wanted to stop working for a change, to leave other people's homes and children. They wanted to stay home and raise their own children, take care of their own houses, have all the things that seemed to be stifling other women. It seemed as if we each wanted what was a burden to the other. For me, therefore, it was hard to engage in the feminist struggle, because the racial struggle was so overwhelming. While sexism certainly existed among Blacks, it was just that I never had that experience because in my household, the man was absent.

I had not encountered any situations where I was told that I could not do something because I am a woman, while I was often prevented from doing things because I am Black. In the first year of *Good Morning*, however, I began to experience a kind of prejudice that made me think differently about the relationship between racial and gender inequality.

As we settled into our production routine, I found myself more and more frequently doing the soft pieces, the fluff. It seemed as if the producers decided, "Oh, Janet, she's cute. She's gregarious. She'll say anything. Put her in the kitchen with the local chef. Put her in the playroom with the kids. Have her chat with the entertainers who came on."

The substantive interviews were always assigned to John. Of course, I had done serious interviews on my own show in Indianapolis. I knew I could do them. It was just a matter of doing my homework, coming up with some questions, having the producer suggest some questions. It was not rocket science. Besides, I only had seven minutes to fill.

Every time I found myself stuck in the studio kitchen while John interviewed another Watergate personality, I wondered whether this was gender stereotyping at play or racism. *Are they saying, "She's a woman, so keep her in the kitchen?"* I would think. *Or is it, "She's Black, so she can't be that smart. Better give her the easy stuff."*

I wanted to be a woman of substance, not just a cutie pie wearing pretty dresses and whipping up biscuits while my serious white male cohost interviewed E. Howard Hunt or Ted Kennedy. I aspired to be like Barbara Walters, who was on *Today* at that time and was an icon for women in television.

I started listening a little more attentively to the leaders of the women's movement, such as Betty Friedan, Gloria Steinem, Germaine Greer, Flo Kennedy, and Angela Davis, who were talking about the glass ceiling, equal pay for equal work and civil rights. I also began to feel a little embarrassed for contributing to and perpetuating the stereotypes. I was not in the kitchen by choice, but I started to come under criticism from both the women's movement and the Black community.

"Why don't you stand up for yourself?" the women were saying. "You're embarrassing us, cooking biscuits."

"Who are you supposed to be, Aunt Jemima?" the Black people would say. "Get out of the kitchen. Prove that Black folks can think."

In a way, it was a wonderful struggle. It made me realize that I had the opportunity to change things for people of my gender and my race. They were beating me up, blaming me for something I had little control over, but they were also saying, "Stand up for us. You can make a difference."

There's nothing that matters more in television than ratings and audience response. So this criticism I was getting helped invigorate my arguments with the producers.

"We've got to do something, here," I would say. "You know, the women are upset with me because I am in the kitchen all the time. The Black people are thinking you've got me cast as Aunt Jemima. I want to do interviews. The hard stuff. I have the ability to do them as well as the entertainment pieces. The versatility can only enhance our ratings."

Over time, I did convince the producers that I could do substantive interviews. Andrew Young, my old friend from Chicago, was a great help to me in winning the opportunity to prove myself.

I had met Andy just about the same time that I met Dr. King and Jesse Jackson at Mahalia Jackson's home in Chicago. Jesse was physically strong and rhetorically gifted. It was clear to all that Jesse was not lacking in ambition and that he would be a forceful voice for the disenfranchised in the years to come.

Next to Dr. King, however, it was Andy whom I admired most. He was soft spoken and unassuming, but was as strong and reliable as steel. I had always had a special fondness for Andy. To tell the truth, I had a bit of a crush on him. Dr. King always teased me about it. Of course, Andy was happily married to a beautiful woman named Jean. So I was content to be friends with him.

After Dr. King was assassinated, our group scattered. Andy was the only one with whom I stayed in touch regularly. He had turned to politics in 1970, running unsuccessfully for a House seat. He ran again and won in 1972. Even though he was very busy, we spoke on the telephone frequently, catching up and sharing stories about Dr. King.

On one of these calls, I asked Andy for help with my predicament on the show. "Andy, I want to get out of the kitchen," I confided. "What do I do? I want to do these Watergate interviews. Can you help me? What's going on down in Washington?"

"Read *The Washington Post*," he said. "It's the best source I know."

"We don't get *The Washington Post*," I said. "All we get is *The Globe* and *The Herald*."

"Well, find a way to get it, because that's where all the stories are."

He hesitated and then added, "Look, there's a young guy from Maine that I work with in the House named Bill Cohen. He's on the Judiciary Committee. He's bright and independent. He's a New Englander, so he's got to be passing your way. Find a way to talk to him. That would really do you a lot of good."

"Oh, he has done the show," I said, remembering a recent production meeting. "I was off that day, I think."

"His district is up there, so I am sure he'll be through again," Andy said. "He's a good friend of mine. Tell him you are a friend, and he can tell you what's going on with Watergate."

A few weeks after that conversation, I came out of our control room and was walking down the corridor toward the studio. We were still operating on a frugal budget and did not have a green room; the guests waited in the hallway, on chairs that looked like they had come from a public health clinic.

I noticed a handsome man in a gray suit standing at the coat rack, digging in his pocket. As I got closer, I saw that he had taken out a handkerchief and was blowing his nose, which looked red and irritated from a cold. He tucked his handkerchief away and turned to look at me over his shoulder. I remember that moment so clearly, his fixing me with the bluest eyes I had ever seen.

At the time, I did not realize who he was and walked on by, nodding hello. A few minutes later, in the studio, I was delighted to learn that the blue-eyed man with a cold was Bill Cohen. He spoke with John about his work on the Judiciary Committee and the difficult choices he and his fellow Republicans were facing in deliberating over the Watergate evidence.

After the broadcast, I went up to Bill and said, "I really wanted to say hello. Andy Young told me that you come up frequently, and I just wanted to say hi."

"I am pleased to meet you," Bill said, smiling a little mysteriously. He had a unique manner. He was not shy or aloof, just different, somehow separate. "Tom Railsback has been talking about you. He's a big fan."

Congressman Railsback of Illinois, who was one of the key Republicans on the House Judiciary Committee, had been on our show a couple of months earlier. I had coaxed him into the kitchen with me to make some soup. We had had a great time laughing and flirting on the air. So I guess he had been telling his colleagues about this Black girl up there in Boston.

I was glad to have met Bill, thinking that now that we had connected, in time, I would be able to call on him to ask for help in pitching Watergate interviews to my producers. However, I was not at all expecting to receive a call from him three or four days later.

The Distinguished Gentleman from Maine

Frankly, I was a little panicked to find a message on my desk saying that Congressman Cohen had called. *Oh, God,* I thought, *what did I do wrong? Why is he calling me?*

To me, a congressman was a figure of legal authority. And where I come from, the only time you got a call from anybody in authority was to reprimand you for doing something wrong. It was like seeing a policeman in our neighborhood. It always meant trouble. Unfortunately the old saying holds true even today: When White people see the police, they feel protected. When Black people see the police, we feel patrolled.

I also remembered the reverence with which my mother regarded her congressmen when I was growing up. She would write to Congressman Andrew Jacobs, who represented our district for many years, collect his replies and place them in a scrapbook. So to me a congressman calling was a very big deal.

"What do I say to him?" I asked my associate producer.

"He's calling you, remember?" she said. "You are just returning his call."

"But what is he calling me for?" I fretted, but finally pulled myself together and telephoned Bill.

"I was up in Bangor the other day and caught your show. I thought you did a great job with Elia Kazan," he said. "It was an excellent interview."

Kazan was a controversial figure. A brilliant theater and film director, he had incurred the condemnation of his colleagues for naming names during the McCarthy hearings into "un-American" activities in Hollywood. It was a truly dark and sinister period in our history. In 1974, Kazan had published *The Understudy*, his first novel, and came on our show to promote it. The book stirred more than intellectual curiosity.

Professor Irwin Corey, a comedian who appeared on the *Jackie Gleason* and *Ed Sullivan* shows was also a regular guest on *Good Day*. Dressed in his "uniform" of tuxedo tails and sneakers, Corey would portray himself as a bumbling genius, with wild hair that resembled an Afro that had just emerged from a wind tunnel. He was a master of zany malapropisms, a perfect caricature of a professor whose brain waves were floating on the wrong frequency. His routine, however, was just that. Behind the clown's mask was a diamond-hard mind—and memory.

When Corey discovered that Kazan was to appear on the show that morning, he burst into the studio, shouting that he would not be on the show with "that man."

Our producer tried to assure Corey that he would not be on the set with Kazan and that they would not meet. He finally calmed down, but his wrath spilled over into the interview he had with John Willis. He was off rhythm, his timing disjointed, his humor flat.

I had received the assignment to interview Kazan. I read enough of the book to get a sense of its major themes, the leitmotif. I do not know if Kazan was surprised that I had gotten the point of the story, or whether other people who had interviewed him had simply not read the book, but all through the interview he kept saying, "Janet, you really got it. You understand what I was saying in the story."

We had a wonderful interview. He was really impressed, and, I think, a little grateful that I focused on the book and did not dredge up any of the past.

Bill Cohen was also impressed. He knew the history and had read the book. And he wanted to talk to me about the McCarthy era that had left its mark on everyone of our generation. He recognized my intelligence and wanted to have an intellectual discussion with me. I could not have been more flattered.

We chatted for ten or fifteen minutes, and I felt so at ease, I told Bill about the difficulties I was having in getting the substantive interviews. Chuck Colson, E. Howard Hunt, Martha Mitchell, John Dean and his wife, Maureen, everybody who had a connection to Watergate was coming to do our show. Some had books in the works, and I was really eager to do some of the interviews.

Bill was very nice about it. He told me that obviously he could not give me any inside information, but that he would be happy to help me understand all the intricacies of what was happening and to sharpen my pitches.

The next time we spoke, I was the one who initiated the call. There was an interview with E. Howard Hunt coming up, and I turned to Bill for help in getting an angle that would get me the assignment. He talked to me at length, always very careful to site public sources, like the *Washington Post* or the *New York Times,* for the information he was sharing with me. When I went into the production meeting the following day, I clearly impressed the producers with my understanding of the issues. I still did not get that interview with E. Howard Hunt, but I did begin to win more respect at the station and with time did get the more substantive assignments.

I stayed in touch with Bill, talking about politics, Vietnam, busing—all the issues that were preoccupying Americans in those days. It was wonderful to be taken seriously by someone as bright and accomplished as he was. I had always had to fight hard not to be treated as a showpiece. I really appreciated a man who was willing to be a friend and to relate to me as an equal.

Several months after I first met him, Bill called me and told me that he would be in Boston the following week and would like to invite me to lunch. I gladly agreed, and we met at the Copley Plaza Hotel restaurant across from Trinity Church. I sat across the table from him, looking into his calm blue eyes and felt that connection I had sensed the first time I saw him in our studio.

There was clearly an attraction, but not so much a romantic one as that of kindred spirits who had found each other. He was married, with a couple of young kids. I was enjoying my single life and popularity on the social scene in Boston. We were happy to just be friends.

At that first lunch, Bill gave me a book of poetry. It was a nice little slim book, one that he had read years earlier in college.

"You might find this interesting," he said. It was one of the Beat poets, Lawrence Ferlinghetti, as I recall, *A Coney Island of the Mind.* Bill thought I would identify with Ferlinghetti's rebellious spirit.

To be honest, I have never been much for poetry. A gift is a gift, though. I read through the book, and I am a little embarrassed to admit it, I thought, *I don't get it. This must be White-boy stuff. I don't get this at all.* Of course, I did not tell Bill this. The last thing I wanted was to seem unintellectual to him.

My admiration for Bill grew even more after the House Judiciary Committee voted for the articles of impeachment against Nixon in July 1974. The stage had been set for that vote when Bill, alone among Republicans on the committee, had voted to demand that the White House turn over its tapes. In July, he was among the six of the committee's eleven Republicans who voted for the articles of impeachment. It was particularly courageous for a first-term congressman from Appalachia's northernmost state to take a stand against the president of his own party.

I called Bill to tell him how impressed I was by his strength and his moral courage. During that conversation he talked to me about his upbringing, the circumstances that forced him to search for an independent path. His father was Jewish, and his mother an Irish Protestant. He was raised in the Jewish faith, in accordance with his father's wishes. However, when it was time to have his bar mitzvah, the rabbi told him that he would not be considered Jewish unless his mother converted, or he went through a conversion ritual that involved drawing blood from his penis.

After consulting with the family, Bill broke with Judaism. However, he still faced anti-Semitism because of his Jewish last name. While pitching at a school baseball game, for instance, he had a parent throw beer cans at him from the stands, yelling, "Send the Jew boy home." Things got so bad at one time, his father encouraged him to change his name. Characteristically, Bill refused.

"I knew that I would always be half of each," Bill told me, "and whole of neither. I knew that I would need to find my own way."

I could really relate to that experience. Even though I am Black, because I am light-skinned, I have always had to deal with the color coding that is so prevalent in our society. I am clearly not White, but more often than not, both Blacks and Whites judge me to be not Black enough.

"Oh, Bill," I said, "that rings so true to me. Living between two worlds."

I told him how, during the early 1950s while visiting my aunt Bertha in Kentucky, I caught more problems from Blacks when I sat in the back of the bus, which was the law.

The Black kids taunted me, saying, "You can't sit back here with us."

"Why?" I asked, "I can't sit up front with the Whites."

"Sit halfway, half-breed," I distinctly remember hearing on more than one occasion.

So, I *did* sit halfway, and *felt* halfway, between two worlds, two Americas. Just as Bill discovered at a young age, I knew that I would need to find my own way as well.

Ironically, it was the Jewish community in Boston that reached out to me and embraced me. The women of Hadassah were just wonderful to me. They made me feel welcome, wanted, and appreciated, even naming me Hadassah Woman of the Year. At a time when I again had to confront hate and racism, they offered me shelter and a sense of belonging, while the Black community remained indifferent, unlike the Black community in Chicago.

My friendship with Bill Cohen also continued to be a source of encouragement and inspiration. When I waded into the racial tensions in Boston and things got very difficult for me, I thought of his courage and determination to walk his chosen path. And I prayed for the strength to continue on mine.

The Good People of Boston

When I first moved to Boston, I had the same preconceived notions about the city as most people who've never lived there. Especially as a Black woman coming from a segregated childhood in Indianapolis, I believed Boston to be the cradle of liberty—the home of the Abolitionists, John Kennedy, Harvard, and M.I.T., the intellectual center of America. I had no idea about the hatred and resentment that roiled under the façade of the city's New England civility.

All that changed in 1974, when mandatory school busing began as a result of a court order issued on June 21, by U.S. District Court Judge W. Arthur Garrity, Jr. Suddenly, that fall children from South Boston, the city's working-class Irish Catholic neighborhood, were taken across town to Roxbury, the Black community and vice versa. What followed was an outpouring of fear, prejudice, and violence. White housewives carrying pocketbooks and rosaries held prayer marches, which sometimes resulted in confrontations with the police. They lay down in the streets to block the buses from passing. More disturbingly, the protesters often resorted to throwing bricks through the windows of the buses carrying Black children. I found it particularly disheartening to see the protesters with their rosaries, standing in front of the cardinal's residence. It was the first time I realized the truth of the slogan: "It's not the bus, it's us."

At first, I simply could not believe that racism was still so virulent in this country, especially in a supposedly liberal place like Boston. This was a northern city, but really just up south. I would look at the pictures on television and flash back to the night at Mahalia Jackson's when we watched Dr. King get stoned at Gage Park. *Was it all for nothing?* I would think bitterly.

But I refused to believe that this was so. These were God-fearing people. They would listen to their pastors. They would see the light. I also felt that I was in a position to make a difference. I had my platform. I had people who were looking to me to be a leader. This was my moment.

I decided to be strategic, to put Dr. King's lessons into action. My plan was simple: I would get to the Cardinal and convince him to speak out against the violence and hatred. To do that, I intended to enlist the help of Father Joe Scannell. Father Joe was a priest at the Roxbury Missionary Basilica with whom I had struck up a friendly correspondence.

Father Joe had first written to me after I had interviewed Maureen Dean, John Dean's wife, about her book *'Mo': A Woman's View of Watergate.* I was very excited to get an interview on anything and was perhaps a little overzealous in my questioning. Father Joe wrote to me and said, "That interview was very good. You might have been a little bit heavy-handed. Mrs. Dean really did not have anything to do with Watergate. She was no match for you. You musn't step on a marshmallow."

I wrote him back to thank him, and after that he often wrote to give me encouragement. So when I decided to reach Cardinal Medeiros, I immediately thought of Father Joe. I called him up and made an appointment to see him the following Sunday, which happened to be Easter. I went straight from the services at my church over to Roxbury Missionary Basilica, still dressed in my Easter best.

The basilica was empty, so I had a clear view of Father Joe as he came down the side aisle, blessing himself as he passed the sacraments. He did not look at all like what I had expected. He came toward me and said, "You're Janet."

"And you must be Father Scannell," I said. "Thank you so much for seeing me."

"Just call me Father Joe," he said and invited me to sit down with him in one of the pews.

"Father Joe," I launched in after some small talk, "I am so troubled by all this violence. I need somebody to help me meet the Cardinal, to ask him to speak up against it. Why is the church silent? This is so painful."

Father Joe sat quietly, even after I had finished talking. He was a man of about sixty, with a sweet, forlorn face and an Irish twinkle in his eyes. He seemed as pained by what I had been saying as I felt. And somehow, without actually saying it, he communicated to me that he could not help me—that the church would not help me. I grasped that there were forces at play that I did not understand. I had watched so many movies about the kindness and generosity of priests and nuns. Ironically, as a young girl, I used to give up my seat on buses to nuns wearing their habits. Had Hollywood portrayed a false image? Had it all been a deception? Or had I simply expected too much from mankind? I left mystified and deflated.

I asked one of my best friends and mentor, Tony Staffieri, who is Catholic, to explain to me why God's representative on earth, who is empowered to tell his followers about their immortal souls, cannot talk to them about the sins of bigotry and violence.

"Look, Janet," he said, "Cardinal Medeiros has his own problems."

"What do you mean?" I asked, confused.

"Well, Father Joe can't tell you this. But I can. Here in this country, the Catholics think only the Irish can be cardinals and popes. Especially in Boston.

"Cardinal Medeiros is Portuguese," my friend continued. "So as far as the Irish Catholics are concerned, he is just a cut above being Black himself. Race is one thing this cardinal is not going to talk about."

Then it all made sense. That was why they were talking about Boston's response to court-ordered busing all the way to the Vatican but not in Boston. Of course, as with the recent child-abuse scandals, the Vatican did not say enough then either.

"Oh my God," I exclaimed before I could catch myself. "Do you White people ever stop dividing yourselves according to pigmentation or how straight your hair is? Or on the basis of what religion you practice? Does this ever end? I thought it was only Black people who indulge in the absurd practice of color coding."

In my world, you were either Black or White. I never understood the way Whites separated themselves from one another by ethnicity, religion, or politics. All I knew was that no matter how different they considered themselves, as soon as one of us showed up, everybody got to be White and that was it. I used to joke during the troubles in Northern Ireland, that the way to solve the problem was to redirect the poor Haitian boat people to Northern Ireland. The Catholics, the Protestants, and the British would all become friends in a hurry, because we Blacks always seem to have a way of uniting White people.

I felt as if I were all alone in the wilderness. It seemed that it was up to me to try to appeal to the conscience of people who were blinded by fear and hate. I remembered Dr. King's belief that by being nonviolent, we would make White people ashamed of themselves. That is precisely what I set out to do.

I went on the air and said, "I have to talk about something that is really important to me. Things are getting so bad with this conflict over busing, I am afraid to live in Boston because I am Black. My mother is asking me to come home to Indianapolis, because she knows I speak my mind against injustice and she is concerned for my safety. But whatever the risk, I cannot remain silent any longer.

"Look, on the one hand you say we're lazy and uneducated and aren't capable of being educated. But when we try to send our children to school, you stone them. I don't understand it. You are supposed to be progressive people here. How can you do this? None of you have the courage to speak out. You ought to be ashamed."

As you can imagine, that little speech lit up the switchboard. They logged more than three hundred and fifty calls from people who expressed a very similar sentiment: "Tell that nigger to go back where she came from. If she doesn't like the way we do things in Boston, the door swings both ways."

My producer, Bruce Marson, came flying up to me after the show. "What did you say?" he demanded. "I have never seen the phones go wild like that."

"What do you mean?" I asked. "I didn't do anything out of the ordinary. You know I always speak my mind about things."

"We got three hundred and fifty calls from very irate people. We've got some threatening to march on the station."

"Well, what are they marching here for?" I asked defiantly. "We don't have any Black children here for them to stone."

"Just calm down, okay?" Bruce said. "We've got to figure out how to smooth this over."

At that moment, Bob Bennett, the general manager, who was a real fan of mine, called me into his office.

"What are you doing?" Bob asked.

"This isn't right," I said. "Somebody needs to stand up to these bigots. The Cardinal won't stand up. The Black leaders don't really stand up. I've got a responsibility here. People listen to me."

"They listen," Bob said, "but they don't think of you as Black, Janet. They don't want you talking that Black stuff."

"What do you mean 'Black stuff'? What do you mean they don't think of me as Black?" I asked, incredulous. "It's television. Can't they see I am Black?"

"Well, they just think of you as their Janet," Bob countered.

"Do they think of me as White?" I pressed.

"They don't think of you as a color at all."

"In a Black and White world, if they don't think of me as Black and they don't think of me as White, they must not think about me at all. That means I'm invisible, and I'm not invisible.

"You know it's wrong," I continued, not letting him get in a word. "We talk about all the other current events—Watergate, the feminist movement, the Vietnam War. The busing issue is happening in our backyard. They're talking about this in Rome. Why can't we talk about it here?"

It was painful to admit, but despite all the opportunities I had gotten and the success I had achieved, I still held bitterness in my heart. I had not yet grasped what Dr. King had begun to address in the last year of his life—that it was the economic and social injustice that isolated and oppressed the poor people of this country, both Black and White. I did not see that the battle over busing was as much about class as it was about race. The poor Whites of South Boston felt that their necks were put under the heel and boot of the upper classes, the liberals who occupied the legal profession and the judiciary, whose children were tucked safely away in posh suburbia. My rage blinded me from seeing their sense of helplessness.

I kept thinking that the only "no" White people ever see is "no parking," "no smoking," "no loitering." "no spitting." We see 'no' everywhere we go, and yet we prevail. You take the poorest White person, dress him up, lose the accent, change the name, give him a chance, and he will blend right in and go right to the head of the class and the country club. We can never assimilate, and despite that, many of us Blacks still manage to make it.

I didn't understand why generations of White people remained poor. They don't have the restrictions we've had to face. What keeps them from being successful? At that moment, I simply was drained of sympathy for the poor Whites of South Boston.

I could only see the rocks they were throwing at our children—at me. For if they are stoning the children because they are Black, the only difference between the children and me is that they were there and I was not.

In my frustration and rage, I was still allowing myself to be blinded by the word *all*. I grew up in a society that divided people into Black and White, and I was having difficulty moving beyond that narrow and restricted view of the world.

Fortunately, yet another teacher appeared to lead me to the next level of understanding and enlightenment. Melnea Cass was in her early eighties when I met her in 1975, and over the next three years she became my mentor and one of the enduring loves of my life.

I had heard legendary stories about Mrs. Cass. She was a Black woman who had lived in Boston since the early part of the twentieth century. Through her extensive civic engagement, she became a force in the city, equally respected by White and Black leaders. Always the voice of reason, she was known as the First Lady of Roxbury, a predominately Black section of Boston, and was very close to then Mayor Kevin White and to a man who remains one of my heroes and dearest friends to this day, Senator Edward Brooke, the first Black United States Senator since Reconstruction. During her lifetime, Mrs. Cass had a street, a swimming pool, and a community center named after her. In fact, while traveling through Roxbury later in life, I remember feeling so blessed as I turned a corner, and there I was, on streets named after two of my greatest mentors: Mrs. Cass and Martin Luther King Jr.

Mrs. Cass came on our show shortly after my outburst about busing, to talk about the issue. I knew right away that there was something magical about her. I got the sense that she knew exactly who I was. Throughout the show, I felt as if she were talking to me alone, showing me how to handle the difficult issue with which we were dealing.

Father Joe wrote me after the interview and said, "I saw your interview with Melnea. It was like watching a bright student learning at the feet of a great teacher."

I was so moved by meeting her, I wanted to spend more time with Mrs. Cass. I was searching for somebody to help me, to give me the tools, information, and support I needed to speak truth to power. All I was doing was speaking out of rage, and the rage was getting in the way of the truth. I saw that Mrs. Cass could teach me how to become an effective leader, how to persuade mountains to move rather than trying to blast them out of the way.

I called Mrs. Cass and asked her if she would give me some time. "Mrs. Cass," I said, "may I take you out to lunch or to tea? Can I come by and see you?"

She was very gracious. "I was hoping you might call," she said. "I think we have a lot to talk about."

We went to lunch and spent more than three and a half hours talking. She told me about growing up in the Carolinas. I told her about Indianapolis and Chicago. Slowly, we worked our way around to what was happening with busing and what the solution may be. We discussed my role, how I could use my voice and visibility to create change. And we talked about how I had tried to make use of what Dr. King had taught me.

Mrs. Cass looked at me straight on and said, "You didn't learn his lesson. You're doing it with violence—with violent words. You're doing it with rage. You'll have to do it with reason. You have to move from rage to reason."

"How do I do that?" I asked, a little stung by the rebuke. "Look at what these people are doing, and nobody's stopping them. The police aren't doing anything."

"They're Irish Catholic too," she said. "The police are no doubt related to many of the protesters and live in the same neighborhood. If they start disciplining them the way you expect them to, it might be hard for them to go home."

"Well," I said, "Father Joe wouldn't help."

"I know Joe," Mrs. Cass said. "He's powerless to do anything. He's reaching out to you and offering you comfort. Accept that as his gift.

"I watch you every day," Mrs. Cass continued.

"You do?" I asked, terribly flattered.

"Yes," she said, smiling. "And I see in you a lot of myself when I was a young girl. I didn't have the audience you have. I had to do it in a different way.

"Along the way I learned that you catch a lot more flies with honey than you do with vinegar. When you speak up, you have to remember a couple of things. One, that it's not your television station, so you can't just say anything you feel like. More importantly, if you want to get people to hear you, don't speak to the White people of Boston. Don't speak to the Black people of Boston. Tell them you're speaking to the good people of Boston. They'll know who they are. And they'll hear you.

"You have a gift of making people forget that you're Black or that they're bigots. Through the sheer force of your personality, you make them connect to you on a human, personal level. You might not like cooking up biscuits and making jam, but that's why they think of you as 'their Janet.' The moment you go out and start telling people that they're bigots, they can't hear you anymore. They retreat into their racism, and all they see is your color. So you've got to try another way. Talk to the good people." It was déjà vu of an earlier mentor's lesson: You can't win with violence and rage.

"Oh, Mrs. Cass, that makes so much sense," I exclaimed, feeling the tightness in my stomach loosen. "How do I do that?"

"I will help you," she said.

From that point forward, we really bonded. It was a soul connection. We understood each other on a level beyond words. And she poured her wisdom, knowledge, and love into me. Mrs. Cass taught me from her own experience. We had become close and had regular evening telephone conversations. During those chats, she told me what it was like for her to be a young Black woman in her time and what it took for her to get to the place where she was so respected and revered by so many people in the city. As I spent time with her, I realized that everybody looked up to Mrs. Cass, Black and White. When she walked into a room, it would hush. The men would stand. It was powerful. Especially since she did not demand it; her presence was commanding enough.

I observed and said to myself, "This is who I want to be. I will be like Mrs. Cass."

Her abiding lesson was about speaking to the souls of people, to their righteousness. In order to do that, I had to move through my anger and learn how to connect with the goodness in people. It was something I fervently wanted to do, but I did not yet realize how deeply the rage was rooted in my being.

Sick with Anger

Around this time, I began to experience serious health problems. I started breaking out in hives and then developed acne. Hair started growing on my face. I felt agitated all the time and was more aggressive. My family doctor sent me to a wonderful endocrinologist at Massachusetts General Hospital, Dr. Janet MacArthur, who diagnosed me with Stein-Leventhal Syndrome, a hormonal imbalance that results from insufficient production of estrogen and overproduction of testosterone.

"This is stress," Dr. MacArthur said. "You're internalizing all your conflicts. That's what's wrong with you. Ultimately, I think you're going to need surgery, because you have just ruined your insides."

"That's impossible," I said. "How can I have done that?"

I have had asthma all my life. So I expected that if I did get sick from the stress, I would feel it in my lungs, where it always went when I was a kid. But it was a different battle that was playing out in my body.

"Illness is a funny thing," Dr. MacArthur said. "There's a whole other level of consciousness that's at play here. Some people take it in their solar plexus, some get migraines. Some people literally lose their sense of reason. You are absorbing it in your gut. And it's going to destroy you."

As I went from one doctor to another and underwent test after test, I kept thinking about what Dr. MacArthur had said. I knew that at some level I was struggling with—rebelling against—the lessons I was trying to learn about moving through the rage.

My mentors were telling me: "Be quiet, be passive. You can be more effective using love rather than violence or expressing rage." At first I thought they were suggesting I turn the other cheek, a philosophy that always ran against my grain. Slowly I understood they were saying to try a more effective way, try reasoning.

"We will defeat racism with kindness. We will persuade White people," Dr. King and Mrs. Cass taught me. "We will speak to the better angels of their nature and make them see the wrongs of their ways."

I understood intellectually that this was the strategic way, the moral way. But I did not want to love the bigots; I wanted to hit them over the head so they would stop. I could not reconcile using the weapons of love to fight something like racism and oppression. I wanted to kill it, and the people I respected most were trying to teach me how to love it away.

What I did not understand was that my teachers were trying to show me how to let go of the rage in order to accomplish my goals. I knew that I could not win through confrontation, but the best I could do was to swallow the anger. And it was, literally, destroying me inside.

It has struck me many times over the years how ironic it is that the illness expressed itself through my reproductive organs. The universe taught me directly that nothing good is born of rage—it is a barren emotion that devours itself.

As my condition worsened and I felt more desperate, I turned to an old friend, Ken Edelin, a doctor I had once dated, for help. Ken was a gynecologist/obstetrician who tested the Roe vs. Wade decision in Boston by challenging the viability of a fetus traditional test of fetal viability at a certain stage of development. He admired me for tackling the busing controversy and the Catholic church's position.

"You're a gynecologist," I said to Ken. "Can't you help me?"

"No, we're too close," he said, "But if you were my wife, there would be only one man I would recommend you go to, Bob Kistner. He was my teacher at Harvard, and he is the best gynecologist in Boston. He wrote the textbook on gynecology and infertility. He is a codeveloper of the Pill. He's a good man and a great doctor. I used to love watching him operate in the amphitheater."

"Oh, I know Dr. Kistner," I said. "He's done our show a couple of times."

I had seen him on the show and remembered his talking about *The Pill,* his book about oral contraceptives. It came out in 1969 at the same time as *The Godfather,* and Dr. Kistner joked that Mario Puzo stole his thunder. He seemed like a very nice man and obviously very knowledgeable.

"Okay," I said to Ken. "So you'll call him?"

Ken called and got me an appointment for the following week. Dr. Kistner could not have been nicer when I went in to see him. He was of the old school, a gentleman physician, but he was not stuffy or pompous.

"My late wife used to watch you on television religiously," he told me as he showed me into his consultation room. "I'd come home from the hospital, and she would tell me who you had on the show and what you talked about. She was such a big fan. She admired your forthrightness."

"I am sorry to hear that she passed away," I said, and then we turned to the reason for my visit.

After he examined me, Dr. Kistner told me that he recommended surgery as the best treatment for my condition.

"Unfortunately, I will have to remove your uterus and one of your ovaries," he told me. "That means you'll never have children."

This was in the summer of 1977. I was just thirty-five. And although I was not even married, it seemed like an awfully big decision to give up the possibility of becoming a mother. Motherhood was such an essential part of being a woman where I came from. It was hard to contemplate giving up even the option of having kids.

"I never wanted children," I told Dr. Kistner, "but I do want to think about this one. I'd just like to have a night to sleep on it."

It was a difficult night. This feeling of looming extinction came over me. *There won't be anything of me to leave behind,* I thought. It had never occurred to me before. I had always done everything I could to avoid becoming pregnant, and now I was faced with making this permanent choice.

However, I did not want to keep living with all the discomfort that I was experiencing. I called Dr. Kistner and said, "I want to feel well again. Do what you have to do."

"I know it is a difficult decision," he said kindly, "but I think it is the right one. You'll feel a lot happier once you don't have the symptoms to deal with anymore."

I had my surgery the day Elvis died, August 16, 1977. I remember coming out of the anesthesia and hearing the news report on the radio. For a while I was not sure if I had dreamed it. I asked a nurse, and she told me sadly that it was true.

The following day, I was still very uncomfortable and groggy from the painkillers. When I woke in the morning, the nurses crowded into my room. They all knew me from television and wanted to chat.

"Dr. Kistner was here three times waiting for you to wake up," the duty nurse told me. "He never does that. Usually, he does his rounds really early, while the women are still asleep, so he doesn't have to answer too many questions."

"Really?" I said, surprised. "Next time, tell him to wake me. Or you all wake me, so I can talk to him. I have a couple of questions."

The very next day, I woke up to find a single lavender rose in a silver bud vase on the table at the foot of the bed. I had never seen a lavender rose before, and it smelled wonderful. It looked so elegant next to the big gift-shop arrangements that are so typical for hospital rooms.

The nurses were in a state of excitement. "Dr. Kistner is in love with you."

"What?" I said. "I've never even see him."

"He comes in every morning—hoping to talk to you. Today, he brought the rose for you. He grows these sterling-silver roses in his garden."

I did finally see Dr. Kistner and thanked him for the flowers. He was very gracious and told me about the different kinds of roses he grew. We also talked about my going home. Dr. Kistner told me that he would discharge me over the weekend.

I was beginning to feel better, so I told my mother, who had come to Boston to be with me but was not very happy about being away from her grandkids, to go back home. I figured I would just take a taxi home from the hospital.

When Dr. Kistner arrived to discharge me on Sunday, he asked who was taking me home.

"I am going by myself," I said in my best independent tone.

"You can't leave the hospital by yourself," he said. "I'll take you home."

He helped me out to his yellow convertible Thunderbird. It was a beautiful summer day. As we set out, Dr. Kistner said, "You know what, why don't you come out to my house? It's a nice drive out to Milton. I'll fix you lunch and show you the garden."

I had gotten the sense that he was a little bit smitten with me, but I was surprised that he was being so open with his feelings. It is unusual enough for a surgeon to bring flowers to a patient. To take her home from the hospital and make her lunch is an outright dramatic gesture.

After a homey lunch, which he made, Dr. Kistner took me all through this huge mansion of a house and the large garden.

"Dr. Kistner," I protested, "I just had surgery."

"Well, you need the exercise," he said dryly and kept going.

Later, he told me that he had wanted me to see the house so that I could see what I could have. He was in love with me, and he wanted to give me everything.

A Promise Kept

Bob courted me in the sweetest, most romantic way. I was cautious, however. Every patient falls in love with her doctor, I figured. Besides, I had just gone through a major life change. I had had the experience of getting married in the midst of emotional turmoil, and I was not going to make the same mistake again. After a couple of months of dating, I told Bob that I wanted some space.

Away from him, though, I realized that I had also fallen in love. I missed Bob and wanted to be with him. I was not going to stand on ceremony, even though it was my rule never to call a man for a date. I was going to a black-tie affair, and I telephoned Bob and asked him if he would be my escort.

He agreed, and we began dating again. We had been seeing each other for about a year when we decided to get married. Although Bob was nearly twenty-five years older than I, I was sure I was making the right decision. He was a kind, dedicated man. I knew that he would be a good husband to me.

I was in Atlantic City to judge the Miss America contest when I called my mother and told her of my plans. I asked her what she thought. Without hesitating, she said, "If you don't marry him, I will." Even Mrs. Cass approved.

It was a bittersweet time. Mrs. Cass had taken ill, and in April 1978, Bob diagnosed her with pancreatic cancer. She had months to live, but she was determined to arrange our wedding. As she became frailer, Mrs. Cass did all the planning from her sickbed. She arranged for the violinist and the preacher. She ordered the imprinted napkins and matchbooks. She selected the catering menu. She purchased the wedding cake.

We were married on November 18, 1978. It was a wonderful ceremony. Bob had wanted to hold the wedding in his favorite place, Acapulco, Mexico. He thought it more romantic than Boston. I told Mrs. Cass of our plans. She was happy and congratulated us, and said she was sorry that she would not be able to go because of her health. Right then and there, I decided that we would get married at the foot of her bed. The location did not matter; it was more important to me that she be there to witness this moment.

"I don't want you getting out of bed," I told her. "We can do it right here in your bedroom."

I had asked her daughter, Marianne, to put a nice bedspread on Mrs. Cass's bed, so she would feel festive. Of course, Mrs. Cass would have none of it. When I arrived on the day of the wedding, she was sitting up in her chair by the window, all dressed up.

"I am not witnessing your wedding from that bed," Mrs. Cass declared, and that was that.

She sat up through the whole ceremony. We staged it so that we were facing her. The preacher stood to the side and conducted the ceremony. We had Bob's son, Stephen, who was his best man; my best man and best girl; Mrs. Cass's daughter; Mrs. Cass's great-grandson who was the ring bearer; and her great-granddaughter who was the flower girl; a violinist; and a photographer. That was all.

The ceremony was brief. I hugged Bob and went over to kiss Mrs. Cass. I was so grateful to her for her friendship and everything she had done for me. I was even more touched by her courage and determination. Mrs. Cass honored me by summoning all her will to get up; putting on her clothes and her favorite antique earrings; twisting her long, silky, black hair mixed with gray into her trademark bun; and proudly sitting through the ceremony. By sitting there, she stood up for me. I felt so loved. She was there to witness me in this rite of passage, the way I had imagined Dr. King witnessing me.

A week or so after the wedding, I sat by Mrs. Cass's bedside and showed her the pictures. When we were all finished, she looked at me contentedly and said, "Well, I got that done."

Mrs. Cass died on December 16, 1978, and all of Boston—including Mayor Kevin White, Senators Ted Kennedy and Ed Brooke, Speaker of the House Tip O'Neill, the governor and past governors of Massachusetts, and even residents of South Boston—turned out at her funeral to pay their respects and to say good-bye.

I mourned her passing yet felt blessed to have known her and to have had her touch my life.

6

All You Have to Do Is Ask

As I was writing this book, I shared the story of meeting and falling in love with Bob Kistner with a new friend, a young Black man. He looked at me quizzically and said, "You know, people are going to want to know about that."

"What are you saying?" I asked, although I had a pretty good idea of what he had on his mind.

"Well, Black people are going to read your story and say, 'You're so full of anger, you came up during the Civil Rights era, you wanted to march, and you married a White man?'"

"Look," I said, irked by the race rhetoric that I have had to struggle with all my life, but also pleased that my friend had the courage and integrity to speak his mind, "marrying a White man didn't erase my Black experience—didn't make me White. It just means that I am not a bigot, a racist. It means that I practice what I preach. I think *character*, not *race*. The fact that I can feel as passionately as I do about wanting equality and justice for my people didn't mean I couldn't love someone who happens to be White. It meant that I actually succeeded in doing what my mother taught me: I avoided becoming a hater and a racist."

I thought back to the day I exchanged vows with Bob facing Mrs. Cass in her chair by the window. In opening my heart to Bob, I had fallen in love not with a White man or a Black man, but with a good man. I felt that our marriage was a symbol foreshadowing what America's future could be. We managed to go beyond race, class, and even age to love each other as human beings. I saw our union as a powerful message about the triumph of the soul over racism.

Bob and I did not go into the marriage blindly. We knew that there would be a lot of raised eyebrows. I was used to shocking people, so I didn't really care about the gossip. I did worry about the risk Bob was taking to his medical practice and teaching at Harvard. I did not want the marriage to affect his career in any adverse way.

"You'll see," he reassured me with a gleam in his eyes. "My practice is only going to grow. Everybody is going to want to see who this old fox is who could woo Janet Langhart."

That was the special quality about our relationship: I thought I got a prize when I married Bob, and he thought he got one when he married me. There was a wonderful sense between the two of us that we enriched each other's lives, and that was all that mattered.

There were plenty of people who whispered behind our backs. If it was not about race, it was about class or our age difference. Bob was significantly older and clearly well-off. Lots of people wished to believe that he wanted a trophy wife, and that I wanted his money. What they did not want to see, of course, was that although Bob definitely had more than I did, having had a significant head start on me, I was doing all right for myself. I had a flourishing career, money in the bank, real estate, and had managed to have retired my mother. I did not need to give up my freedom to have someone take care of me.

I have to admit that it frustrated and angered me to think that people were making judgments about me based on appearances. *They don't know what heart beats in here,* I would think sometimes. *All they see is the color, the gender, the looks, the TV personality. Where would I be as a person, as a spirit, if I were only those things?*

It would be some time still before I realized that what I was struggling to be was Janet. My heart yearned for a place where I could simply be myself, without the burdens of all the constructs into which society, Black and White, wanted me to mold myself.

From the moment I was old enough to ask the question Who am I?, I heard, "You are a little colored girl." My Blackness is essential to who I am, but it is not all I am. My culture—the experience of my people—has shaped me, but there has always also been my own soul whispering "I am." The rage that racism stirred up in me was not only the indignation at the oppression of African-Americans by White society but also the rebellion against the oppression of my soul by narrow social definitions of who I should be. In many ways, my marriage to Bob Kistner was the beginning of my journey back to myself.

Big Time

Bob had an incredible work ethic and a really distinguished career. He always told me that one of the things he especially liked about me was that my ambition and discipline matched his. He was unfailingly supportive and encouraging about my career. It was so touching; Bob even kept a scrapbook of all the magazine and newspaper articles in which I appeared.

At the time we met, my career was really taking off. Once I got the opportunity to do interviews, I proved that it was something at which I was highly skilled. And the more I did, the better I became. I realized that I could create drama and excitement by simply bringing my natural curiosity and interest in people into the studio.

I no longer needed gimmicks. I was creating interesting television by being myself. I talked to Gloria Swanson about her sex life, for instance, and asked her whether she felt it was "healthy." I interviewed Betty Friedan and pressed her about her views on the differences in the ways in which society oppressed women and African-Americans. Much to the consternation of the Catholics in our audience, Betty likened the hierarchy of the Catholic Church to the Ku Klux Klan. The audience was moved in a different way when Ted Kennedy, during the celebration of America's Bicentennial, choked back tears on camera in response to my asking him how he felt about losing three brothers—Joseph, John, and Bobby—in the service of their country.

My audience came to expect that I would show them a different side of the person I was interviewing; that I would get beyond sound bites and rehearsed spin to a more intimate insight. I was not trying to be a tough cookie, but I did ask questions that had an edge to them. I probed, and not all of my subjects understood or appreciated my efforts.

One instance that stands out was the national controversy I generated with what *Newsweek* called my "provocative questions" to Lauren Hutton.[1] Lauren was one of the first supermodels. She had

[1] "Newsmakers," Bill Roeder, *Newsweek*, April 25, 1977, p. 72.

appeared on more than twenty covers of *Vogue* and had recently signed a major contract with Revlon to promote the company's newest lipstick. This was unprecedented, and I wanted to find out to what she attributed her success.

I had modeled myself, and I knew how tough that business was. You really had to have something special to make it as big as Lauren did. In the back of my mind, I saw a real parallel between us. She was an ordinary White girl from West Virginia, and I was an ordinary Black girl from Indiana. We had both made it in our own way, and I wanted to know how she had done it. To me that was what was interesting, not what shade of lipstick she preferred.

"How do you get from West Virginia to Manhattan?" I asked Lauren. "Why Lauren Hutton on over twenty *Vogue* covers? Why you with the big Revlon contract? Why you among the many beautiful girls in New York?"

Lauren looked at me through unblinking, hostile eyes and said, "I fucked around."

I almost fell out of my chair. All I could see was the switchboard lighting up. I had once slipped up and said "Christ Almighty" after watching a clip from the movie *The French Connection* and had people calling the station threatening to have our license revoked because I had used the Lord's name in vain.

The director said in my ear, "Go to break."

I composed myself and said, "We'll be right back."

At the commercial, I said, "Lauren, do you realize what you just said?"

"Well," she said with a wave of her hand, "you can just cut that out."

"No, we can't," I said, shocked that she did not realize she was on a live broadcast. "We just went live all over New England."

"Oh my God," Lauren exclaimed. "I am going to get fired."

We did get hundreds of complaints at WCVB-TV. In fact, the incident attracted national attention. There were stories in newspapers across the country. Lauren was not very gracious in explaining her behavior. She said that I had baited her because I was envious. Besides, she added in the *Newsweek* interview, "There's no such thing in any business as sleeping your way to the top."[2] She blamed me for what came out of her mouth.

[2]Ibid.

Despite the complaints, the episode did not hurt Lauren's career or our show's ratings. The audience appreciated the spontaneity of our format and the surprises it produced. Even my staid cohost would occasionally loosen up and serve up an unexpected question, like the time he asked Jerry Hall, another supermodel, whether she ever felt ugly.

John managed to spark a controversy of his own, but one that inevitably drew me into its flame.

When questioning Bobby Seale about the Patty Hearst abduction and membership in the SLA (Symbionese Liberation Army), he mistakenly assumed that Bobby's Black Panthers and the SLA were one and the same.

The Black community interpreted his confusion and inability to distinguish one Black group from the other as symbolic of Whites saying that all Blacks look alike.

His error prompted a number of protest calls from the Black community to the studio. On the air the following day, I allowed that it was an "understandable mistake" on his part, and by doing so, validated his innocence.

At the conclusion of the show, I was summoned to a session including all of the Black employees at the station. I was happy to finally be acknowledged by them. Naively, I assumed they wanted me to be a part of a group discussion over the busing controversy. As soon as I walked into the room, I sensed hostility—not directed toward John, but toward me.

The busing controversy had placed me at odds with many in the Irish community in South Boston. "Tell the nigger to go back to Africa" was a consistent refrain. I tried to deposit the hate mail in a virtual toilet where it belonged. While I never let on publicly that I was bothered by the virulence of the criticism, I internalized the stress, which led to my medical problems.

In raising the issue of people displaying rosaries while marching with hate mongers, I discovered that I was out on my own. Those Blacks who worked at the station remained silent when it came to defending my comments. That is, until they thought that I had been "too soft" in commenting on John's statement. Now, it seemed I was not Black enough to suit them.

The self-annointed leader of the group was a very light-skinned Black woman. I had heard rumors that she and her family had on occasion passed for White until it had become fashionable to be Black.

She began to chastise me for going easy on John. My blood went up immediately. No one was going to play the race card against me, be they Black or White. It was time for more "bandana talk."

"Listen," I said angrily to my accuser. "Who do you think you are? I understand that for years you straightened your hair and walked around Cape Cod trying to pass for White. Now that Black is in, suddenly you've decided to grow an Afro and an attitude."

I had always tried to be pleasant and gracious to everyone at the station, but they misconstrued my behavior as passive, and me as a pushover. They were completely stunned by my sudden aggressiveness and use of less-than-refined language.

"And for the rest of you, I've been here nearly six months and not one of you has had the decency or courtesy of welcoming me to this racist town or to the station—or offering to support me when I took on the Catholic Church and all the bigots out there. Now, suddenly, I tell my cohost that he made an innocent mistake and you want to pull my credentials to the race.

"Well, I've got a job, and I'm working really hard to keep it. I'm not the master around here on this plantation. If you've got a problem with what John Willis says, then you go to John or to the boss, Bob Bennett. But I doubt if any of you have the courage to crawl out the crab barrel and confront Bob Bennett because you know that all he'll do is pat the men on the head and the women on the ass and send you back to the field. And that's why you're coming to me. But I want you to hear me: Don't you (expletive deleted) ever speak to me this way again!"

Once again, I found myself confronting a case of plantation mentality. I had received a size eight dress by getting the show and being successful and the other slaves resented my wearing it. My outburst had a salutary impact, however. After the meeting, several of the men came to me and apologized. "Hello, Janet," one of them said. "Welcome to Boston."

Despite my involvement in the busing controversy, Boston embraced me with a passion that remains to this day. I appeared on the cover of *Boston Magazine*. I was frequently mentioned in a positive light in the society and gossip pages of both newspapers. My face appeared in the terminals of Logan Airport in a national advertising campaign for *U.S. News & World Report,* and our show retained its preeminence throughout New England. Even to this day when I return to Boston, I am treated like a Homecoming Queen.

John and I were a real force in television at that time. Our show was a required stop on any promotional tour, whether you were a politician, an author, entertainer, or movie star. In the five years that I was with *Good Day,* we interviewed thousands of notable people. There was a time when I could not watch television or see a movie without coming across someone I had had a chance to get to know in the studio.

Marian Anderson exuded such grace during an interview that I taped one afternoon. I was excited about the prospect of meeting this great lady who had been treated with absolute reverence in our household. Whenever we heard her powerful voice on the radio, my mother would insist upon total silence. Her pure contralto was a gift from God, a voice that Arthur Rubenstein said comes only once in a lifetime.

Marian Anderson had performed at the White House, had toured and taken Europe by storm, and had reportedly been embraced by a prominent European who said, "My roof is too low for you." The Daughters of the American Revolution (DAR) felt otherwise. In their jaundiced eyes, the roof of Constitution Hall was too high.

They either were ignorant of, or indifferent to, the fact that Crispus Attucks, a Black man, was the first to fall in the cause of freedom in that revolutionary war that they were the daughters of. These self-anointed descendants of "White revolutionaries" decided that, talent be damned, no Black woman was worthy of performing on the stage of the building that bore the name of our Constitution. America is full of such ironies, contradictions and hypocrisies.

What rescued America from the obscenity of that decision was the courage of another great woman, Eleanor Roosevelt. The First Lady promptly resigned her membership in the DAR and arranged for Ms. Anderson to perform on the steps of the Lincoln Memorial. More than seventy-five thousand people lined the Mall to hear her performance. Millions more listened to the power and purity of her voice on the radio.

On a cool Easter Sunday in 1939, she stood wrapped in a fur coat at the feet of "The Emancipator" and sent forth a message that no hatred was strong enough to contain.

That triumphant moment entered our history books, but that event did not change the rules of racism. For years to come, Ms. Anderson would perform to sellout crowds in the South, and yet be barred from its restaurants and hotels. German soldiers captured and transported to America to be held as prisoners of war were given amenities denied to her, as well as to America's Black soldiers who had served so bravely.

I was anxious to explore her feelings about how she had been treated, whether she harbored anger and resentment for those who had denied her humanity. As she sat across from me, I was struck by her beautiful cheekbones, regal composure, and equanimity of presence.

In response to my questions, she refused to express any bitterness. She remained serene, outwardly kind, and free of recrimination. She said she had been forewarned at an early age of the unkindness that awaited her. She believed that she must transcend the ugliness and humiliations that were sure to come.

She reminded me of my mother's advice that, "People will hate you because you're colored, but you mustn't hate them." I envied her generosity of spirit, hoping the day might come when my own rage would be as leavened with such grace.

Years later, I had the opportunity to interview Rosa Parks on *Black Entertainment Television* (BET). Rosa Parks reminded the world that moral courage is not measured by the size of an individual, but by the strength of one's character.

Dr. King often cited her as the mother of the Civil Rights Movement. After she exhibited such courage in saying no to a bus driver who demanded that she relinquish her seat to a White man, he could not possibly say no to a call to duty. He knew the risks involved, but he was inspired by her sheer bravery.

During my interview with Ms. Parks, I had to maintain the appearance of dispassionate professional even though I felt a sense of rage welling up inside.

How, I silently asked, *could White people be so mean, so lacking in humanity? They claim to be a "superior" race, but what is superior about abusing a Black woman, of trying to humiliate her by asserting the raw power simply because they can? Can they only feel big by making others feel small? Is their hatred born of fear? Exactly what is the basis of their fear; that if Blacks were to enjoy equal rights, we might seek revenge for their sins? Or do*

*they view it as some twisted zero-sum game that if we were equal,
they lose?*

What prevented my anger from spilling into public view that day
was Rosa Parks's quiet grace, her gentleness, her refusal to indulge in
verbal retribution. Her power was that of the flower that quietly
forces its beauty up through the layers of brick and cement into the
sunlight.

On the darker side, there was David Duke who was coming to
Boston and was scheduled to appear on our show.

Having been told to stay away from racial politics, I nonetheless
lobbied for the chance to interview him. One of my producers who
usually balked at allowing me to engage in politically charged interviews decided to grant me the opportunity to do so, if only to prove
that I was incapable of remaining coolly professional.

My buttons were easily pushed on the subject of race in those
days due to the community's reaction to court-ordered busing. That
producer in particular liked to push my "race button" by frequently
using the word 'nigger' in the context of recounting the sentiments in
South Boston. I felt like she was deliberately pouring salt in a wound.

So when she said, "Okay. You always want substantive interviews. You got it."

"David Duke is not substantive," I retorted. "He's just White
trash and an example of the worst of you."

My response sounded more intemperate than I intended. I realized that I would have to remain "politically correct" if the interview
was to be seen as successful. I did my homework, reading every absurd remark he had made about White supremacy and "Negroes and
their rights."

When we sat down on the set, I was on my best behavior. Duke
was quite young at the time, perhaps in his early twenties. He seemed
proud to admit he was a racist and wanted the world to know that
he was a member of the Klan, and that it was alive and well.

I cruised through some preliminary questions to give the impression that he was not in for a rough interview, and then asked him to
explain how he reconciled the superiority of the White race with the
existence of poor Appalachians or White beggars on the streets of
our urban centers.

He became flustered.

"I've heard that you consider Black people to be inferior, right? Then how do you reconcile the success of many Blacks with so many poor Whites, when we all live in a society that is designed for Whites to win? The playing field has never been level."

Again, his answer was bumbling.

"Are you proud of the Klan's history?"

"I'm not against Negroes. I'm just for the rights of White people."

I had one eye cocked on the control room, anticipating that I would get the cut sign from my producer. The allotted time was about to expire when I asked him directly, "Do you feel superior to me?"

"No," he said quietly. Realizing the import of his denial, he awkwardly tried to qualify his answer. Too late, the interview was over.

As he departed the set, I thought him to be naive and ineffectual. He, like so many of his ilk, could hold his head high by stepping on the necks, not of the inferior, but of the powerless. His Klan hood, like those I had seen as a child, was a mask that hid weakness and cowardice.

Years later, after undergoing what appeared to be considerable physical make over, Duke emerged to run for the United States Senate. While his appearance had changed, his heart had not. No amount of cosmetic work could sever the mark of evil. His manner was more sophisticated, his rhetoric more polished, but the message remained the same:

> *If you're White,*
> *you're alright;*
> *If you're Black,*
> *get back.*

Yul Brynner was a White man who always wore black. I first saw him on the screen as Ramses in the movie *The Ten Commandments.* While the world anointed Charlton Heston as a demi-god for his portrayal of Moses, I thought Brynner was more charismatic. Whatever the movie role or genre of film, he was the star.

In *Magnificent Seven,* he was the most magnificent of all. In the *King and I,* he was truly royal. The stage production came to Boston. Boston was historically the tryout town before shows traveled to New York City to Broadway. I saw the performance and thought him to be just as riveting on the live stage. I remember during my interview with him, I commented that even when he was standing still with his back to the audience, with the child actors dancing around him, to me, he was still in motion. I stayed focused on him. He didn't seem surprised at the remark. He acknowledged that others had made the same observation. He said that just because his back was to the audience and he wasn't moving and was silent, he didn't stop acting. The wheels were still turning. He was still acting. And we felt it.

He and his wife invited me and my friend, Tony Staffieri, to another performance. In fact, I saw the musical three times. The last time, he invited us backstage. He had requested that the theater (and every other theater he performed in) paint his dressing room a chocolate brown. Candles were burning. It resembled a small, warm prayer room—quiet, dark, and glowing with votives. He had Christian artifacts and icons adorning the walls and tables.

At dinner he told me he was a gypsy—a Russian gypsy. He had run away as a youth to join the circus as a trapeze high-wire artist. He said he had always been superstitious like many in the theater and circus. Once, at age seventeen, he fell off the wire and broke his back and lay in a hospital in traction for nearly a year. Not one person from the circus came to see him. I asked why and he said that they were superstitious—that if they came to see him, it meant bad luck for them. I remember at dinner he ate raw liver and sliced Bermuda onions. His skin was tan—an even tan as though it was not from the sun, more of an ancestral gift. His eyes were dark and piercingly intense.

I was clearly mesmerized by Yul, his adventures and philosophy on life. He believed there are certain rituals one must practice to stay in balance and maintain harmony. It was important to create an environment that is comfortable and soothing—drink pure water, exercise the body, and keep the mind clear of dark thoughts.

Looking back, it was my first exposure to the holistic and the metaphysical. Several years later, I would recall Yul's words when I began a journey into myself. As I rode the stationary bike he sent me as a gift for my kindness to him, I remembered him saying on the note that accompanied the bike, "You have been blessed with a good mind—one way to sustain it is to keep your body fit." Being thin in my earlier days, I never felt it necessary to work out. Yul advised me not to exercise to remain a certain size, but to attain a higher consciousness, to connect with the infinite.

He would call me frequently. I loved our discussions, and I loved his views on life, death, heaven, earth, humanity, and inhumanity. When I heard he had died, I felt the world lost a great actor, a very unusual being. Yet, I felt his star surely fit perfectly in the heavens.

Several years later, I had the opportunity to interview another major star, Richard Burton. I was fascinated by him and Sean Connery. Maybe it was the richness and lyricism of their voices, but I found both to be manly and magnetic.

Although Burton was divorced from Elizabeth Taylor at the time, the two came to Boston to appear together in Noel Coward's *Private Lives*. Burton's new wife, Sally, also accompanied him on the tour.

After discussing his many films and which were his favorites, I asked him what it was like to act with Elizabeth, to whom he had been married twice, with his new wife in the audience.

"It's not difficult at all," he responded. "Sally understands completely. We're all great friends."

I wasn't sure that I would be quite as gracious as Sally, but decided not to challenge matters of the heart.

As a final question, I asked him, "Do you like being famous?"

"Yes," he replied, "but I don't like being recognized."

"I'm not sure I understand."

"Well, I'd like to be like the famous author, John Steinbeck. Everybody knows his name, but few people would recognize him. He could call and get a table at any restaurant just on his name alone."

It may have been Burton's cross to carry, but few in the world did not recognize his powerful face and the clarity of that extraordinary Welch voice except, perhaps, for me. I need to explain.

That evening after attending opening night of the play, Burton joined me; Elizabeth Taylor; his wife, Sally; Joan Kennedy; and my husband, Bob, at a black-tie dinner. All of Boston's theater crowd attended the gala and flooded the dance floor. Elizabeth was charming and complimentary. Burton's wife, Sally, seemed quite shy. Joan Kennedy and I were acting like schoolgirls over Burton's charm.

Bob and I had just finished dancing when Bob left for the bar to get me a drink. Burton came over to me and whispered something in my ear. The decibel level in the ballroom was so high that I could not make out what Burton had said.

Easter Sunday, 1943, with me
(on the right), my mother,
Louise Stamps, and sister, Myrna.
(Photo courtesy of author's archives)

School photograph of me
at age seven.
(Photo courtesy of author's archives)

My mother, Louise Stamps. Photo was taken in 1982.
(Photo courtesy of author's archives)

Mrs. Melnea Cass, with
her great-grandchildren,
on my wedding day to
Robert W. Kistner. Mrs.
Cass was an inspiration to
me during the racially
charged days in Boston.
*(Photo courtesy of author's
archives)*

Robert W. Kistner and me.
*(Photo courtesy of author's
archives)*

Louis Armstrong and me, taken after he crowned me "Miss Chicagoland" at McCormack Place in Chicago, 1966.
(Photo courtesy of Johnson Publishing Co.)

On the polo field with my polo pony, Delta.
(Photo courtesy of author's archives)

In the kitchen with Academy
Award-winning actor Joel Grey on
the *Good Morning Show*.
(Photo courtesy of author's archives)

Dancing with the legendary
Duke Ellington.
(Photo courtesy of Johnson Publishing Co.)

Muhammad Ali instilled in me the will to never place ambition over principle. Muhammad and me at the NABOB dinner in Washington, D.C., 1992.
(Photo courtesy of author's archives)

Interviewing the mother of the civil rights movement, Rosa Parks, for BET in 1993.
(Photo courtesy of Robert Brooks, BET)

Civil rights leader and Chair of NAACP, Julian Bond, and me as co-hosts on the set of *America's Black Forum* in 1993. *(Photo courtesy of author's archives)*

Andy Young, former congressman and U.S. ambassador, discussing Middle East politics on *AM New York*, 1979. *(Photo courtesy of author's archives)*

Bill and me on our wedding day, February 14, 1996, in the Mansfield Room in the U.S. Capitol. *(Photo courtesy of author's archives)*

Marion F. Hutchisson, "Hutch," with Bill and me at our wedding in 1996.
(Photo courtesy of author's archives)

Me and my Maltese, Lucky.
(Photo courtesy of author's archives)

Walking the halls of Congress with President Nelson Mandela, Senator Bob Dole and my husband, Senator William S. Cohen. *(Photo courtesy of* The Washington Post*)*

Bill and me with Secretary of State Colin Powell.
(Photo courtesy of the Department of Defense)

My husband, Bill Cohen, being sworn in as Secretary of Defense in the Oval Office, January 24, 1997. President Bill Clinton and Vice President Al Gore look on.
(*Photo courtesy of the White House*)

One of my dearest friends,
F. Lee Bailey.
*(Photo courtesy of author's
archives)*

Staring across the DMZ from Camp Bonifas, Republic of Korea, in May 1997. We observed the North Korean observation posts while in turn being observed by North Korean border guards. On the right is General James L. Jones, now Supreme Allied Commander, Europe (SACEUR) and the Commander of the U.S. European Command (COMUSEUCOM).
(Photo courtesy of R. S. Ward, Department of Defense)

Interviewing President Bill Clinton aboard Air Force One. The televised interview was broadcast over the Armed Forces Radio and Television Network (AFRTS).
(Photo courtesy of the White House)

Hillary Clinton and me during the Change of Command ceremony for
General John M. Shalikashvili at Ft. Myer.
(Photo courtesy of the Department of Defense)

Bill and me meeting with China's President Jiang Zemin, in Bejing, June 2000.
(Photo courtesy of Helen C. Stikkel, Department of Defense)

President Clinton greeting my mother. Oval office, December 22, 2000.
(Photo courtesy of the White House)

Speaking to U.S. Marines awaiting deployment during a meet-and-greet visit to Camp Pendleton, 2001. (*Photo courtesy of HQMC*)

Bill and me with the Clintons during the holiday season, 1997.
(*Photo courtesy of the White House*)

Meeting America's finest during a visit to Taszar Air Base, Hungary, July 10, 19▪
(Photo courtesy of Helene C. Stikkel, Department of Defense

Bill and me meeting U.S. troops stationed in Tuzla, Bosnia and Herzegovina during a Christmas tour on December 24, 1997.
(Photo courtesy of Sgt. James F. Thompson, U.S. Army)

Bill and me touring a Jewish cemetery overlooking the war-torn city of Sarajevo in 1999.
(Photo courtesy of Helene C. Stikkel, Department of Defens

I thought that he had offered to get me a drink. As Bob was on his way to the bar, I shook my head and politely said, "No, thank you."

As Burton moved on to the next lady at the table, Joan nudged me and said, "Well, that took restraint."

"What?" I asked, puzzled. "Bob's already getting me a drink."

"He didn't offer to get you a drink," Joan said, laughing. "He asked you to dance!"

As I watched him dance with the woman who heard his request, I vowed to have my hearing checked. Talk about missed opportunities!

Over the years, I had watched Dan Rather, CBS's new anchor, brave hurricane winds; get punched to the floor by Mayor Richard Daley's man during the 1968 Democratic Convention in Chicago; and press the politically powerful to the wall with the force of his questions.

What has always stood out in my mind has been his decency and integrity as a person. As a young man, Dan had served in the Marine Corps and the experience left its indelible mark on him. As a journalist, he would travel to Vietnam five separate times, having stayed once for nearly a year to cover the action.

During the interview, I asked him about the role that race played in our military. His answer was characteristically pithy, and memorable.

"Same mud, same blood." He then explained that in combat, when blood begins to flow, skin tends to matter less.

The honor and horror of war has touched him profoundly. So too has the art and humanity of his talented wife, Jean.

It's been my good fortune to call them both friends.

Of all the personalities I encountered, the most unlikely had to be William Loeb, the publisher of New Hampshire's arch-conservative newspaper, *The Manchester Union Leader.* This was a man who had the power to make or break politicians who held or aspired to the highest offices in the land as Senator Edmund Muskie, and so many others discovered. Loeb was a man who saw the world in terms of black and white. No shades of gray existed. He lashed out at any political figure who strayed from his rigid conservative ideology. He had called President Dwight Eisenhower, "Dopey Dwight," and turned against Richard Nixon when Nixon traveled to China. He vilified communists, liberals, intellectuals, and anyone who thought that raising taxes was a responsible act of government.

He had editorialized against passage of the 1964 Civil Rights Act, saying it was the work of communists who were intent on imposing a totalitarian government on all freedom-loving Americans. Although I didn't know at the time that he was so angered over Muhammad Ali's refusal to be inducted into the army that he refused to allow any coverage in his paper of Muhammad's fight with Joe Frazier in 1971, I knew that he was not a man who shared any of my views.

I was, therefore, stunned to receive a letter from Mr. Loeb, printed on *The Manchester Union Leader*'s red, white, and blue stationery. In the letter, he wrote that he watched our show regularly and had become a big fan of mine. Frankly, I didn't know whether it was all a prank. New Hampshire, after all, had emblazoned the state motto on its license plates: LIVE FREE OR DIE. I was convinced that the motto's originators did not have my freedom in mind.

Several letters followed the first one before he invited me to visit with him and his wife, Nackey, at their home in Prides Crossing, Massachusetts.

I was intrigued. Why not? An interview just might set off a few sparks.

My director/producer, Bob Loudon, and I drove to Prides Crossing and were invited into a stately, thirty-room manor that was guarded by a German shepherd and Doberman pinscher. They were a visible reminder to anyone who had trespass in mind that they would not receive a hospitable welcome. A servant greeted us at the door and escorted us into a large study. Moments later, Mr. Loeb joined us. He was a bald man with bushy eyebrows whom I was prepared to find irascible and disagreeable. To the contrary, he was most gracious as a host. I detected in him a genteel, almost Southern manner, although I assumed he was very much a New Englander. We engaged in some small talk about his background and how he got started in the publishing business. Although he gave the impression in his newspaper that he was just an average citizen, his education and lifestyle were very much that of an elitist.

Nackey soon joined us and beckoned us to follow her to the dining room for lunch. Nackey Loeb was the former Nackey Scripps

Gallowhur, an heir to the Scripps Howard publishing fortune. She, like her husband, was most charming and engaging. As the meal was placed before us, Mr. Loeb said grace. It was a ritual that my mother had faithfully performed in our home.

After lunch, Mr. Loeb invited me to join him on his shooting range. I had read that he frequently carried a firearm. He handed me a German Luger pistol, instructed me how to line up the target in the gun sight and smoothly squeeze the trigger. This was the first time I had ever fired a revolver, but I was determined not to show any fear. I fired off a round and to his—and my—surprise, hit the bull's-eye.

"Dead Eye Langhart," he happily proclaimed. "From now on, that's what I'm going to call you!"

That's precisely what he did in the correspondence we carried on from that day forward. We stayed in touch regularly and called each other on our respective birthdays, mine on the twenty-second of December, his on the twenty-sixth. One of those calls, which I'll always remember, came just after his birthday. He had had an accident while driving on an ice-slicked road out West. Although he was uninjured, Nackey suffered serious injuries, resulting in a permanent, partial paralysis. Mr. Loeb was grief stricken, blaming himself for inflicting such a cruel injury on the woman he so deeply loved. I tried to console him, accentuating the positive that Nackey was very much alive and that the accident could have been far worse for both of them. By the time we finished the conversation, he seemed relieved.

It was all very curious. William Loeb was a man who detested liberals and the cause of civil rights for Blacks. Yet he had befriended me and welcomed me into his home. He had even written to ABC in New York urging them to hire me as a talk show host. If he was a bigot, he never displayed his prejudice to me. Perhaps he was, in the lyrics of a Kris Kristofferson song, "a walking contradiction, partly truth and partly fiction."

Good Day's success and my popularity gave me a lot of confidence. I had always been very clearheaded about the business end of show business, and I understood the relationship between ratings and revenues. I knew from looking at the station's bottom line that our show was underwriting the news. That is highly unusual, because the news is typically the moneymaker in any lineup. It was clear why the general manager had blocked my moving to the network when the first opportunity presented itself: As a good businessman, he was not going to part with his cash cow. But I wanted a bigger stage on which to perform, one that only a network program could provide.

When, in 1978, NBC approached me about doing *America Alive!*, I played my hand closer to the vest this time. I had been on *Good Day* for five years, and I was ready to "go network." It was a big risk. You could do local television for life once you were established. It was much harder to break through on the networks. Shows come and go. Formats change. The competition is intense, and the egos are enormous. All of which make it extremely difficult to reach the status of a network "personality."

I was ready, however, and Bob was very supportive. In fact, I made the move to *America Alive!*, which required me to travel all over the country, just as we were getting ready to marry. I was one of several hosts on the show. Bruce Jenner, who had won the gold medal in decathlon in the 1976 Olympics, was the headliner. Jack Linkletter, Art Linkletter's son, was also one of the hosts. David Horowitz, who does consumer affairs in Hollywood now, was on the show, along with David Sheehan, a celebrity reporter, and Pat Mitchell, a former Boston media star, who became president and CEO of PBS.

It was on my first appearance of *America Alive!* while interviewing Julia Child in her famous Cambridge kitchen, that she announced my impending marriage to Bob. It seemed everyone I knew in the country watched the show that day if you measured the responses of shock and congratulations.

One of the things that made *America Alive!* so attractive to me was that NBC offered me the opportunity to report on hard news, which I had always wanted to do. I quickly discovered, though, that reporting and news gathering was not really my strong suit. I was not particularly good at it. My strength was interviewing people in a studio setting or on location.

The show, although the first to do live feeds coast to coast, was not a hit. There was enough star power to be sure, but the show just didn't hang together. Whether the fault lay in the program format, incompatible personalities, or inadequate promotion remained unclear. I think it was the competition. We were lined up with the popular, well-entrenched soaps. Whatever the reason, the audience was tuning us out. So before I had a chance to fail, the show was cancelled. The highlight, however, was to have *Washington Post* television critic Tom Shales mention me favorably in the show's critique.

Bob encouraged me so much through that time. He relished seeing me on television. He kept telling me to stick with it, to take risks. "You are not going to hit it on the first try, Janet," he reassured me. "Just keep going." I appreciated his support so much, especially since pursuing my career ambitions meant that I was often away from our home in Boston.

After *America Alive!* went off the air, I got a show in New York, called *A.M. New York*. My cohost was Clay Cole. The show was a precursor to *Live with Regis and Kathie Lee*. Even though I was back to commuting several hundred miles a week between my home in Boston and my job in New York, I loved that show. It was 1979, and I interviewed a wide variety of people from the Harrisburg, Pennsylvania, residents confronting the near meltdown at the Three Mile Island nuclear power plant, to pundits on the Iranian hostage crisis. Two of my personal favorites were the talented and gifted Sammy Davis, Jr., who watched the show when he was in New York, and one day, he just decided to come unannounced to the studio. It was so fantastic. I had read his book, *Yes, I Can,* which has remained an inspiration. The other was Father Louis Gigante, whom federal prosecutors were trying to force to turn state's evidence against his brother, Vincent "The Chin" Gigante, the Genovese crime family boss.

One of the most exciting people to get to know was Francesco Scavullo, the famed photographer. I had interviewed him previously on *A.M. New York*. He is a kind man, and obviously very talented considering all the glamor covers he shot for *Cosmopolitan* magazine.

He knew that I modeled earlier before my TV career and offered to photograph me for his upcoming book, *Scavullo Women*. I was flattered to be in the company of women I'd long admired. Lena Horne, Brooke Shields, Elizabeth Taylor, Sophia Loren, and others.

I was in makeup, which seemed like forever. Then it came time for hair. While on set, Scavullo thought I should have a more natural look. The hairdresser was Andre Douglas, famed wig designer. Scavullo said to take off the wig, "let's see her real hair." It was braided underneath. He suggested it be unbraided. I protested, saying I needed a perm. It was wild and thick, and he liked it! "That's the look I like that—it's more natural."

I remember Andre mixing a bottle of baby oil and water and

spritzing it onto my hair to keep it down, for as it dried it would rise like yeast. The experience reminded me of those hot, humid nights growing up in Indy—as soon as Mother would press my hair, it would go back. I chuckled to myself.

Scavullo was right, though. When he sent me an advance copy, I was amazed. He had worked his magic.

Considerations of beauty were a mere diversion from the more serious issues that were dominating the news at the politically turbulent times. The Middle East, once again, seemed on the verge of exploding. And my old friend Andy Young, who had been appointed U.S. Ambassador to the United Nations by President Jimmy Carter, seemed to be at the center of the storm. At issue was a proposed U.N. resolution that would recognize the rights of the Palestinian people more explicitly than the resolution that was then on the books. I called Andy to find out the ins and outs of the politics, as I had done throughout the course of our friendship.

"This is a hot one, Janet," Andy warned. "Stay away from it."

I heeded his advice and did not raise the question on the air. However, when Andy was forced to resign in late August 1979, because he had met, allegedly on his own initiative, with the Palestinian Liberation Organization (PLO) observer at the United Nations, I could not remain silent. I publicly joined the sizable chorus of Black voices questioning why opening a dialogue that might lead to a peaceful solution to the impasse in the Middle East was considered such an unpardonable offense.

As it usually happens with issues where Blacks and Whites are concerned, Andy's resignation became a question of race. I had again asserted my Blackness, as I had done over busing in Boston, to an audience and an establishment that preferred to ignore the fact that I am African-American. So in addition to the competitive environment at the networks, I faced an extra obstacle to getting ahead: I insisted on principle. Unfortunately, as rumor had it around the station manager's office, the price of principle was my job. Although the show was getting good ratings (we were starting to beat *Donahue*), ABC cancelled it.

Job opportunities became harder to come by. Somehow, I just could not find the right fit. Everyone seemed to want to have me fall into one category or another, in which they believed I belonged. Some wanted me to be a field reporter. Others thought I should sit behind a studio desk and read the news from a teleprompter. But my talent is that of an interviewer who relates and reacts to a guest with complete spontaneity. The spirit that I bring to an interview is strangled by prescripted comments drafted by some recent college graduate who owed her job to her father's connections.

Trouble is that I simply don't conform well to stereotypes. This creates cognitive dissonance for people. I do not satisfy their preconceptions of who I am, and a lot of people can't accept. They feel challenged in a way that is uncomfortable, that puts their construct of the world into question. To deal with it, some simply dismiss me, others withdraw, and still others get angry.

I remember a lunch I once had with a man who worked on *60 Minutes*. We met at some professional function, and he invited me to meet him to talk about the business. When I saw him next at one of B. Smith's restaurants, I immediately sensed that he was interested in me for other than professional reasons. While I wanted to talk about politics and world events, he kept steering the conversation to more personal matters. I politely parried and continued to try to engage him in an intellectual discussion. It was painfully clear that that was not the kind of stimulation he was interested in. With every question about the Middle East or the Iranian hostage crisis that I raised, I could see him getting more and more listless. We finished lunch, said our good-byes, and never spoke again. Later, in describing the meeting to a girlfriend, I said that I felt as if he had looked under my dress and found something very unattractive—a brain.

Fortunately, I had earned and saved a considerable amount of money while I had been at the networks, and I could afford to keep pursuing my aspirations without having to rely on my husband for financial support. I was especially sensitive about that because of the assumptions that people made that I had married Bob for his money.

I began to realize that I was in for a long fight. I did not give up on my hopes of making it big in television, but I saw that I would need time to regroup, to plan my strategy. I wanted to work, and I missed Bob. We had had little time to settle into married life; our careers had always taken precedence.

I returned to Boston, my mind set on getting a job and on making a home for Bob and myself. Work was paramount, however, since I have always insisted that you have to carry your own weight. I have always believed that you must be productive and self-sufficient.

I was determined to work at whatever I could get. So when my old network WCVB-TV offered me a small job on a show called *Sunday Open House,* I was glad to accept. What I did not realize was how much resentment there was at the station because I had left to pursue network opportunities.

"You left this station high and dry," the general manager Bob Bennett said to me after I had signed the contract. "But you know what? I got you back, and I bought you dirt cheap."

It felt as if he had slapped me across the face. From that day forward, I swore that I would never undersell myself. People seem to respect you more when they pay top dollar for your services. What Bob Bennett didn't know, however, was that I did the show this time so that my husband could take delight in seeing me work, just as my mother had in Indianapolis. The truth is, I would have done the show for nothing. In Aretha Franklin's words, just who was zooming who?

At that time, I also signed on to do a column for the *Boston Herald.* It was called "Janet's People" and ran in the Sunday paper for two years. I interviewed people such as Larry King, Oprah Winfrey, and George Clooney's father, Nick, who hosted a local radio show and whose sister was Rosemary Clooney, one of my all-time favorite singers. I did soft, feel-good interviews that let my subjects shine. It was a pleasure to work on them. Print was a discipline that was very different from television, and I was grateful to Rupert Murdoch for giving me the chance to grow. I loved the newspaper challenge of meeting a deadline; however, my first love was television.

You Asked For It

I grabbed whatever was available, including a globetrotting syndicated show called *The New You Asked For It.* It was a revival of a show that had been hosted by Jack Smith and Art Baker during the 1950s and 1960s. The comic and impersonator, Rich Little, hosted our show. The correspondents were a diverse group of dazzling women, ranging in careers from reporters, talk show hosts, and aspiring actresses. We were cast in the mold of *Charlie's Angels,* traveling to all parts of the world, finding stories (mostly bizarre) that viewers asked to see, such as: the Burmese woman who kissed a

cobra and lived, the flying bats of Brunei, the migration of the wildebeest, and the snake man in Malindi.

In my earlier years, I had dreamed of being a missionary to my ancestral home of Africa. I always thought that the more poor and
needy they were, the more I could help. But my first trip to the continent would not be one of service, but one of adventure.

In the summer of 1981, the television crew and I flew to Kenya to
cover a safari. We landed at Nairobi and, unexpectedly, spent nearly
a week at the InterContinental Hotel waiting for our video equipment to be released. It seemed there was a matter of some bribes that
needed to be paid to some unsavory folks before technology could be
reunited with the talent.

We spent the downtime actively exploring the city in search for
potential segments to tape once the video equipment was in our
hands. Being great people watchers, we also played the game of
Name that Tribe. Most of the people we encountered in the city were
Black, but the differences in their size, shape of the head and body,
and style of clothes could be traced to specific tribes, such as:
Kikuyu, Luce, Mero, and Masai.

During the course of our visit to Kenya, I would take note of
short, almost squat women who looked like a lot of the women in
my family. A few miles away, there were women who were tall and
lean, virtually free of any body fat.

There were just so many striking variations upon a theme, much
like Africa itself. The topography runs from spectacular mountains
to shimmering grasslands to arid plains. The flora, fauna, birds,
beasts, and reptiles are kaleidoscopic in variety and beauty.

Our first stop was the Giraffe Centre located at the Nairobi National
Park. We ate lunch at a manor that was the private house of the
Leslie Melvilles. There, we were treated to the sight of Rothschild giraffes suddenly swinging their heads through open windows into the
dining room.

The only giraffes I had seen previously were in magazines or movies.
They were huge animals, standing eighteen feet tall and weighing
twenty-seven hundred pounds. The Rothschild giraffes, I was told,
differ from others in the color of their coats and the shape of their
patches, which tend to be less jagged. They are exceedingly strong,
possessing a powerful kick that wards off most predators—except
when leaning down to drink water. Then, they are vulnerable to
lions, leopards, and hyenas.

After lunch, we went outside and stood on a raised platform and watched a woman place a carrot in her mouth and have it snatched away by one of the giraffes. My crew encouraged me to follow suit. I was apprehensive over the prospect of such a gigantic animal coming close to my face, but finally relented.

I clamped the carrot between my teeth and waited. Nothing happened. The giraffe ignored me and turned away. Frankly, I was relieved. Then, without warning, the giraffe swung its neck around and snatched the carrot from my mouth with a long (seventeen-inch) black tongue that unfurled like one of those paper whistles that we blow at New Year's parties.

The giraffe's face was so close; I could feel the velvet soft folds of its lips touching mine. But what was most memorable was the rush of warm air that it exhaled through its nostrils. I detected the smell of minted leaves.

It was all captured on video, including my surprise and spontaneous laughter. Fortunately, our cameraman got it on the first take. I was not eager to undergo a repeat performance. In fact, it was an experience I would not repeat until a decade later when I visited Michael Jackson's ranch high in the hills of Southern California.

Late that afternoon, we arrived at our designated campground. It consisted of a number of tents and a single, thatched-roof, columned building that served as the lodge and dining area.

Rudimentary tents were reserved for the most recent arrivals. Each time a party moved on to another camp, their tents, somewhat more elaborate, were taken by those next in line. Hot water was in short supply. Each morning, those first to come were the first to bathe. A premium was placed on early risers, of which I decidedly was not.

Early in the evening, I noticed that a goat was tethered within thirty or forty feet of my tent. I asked our guide why the goat was there. The answer was that he served as a delectable diversion. If any of the women were having their menstrual period, it could attract a lion or other predator. The goat would be a preferable alternative meal.

I checked on the goat for several days, uncomfortable with the notion that he was an involuntary member of our safari's food chain. Fortunately, he was still alive when we moved on to our next destination.

During the second week on the safari, we visited a witch doctor. I had confided to our crew that I was concerned that the vegetation and animals might aggravate an asthmatic condition that continued to afflict me.

My producer had researched the subject and learned that a Masai witch doctor had a cure for asthma. She suggested that it would be a great piece for the show to reveal the power of tribal medicine. I thought it preferable for him to stir up something for the fly-infested, diseased eyes of the infants in his tribe. I was, however, willing to be a sport about it all.

Actually, at the time, my breathing was fine. Until, that is, I saw the ingredients of his potion.

Earlier that morning, our interpreter, a Masai warrior, dressed in traditional tribal garb, with ocre hair, a beaded necklace, and a bright red shawl draped across the shoulder, took us to witness another young warrior shoot an arrow into the jugular artery of a white ox. Blood immediately spurted out, but was captured in a leather pouch. Mud or dung was quickly packed into the wound, stemming the flow of blood. The ox then trotted off nonchalantly.

I was horrified at the sight and thought the act was cruel. Our interpreter saw that I was distressed by what I had just seen.

"You need not worry," he assured me in perfect Oxonian English. "No harm has been done."

I wondered whether he was a Hollywood actor, who after playing the part of a Masai warrior to the video cameras, would change into a pin-striped suit, pack his leather luggage, and catch the next plane out of Nairobi back to Los Angeles.

"Where did you learn English?" I asked, still not sure that I wasn't the victim of a practical joke.

"From the missionaries. Years ago."

After spending a few minutes of small talk inquiring about his family and future, I returned to the subject of the ox.

"What is the blood used for?"

"Oh," he intoned, "for the Masai it has many uses."

A perfectly ambiguous and unsatisfactory answer. I was soon to discover, however, one very specific application.

The witch doctor took a large gourd that contained milk from the ox and poured the blood that had been extracted earlier. He sprinkled in some weeds or herbs into the mixture while huge flies swarmed all around us. Then he erupted like some violent volcano and coughed up a ball of yellow phlegm and added it to the concoction. Finally, he took a flask made from some part of an animal—a scrotum, the crew joked—and poured out a small amount of liquid into the gourd. I feared it might have been urine.

With each ingredient added, I felt faint. I considered announcing that I no longer had asthma, but feared that I might break into a psychosomatic-triggered attack that would expose the lie.

The witch doctor mumbled some unintelligible words over the mixture, then using his hands, he smacked my forehead, back, and chest. Gesturing, he insisted that I drink the potion.

The interpreter translated the witch doctor's instructions, the last being for me to drink the entire contents of the gourd without stopping. As the vessel was handed to me, I tried to prevent a gagging sickness that I felt from showing by smiling at the witch doctor. I noticed that the camera positioned on a tripod behind him did not have its light on. I tried to stall, yelling, "The camera's not working." I prayed for that to be true. Tom, the cameraman, smiled gleefully, hoisted the camera off the tripod and onto his shoulder. A light clicked on and he shouted, "Rolling."

I took the gourd from the witch doctor and looked over to my producer, hoping to find in her my salvation. I prayed she would yell, "Out of tape," "Cut," or "Stop." No luck.

I was mindful of the briefing we had received about the Masai. They were noble, honest, proud people who were easily insulted by any disrespect shown for their customs or hospitality.

They could be said to be traveling "the last mile" of hospitality by offering to cure my asthma. Who knows, maybe it would produce a miracle. I thought back on all the horrible nights that I had suffered in childhood and all the dreadful gasps for air I would know in the future. *Oh hell,* I thought.

I lifted the gourd to my lips, threw back my head and swallowed the slime in one long gulp. Then I nodded to the witch doctor, took my middle finger and ringed the gourd as if taking my last taste, put my finger to my lips, and licked.

I actually licked my index finger and not my middle one. It was an old trick and one that served me well. I did it to fool everyone in a gesture of one-upmanship so I would not be the brunt of everyone's jokes during our usual evening ritual around the campfire.

I had pleased the Masai and dazzled the crew with my bravado. They later asked what it had tasted like.

"I can't describe it. There's nothing to compare it to, but I'm breathing even better than before," I said with a straight face.

As I walked back to my tent, I held my breath, and when alone, rushed to the basin and used soap to scrub my tongue and teeth. I even swallowed the soapy water, terrible in its own right, hoping it might kill anything squiggling in my stomach.

Later that evening I went into the tent of John Brown, a stiff upper-lipped Englishman who served as our soundman, and asked for a swig—actually a huge gulp—of Hennessy, a staple that he kept in ample supply.

The next morning I awakened, surprised to find that I was still alive. As we gathered in the village to exchange good-byes, one of the Masai women present suddenly reached out and grabbed my arm. It was not a friendly gesture. The other women stood in a circle, giggling, but their giggles were devoid of any pleasantry. Then she pulled a bracelet I had purchased in Nairobi off my wrist.

Again, we had been told that the Masai were noble and honest and would never take anything from us unless they offered something in return of equal value.

The woman gave me nothing. She simply put my bracelet on her wrist. The women continued to giggle but their eyes were full of dare.

My first instinct was to retrieve the bracelet, but an inner, wiser voice counseled me to let it go.

Later, we learned just how wise a decision that was. As we traveled through the Liki North Valley, we learned that a Swedish crew that followed us three days later had a similar experience. One of their crew members was found murdered.

An experience nearly comparable in excitement occurred after we videotaped the annual migration of the wildebeest—the principle reason for our venture to Kenya.

Each year from July through September, the wildebeest, nearly a million in number, along with thousands of zebras, make the long trek from the Serengeti in Tanzania to the Masai Mara along the Kenya border. It is an incredible sight. The shaggy-headed, thin-legged wildebeest, almost iridescent pewter in color, move en mass in an erratic fashion, consuming grass and vegetation along the way.

In order to catch the epic scope of the migration, our cameraman, Tom, hovered high over the herds in a hot air balloon. I decided to join Tom in the balloon so that we could use the spectacular vistas as a backdrop for my commentary on the phenomenon with the tagline: "You're seeing the migration of the wildebeest because . . . you asked for it." On more than one occasion, however, the best-laid plans managed to go somewhat awry.

Early in the day, the temperature was relatively cool. As the sun continued its ascent, the heat, humidity, and gravity forced our balloon in the opposite direction.

Despite every effort to fill the balloon with hot air, we continued our descent and landed on the rolling terrain of the Masai Mara.

Our safari crew had faithfully followed our flight path in a Land Rover and came racing toward us as the balloon's basket touched down. Almost immediately, they began to set up a picnic lunch, laying out a linen tablecloth on the ground in the grass along with china, flatware, and crystal glasses. For lunch, white-gloved servants set forth cold chicken, chutney, pound cake, and tea.

It was completely bizarre to be sitting cross-legged on the perennial grounds of the Serengeti and be feted as we had been in our base camps, as if we were lounging about at a four-star hotel. The juxtaposition was, well, jarring in a strange, exotic way.

While engaged in a discussion of the day's experience, I noticed something moving in the tall grass. It was a stealthy lioness, followed by her two cubs. Then the massive head of a lion appeared, his gaze fixed directly on us. We had landed in a lion's pride and disrupted the tranquility of their habitat.

I fought back a growing sense of panic. We were completely defenseless. No one, including our guides, was allowed to carry weapons.

"Relax," I was told. "You can see that they've eaten recently. Absent any provocation, they're unlikely to turn to us for dessert."

And they didn't.

Hunger and its satiation is the elemental code of conduct that governs Africa's animal kingdom. Ethics and morality are totally antithetical to the Darwinian struggle for survival. Truth and consequences. Stay out of the path and sight of anything bigger, stronger, quicker—or hungrier—than you or end up as oatmeal in the belly of the beast.

Actually, it was not the belly of a beast that I would soon fear, but that of a ten-foot python.

After leaving the Masai Mara, we returned to Nairobi and then boarded the midnight train to Mombasa. It was an old train that offered private compartments and a more than adequate menu. It was straight out of the Agatha Christie novel, *Murder on the Orient Express*.

After rocking along through the night, we finally arrived around daybreak in Mombasa. From there, we boarded a ferryboat to Malindi, an island off the coast of Kenya.

We were given a quick tour of the slave quarters there, along with a brief history that revealed that the Arabs may have been Africa's first slave masters. I couldn't wait for the opportunity to call Muhammad Ali and tell him that he had simply exchanged one slave name (Cassius Clay) for another!

Then our guide, a tall, thin, White Kenyan named Mark, had us assume seats in a small canoe that threatened to tip over whenever one of us shifted our weight.

"Be careful," he warned us as we slipped into a murky river. "There are a lot of snakes in the water. Keep your hands inside the canoe, and don't rock it."

While Mark was supremely self-confident, I began to question whether I had taken leave of my senses. What exactly was I doing here?

In ten minutes or so—it seemed like hours—we arrived at our destination. There we were to capture on camera python snakes in all of their power.

As we moved through the wooded area into a clearing, one of the African men shouted something in what I assumed was Swahili.

They then pointed to a python lying, panting in the sun. We could see a very large bulge in its belly. He had just swallowed his meal for the day.

Mark decided that if we traveled all the way to Malindi, we should want to give our viewing audience "a bit of a show."

Barking orders to two men to lift the tail of the snake while he grasped its head, he asked me to hold up the snake's middle.

"Are you sure it's safe?" I asked, surprised that I was not semi-hysterical at the thought.

"Trust me. He's harmless right now." The qualification of *right now* was not a confidence builder.

Not wanting to look frightened before our crew, I lifted up the python's middle section. The skin was cool, smooth, and not at all slimy, as I had expected.

Then Mark instructed the two men to let the tail wrap around me. Screaming or running at this point was out of the question. I was game.

While Mark held the snake's head in an arm lock, the lower half of its body began to curl around me.

The camera was rolling.

"Don't worry, Janet," Mark said. "We won't let it crush you."

Suppressing all fear, I smiled straight into the camera and said, "We are here in Malindi, playing with a ten-foot python, because you asked for it!"

Later that night, we were dining in a restaurant, drinking wine, recalling the day's events, when two African waiters came rushing over to our table and shouted something that sounded like Hollywood's equivalent to, "Bwana! Bwana!"

I immediately flashed back to my childhood days at the movie theater when I watched *Tarzan, the Ape Man*. It was always curious to me how Africans who have lived and survived for centuries in the jungles of Africa had to call upon a White man to rescue them from the crisis of the moment. It was déjà vu all over again.

We got up from the table and were led to the area that had produced such excitement. A python was on the restaurant's roof and was dangling outside one of the windows.

Mark shouted, "Quick, get me a flashlight and one of those large garbage cans and its cover."

The men dashed off and returned with Mark's weapons of choice.

Calmly he shone the light into the python's eyes and then led the transfixed snake directly into the garbage can. Just as the two men started to slap the cover on the can, we heard a great *whoosh* sound. The python had released the contents of its stomach all over Mark!

I was stunned by the sight (and smell) of what had just happened. Mark, however, dismissed the episode with aplomb worthy of a seasoned Shakespearean actor. "Nothing to fret over," his manner said. Grace under pressure, after all, was the hallmark of the Englishman.

I suspected, with the exception of the python's elimination spasm, that the snake's capture had all been planned to add a little spice to our final day of the excursion. I even speculated that the python may have been Mark's pet, the same one who had wrapped itself around me earlier that day.

Real or staged, it was great theater.

* * *

In recalling the safari experience, I found the most instructive lesson for me was not only the need to adapt to the environment, but that I had the ability to do so.

Prior to Kenya, my idea of "roughing it" was a weekend at The Ritz. Out on the Serengeti and Masai Mara, however, amid the wildebeests, elephants, zebras, lions, witch doctors, and pythons, I discovered the hard truth that it is the strong that, indeed, do survive. That strength is not measured in power alone, but in the cunning and capability to move synchronically with the unwritten rules of the universe.

Adaptability means survivability. It was a mantra I would carry with me into territory that would prove just as viperous and dangerous as existed in Africa.

August in Paris

Sandy Frank, the owner of the The New *You Asked For It* show, would frequently hire different producers and film crews in various parts of the globe, and then his "angels" would simply fly to the location and join up with them for the shoot. While this arrangement may have had its economic merits, it occasionally led to friction and misunderstanding.

I had gained a reputation with Sandy and his producers for being willing to try almost anything. But I knew the difference between boldness and buffoonery, between courage and stupidity.

Shortly after returning to Boston from the trip to Africa, I set off again, this time to France. In the Camargue in the south of France, I participated in the local custom of riding a horse through the narrow streets of the village while the residents slapped the horse's chest with sacks of flour. It wasn't quite the running of the bulls at Pamplona, but it had its element of excitement. Plus, the flamingoes were beautiful.

It was in Paris that I decided to draw the line. The local producer decided that our viewers would be eager to see me water ski on the River Seine. The problem was that I couldn't swim, and there were no life jackets available. Moreover, I was dressed in a fashionable pair of slacks and blouse, not a swimsuit.

"All the more interesting," the producer shouted as he smoked his Gaulois cigarette and gazed into the eyes of some Spanish girl he was romancing at the moment.

Leaning against the shore and fumbling with the skis, I saw Andre, a member of the crew, shake his head and say with his low Corsican accent, "The water is so toxic. You'll be dead before you can drown."

Unlike many other crew members I had encountered, Andre wasn't trying to goad me into action. He wasn't kidding, the water looked putrid, even toxic.

"This is stupid and dangerous." I threw down the skis and walked away from the shoreline. "I'm not going to do it."

"Don't be silly," came the producer's retort. "It's perfectly safe. You can't get hurt."

All I could creatively visualize at that moment was my taking a spectacular spill while traveling thirty miles per hour behind a speed-boat, into a rancid river. To what end? To garner the plaudits and laughter of some anonymous couch potatoes. "Isn't she cute?" "Isn't she daring?" "Isn't she stupid!"

"No," I shouted back. "You can get someone else to do it, because I won't."

"I'll call Sandy and get you fired for walking out on this!"

"Great. You do that. I'd rather have you call him than call my mother and tell her why I just drowned!" With that, I walked off the set and caught a cab back to the Left Bank to the apartment that Sandy had been renting for us.

Before entering my room, I stopped at a local bookstore and picked up a copy of Oriana Fallaci's *A Man*. Knowing how contemptuous the Parisians are toward Americans who can't speak French, I was surprised to find that the book was printed in English. I had interviewed Oriana during one of her visits to Boston and admired her fiery spirit and willingness to flaunt her independence. I spent the rest of the day reading the book, not experiencing any doubts about my decision or my future.

Sandy Frank, I was convinced, wanted video angels, not real ones.

He imposed no penalty for my display of common sense and independence.

*   *   *

Upon my return from Europe, I was called upon to judge the Miss America Pageant for the second time. That was a lot of fun, actually. It felt so good to see how far I had come from a young Black girl who could not even dream of being Miss America to being a television celebrity judging the contest again. I went out of my way to treat the women as more than just beauty queens. I asked questions about the presence of Soviet troops in Cuba and about premarital sex. I asked one of the contestants, a pretty blonde who represented one of the Carolinas whether she approved of interracial marriage. Without any pretense of thoughtful hesitation, she responded, "It's a sin." When I asked why, she said, "In the Bible, Jesus says that the mixing of the races is a sin." After she departed, NBC talk show host and fellow judge, Tom Snyder, turned to me and laughed. "Guess I know one vote that she's not going to get."

She would not lose my vote simply because of that response, but I was surprised how little had changed in the racial attitudes of the younger generation from the South that she represented. I along with many other Blacks assumed that we simply had to wait for the older bigots to die off. It was clear that it would take more than the passage of time to change attitudes. While I tried to repress the thought, I could not help remembering my aunt Leola's warning that the little blond baby that I once cuddled would one day grow up and call me a nigger.

Ancient Paths

In October, Sandy Frank's angels were back in the air, and this time, we were on our way to the Middle East. We landed at the David Ben Gurion Airport in Tel Aviv, and as we stepped out from the baggage claim area into the teeming street outside, we moved into a sea of Semitic faces. While I never sensed that we were in any danger, there was a palpable sense of anxiety that seemed to hang in the air.

Our Israeli escorts took charge immediately and made all the arrangements for us at our hotel. Efficiency and security were their trademarks.

After a restful evening, we started out the next day to tour the Old City in Jerusalem. We visited the Western Wall of the Temple Mount (the Wailing Wall). The Temple Mount is believed by the Jewish people to be the place where Abraham offered up his son to God. It is of equal religious significance to Muslims. According to the Koran, it marks the place from which the Prophet Mohammed, accompanied by the Angel Gabriel, rode his winged horse to the Throne of God. As non-Muslims, we were not allowed to enter the grounds of the Temple Mount, but stood in awe of the architectural beauty of the Dome of the Rock, a shrine that remains the third holiest place in Islam, after those in Mecca and Medina located in Saudia Arabia.

We traveled north where we stayed for two nights in a kibbutz owned by a man from Texas. We then met with famed archaeologist and warrior statesman, Yagal Yadin, at the Sea of Galilee in Nazareth, where according to the Bible, Jesus walked on water. Later we floated in the salt-ladened waters of the Dead Sea, the lowest point on earth.

As a final treat, we climbed Masada, the mountain fortress built by Jonathan around 37 B.C. during the Hasmonian Revolt as a rather elaborate retreat. It was here that more than a thousand men, women, and children committed mass suicide rather than be taken captive or killed by the Roman Tenth Legion.

That story reminded me of one often told in my family of a Kentucky slave woman who had given birth to twelve children, killing each one of them with her bare hands soon after they were born. She preferred death for them, rather than bondage. It seemed the commonality of the two stories was an extraordinary commitment to freedom.

After leaving Israel, we flew to Egypt so we could shoot the Great Pyramids in Giza. While we were there, in the shadow of the massive and weathered face of the Sphinx, another shooting was taking place. President Anwar Sadat, an extraordinary leader whom I had made arrangements to interview, was gunned down while attending an outdoor ceremony.

I was staying at the Heliopolis Hotel in room number 1006, a number that corresponded to the date of his assassination, October 6. I may have only imagined it, but even my key seemed to be cast in the shape of an automatic weapon.

What was not imaginary, however, was the reaction of the Egyptians I encountered after President Sadat's death.

"This is a terrible tragedy," I said to the hotel's concierge.

"Not really," he said, shaking his head in disagreement.

Others at the hotel were completely nonplussed. There were no tears shed, no wails of grief to be heard. The man that so many Americans admired for his courage and statesmanship in making peace with the Israelis was seen by many of his countrymen simply as a traitor.

I left Cairo depressed. The refrain from a song about John, Martin, and Bobby kept playing over and over in my head. A trio of heroes who fired the imaginations of people the world over—all cut down by the bullets of assassins. Now Sadat. Would the violence ever end? I wondered.

The answer came years later when another towering figure, Israeli Prime Minister Yitzak Rabin, was taken from us by another armed fanatic.

As exciting as the travel was with *The New You Asked For It,* the work was only part time. I spent the next two years traveling back and forth between Boston and New York making spot appearances on various programs. I wanted very much to work full time and had called my agent to inquire why there seemed to be no movement on the job front. He professed, lamely, that the networks were having difficulty locating me because I traveled back and forth to Boston so frequently. Shortly after that conversation, I received a call from CBS. It was not a welcomed one. I was excited, thinking my agent had become energized on my behalf. The excitement turned quickly to disappointment. CBS did not want to hire me, but simply use me.

When Vanessa Williams had her Miss America title stripped away because it was discovered that she had once posed for some provocative nude photographs, CBS wanted me to go on camera to express my thoughts on whether Vanessa was worthy of holding on to her crown. I was furious with the entire situation. When Vanessa won the title, I was excited for this beautiful, talented young Black woman. Finally, I thought, America had arrived. Now, what she had worked so hard to achieve was about to be taken from her.

I have found over the years that whenever a Black personality's head is about to fall under the guillotine, the media drags out another Black person to set the blade in motion. It's always a catch-22. If you condemn the conduct in question, you are seen by other Blacks as a Judas, being trotted out by Whites to prove their point. If you defend the conduct, the White community believes that your racial allegiance blinds you to truth and justice. Disloyal Black or

Unprincipled Apologist. Pick your poison. I refused to play the game that masquerades as the media's disinterested search for balance and fairness. I did not judge the pageant in which Vanessa won the title. She was one Miss America whom I was not now going to judge in public.

Around this time, I also finally got to meet Bess Myerson. I served as the mistress of ceremonies at the twenty-fifth annual Israel Bond Fashion Show and Luncheon at the Waldorf-Astoria in New York. Ms. Myerson was the special guest, along with Representative Elizabeth Holtzman. Marvin Hamlisch provided the entertainment, and a constellation of socialites and stars participated in the fashion show. I had been invited to host the program by Ruth Brown, a prominent woman in the Jewish community. She took me by the hand to introduce me to all of the important public personalities who were in attendance.

It was wonderful to know that I continued to be so popular. However, in spite of my celebrity, I could not find full-time work in television, either locally in Boston or on the national scene.

I was not happy about not working full time, but I did now have more time to be with Bob and to build our life together. Bob loved to go out. He was good-looking and dapper, a terrific dancer, and a consummate extrovert. "You would go to the opening of an envelope," I used to tease him. But we had a wonderful time together, dressing up, going to parties, and dancing.

We had purchased a condominium at the Ritz in Boston and often stayed there several days a week. The rest of our time we spent at the house in Milton. It had beautiful grounds, with lovely gardens and a tennis court. It was a very special place.

I had had to make an effort to feel comfortable in it. Bob's late wife, Georgia, had died decorating that house. He had told me how, sitting in his study, he heard a terrible thud at the top of the stairs and knew that she was dead. Georgia was a heavy smoker and had high blood pressure, and Bob's instinct told him that she was gone. He went up to where she lay, carried her into her bedroom, and laid her out on her bed. It was a terrible loss for him and their four children.

I felt Georgia all around me in that house. She was talking to me through the fine upholstery she had picked out, the lovely things she had collected, the placement of furniture. Bob augmented my sense of her presence by telling me stories about her. How politically active she was in the Republican Women's Committee. How she had fought to get her children the best education. She did it all—a strong woman with whom I felt a great affinity.

So I felt her in the house. Not in an eerie way, as if she were haunting me, but enough for me not to like to stay there alone. I was not hearing voices or seeing anything out of the ordinary; I simply could not feel at home. I knew what I needed to do was to speak to Georgia out loud, to connect with her spirit.

I waited until Bob went off to a professional conference and went out to Milton. It was winter, and it had started getting dark early. I was on the telephone with a friend one night. "Oh, I've got to go," I said. "I have to turn the lights on in this house." I meant all the lights. It took me about twenty minutes to turn them all on, and then I went downstairs to a little vanity room that Georgia had built for herself next to Bob's study. I paused by the entrance, took a deep breath, went in, and closed the door behind me.

"Georgia," I said, "I want to have a talk with you. First of all, I want to thank you. You shaped this wonderful man who is now my husband, and you reared four wonderful children who are so nice to me.

"I also want to thank you for this beautiful home that you prepared. And I'm sorry you didn't get a chance to enjoy it.

"I promise you that I will take care of your husband, because he needs care. I will love your children as much as they will allow me to. And I will take care of every precious thing in this house."

When I left the vanity room, I went upstairs to Bob's bedroom and took out photographs of Georgia that I had come across in one of his drawers one day while putting away laundry. I took the pictures and put them out in the living room and the study.

After that, I was at peace in that house. I still did not like to stay there alone, because it was big and quite secluded. But I felt that it was my home.

When Bob returned and saw the photographs, he was speechless. "This is her house," I told him. "When her children come home to see their father, they should see their mother's picture here."

Bob was moved almost to tears. He understood that I felt camaraderie with her spirit, and that this was my way of showing it. We did not talk about it again, but somehow we moved even closer to each other in our relationship.

Bob was a mystery to me in some ways. He had his doctor's nononsense, pragmatic view of life, but also a deep spiritual side, which he hid from everyone, including himself. I discovered it by accident. We were in New York at Christmastime, and I dragged Bob into St. Patrick's Cathedral. I have always loved Our Lady's Chapel, the small, quiet space in the back of the immense building.

We sat in one of the pews, and I closed my eyes to meditate. Suddenly, I felt the pew trembling. *Oh my God,* I thought. *Are we having an earthquake in Manhattan?* I opened my eyes and saw Bob, with his head in his hands, crying and shaking uncontrollably.

I said, "Honey, what's the matter?"

"Just give me a moment," he stammered. Then he leaned forward onto the kneeler.

Is he having a heart attack? I wondered, never having seen him so emotional.

I kneeled with him and held his hand. "What is it?" I asked again.

"The smell of the incense, this building, the sacraments," Bob said. "It all just reminded me so much of going to church with my mother and father when I was a little boy. I haven't been in a church for so long."

I was stunned, for he had told me prior to our marriage that he was Episcopalian. I learned that he and Georgia had converted because it was more socially acceptable in the elite circles of Boston not to be Catholic.

I tried to encourage this softer, more emotional side of Bob. I gave him the woman's perspective to help him be more compassionate toward his patients. All he could see was that he was working to ease their suffering. He could not empathize with their sadness and anger about their inability to reproduce.

"Honey," I would tell him, "you know you are brilliant. But they are the ones putting their lives in your hands. It is natural for them to be scared."

I remember the evening when Bob understood his patients' fears. We were at the Ritz and went down to the Grill for dinner. To my surprise, Bob proceeded to get a bit tipsy—something I had never seen him do before.

"What's the matter with you?" I asked. "It's a good thing you don't have surgery tomorrow."

"No," he said, tipping back another Tanqueray gin and tonic. "I have a root canal tomorrow."

I could have burst out laughing, but I did not want to offend him. I suggested we walk around the block to clear his head. With my arm through his, to give him support, I walked Bob down Newberry Street to Berkeley, then along Commonwealth Avenue to Arlington. We crossed Arlington to sit on a bench near a weeping willow tree in the Public Garden, before returning home. I could not resist ribbing him just a little.

"You were getting yourself ready for a root canal, Dr. Kistner?" I said. "What would you have done if you were going in to have your uterus removed?"

I don't think he found it funny at the moment, but he did seem to become a little bit more empathetic. At least, he seemed to understand the fear his patients had of surgery.

A Passion for Ponies

Even during this time when we were settling into being a couple, Bob and I continued to lead independent lives. He devoted himself, as he always had, to medicine, and I kept working at maintaining my career. The jobs were sporadic. However, I refused to be idle. I wrote, I did television, I developed creative ideas, I built my skills, and I pursued my interests. This was the time I discovered my love of horses. The man from whom we had purchased the condominium at the Ritz, Charlie Downer, was a polo player, and he introduced me to the game. From that day on, I spent much of my free time at the stables.

I started to learn to ride in the winter of 1982. The mechanics of riding was only part of the challenge that I had to face. From the days of my early childhood, I had associated horses with a profound sense of danger. During one of our frequent summer visits to my aunt Bertha's home in Hopkinsville, Kentucky, I was playing in the loft of her small house with my cousins, wearing a sleeveless, cotton nightdress that my mother had sewn for me, cut from a flour sack. The adults who were gathered below suddenly stopped talking and joking. In the distance, I could hear a sound that was unfamiliar to me, but one that sent a wave of terror through the house.

Aunt Bertha shouted up to us, "You young'ns be quiet up there! Be quiet!"

The sound grew louder. It was not a violent, summer storm approaching, but the thunder of shod horses galloping along the paved road just a few feet from the front door of the house.

"Blow out the lamps!" Aunt Bertha shouted. "Blow out the lamps. Get down, get down."

The men on the horses, members of the local Klan, rode by shouting something unintelligible. They fired no shotguns into the house as other night riders had done to some in the neighborhood on past occasions. But their objective of instilling fear had been achieved. I found myself hyperventilating, gasping for breath, which was not healthy for an asthmatic.

For years, I repressed the memory of that experience, while ironically associating the fear of that night with the sound of the galloping horses rather than the twisted men who rode them. For me, climbing onto the saddle of a horse represented conquering more than simply the fear of falling.

The first horse I rode was this beautiful old black horse named Bridget. I had not realized how deep a relationship I could have with an animal this large, despite having loved my other pets—dogs, cats, birds, and rabbits. But I absolutely fell in love with Bridget. I would worry about her standing in that poor, cold stable. On days I did not ride, I came out to walk Bridget to keep her warm. I even stayed overnight with her a couple times.

After I felt comfortable riding, I went through polo clinic and learned to ride and hit the ball. I did not rate very high in the amateur standings, but I was good enough to play with the men's clubs. At that time, the women's clubs were not taken seriously, and I refused to be marginalized, even in sport. Polo is a physical game, and you can get hurt. That was the argument the men used to keep us off the field. *Hey,* I thought, *the pony equalizes us. It doesn't matter what my gender is, as long as I can ride. And, I have a good pony. I can be as tough as any guy.* My budding love affair with polo was an exotic and dangerous experience. It was the equivalent of playing hockey on horseback. Raw violence, spirited competition and pure exhilaration. The only thing missing were the fistfights and brawls

Actually, I loved the riding and the pageantry of the game much more than I loved polo itself. Gradually, I started becoming interested in other equestrian sports, such as dressage and jumping. I decided to go to Europe to study the different styles and disciplines of riding.

Bob was remarkably giving and understanding. Many men would not have been happy about their wife going off to another continent for several weeks to pursue a hobby. Bob said, "Look, I'm doing my medicine. This is my life. My hand is complete when the scalpel is in it. I want you to be complete too. If that means going around the world to learn how to ride horses, I want you to go. Just make sure you come back."

I packed up my boots, my britches, a couple of dresses, and a few books and went to Europe. My girlfriend came with me, and we traveled everywhere—Italy, Switzerland, France, England—just riding horses. In England I felt that I had found the milieu for which I was searching. The British have a real horse culture, and I wanted to stay there and learn. My girlfriend went back to the States, and I got a flat in London and began my studies. In the beginning I would take the train each day from Charring Cross to Kent, which is near Beneden. I soon decided that I was wasting too much time commuting. I rented a small room at a bed-and-breakfast in Beneden so I could spend more time riding.

I rode every day at a place called Moat House Stables, which ran a school, mostly for wealthy young girls who wanted to learn to be riders. It was hard work. We rode three hours a day and cared for the horses, cleaned out the stalls, took care of the tack—learned everything there was to learn about horses. I would get back to my room and just pass out.

I was becoming an accomplished rider, however, and I was augmenting my love of horses with a real understanding of these magnificent animals and their behavior. I was also meeting a lot of interesting people with whom I shared my passion for horses. Lord Patrick Beresford, the younger brother of the Duke of Waterford, became a particularly close friend. He was so lovely to me, such a gentleman. Through him, I got the chance to see the English "horsey" class up close and to participate in some of its rituals.

That was how I got to meet Princess Anne. Patrick invited me to go riding at Windsor Palace. Naturally, I jumped at the opportunity. Patrick lent me his beautiful buff-colored horse, Buck. He mounted one of the Queen's horses, and the four of us went off for a ride across the lush English countryside. Up on a hill overlooking the palace, we paused and looked down at the breathtaking views.

After the ride, we went off to the estate of one of Patrick's friends that was next door to Windsor. Because of our muddy boots, we went through the kitchen. As we walked in, I noticed this beautiful woman in expensive, well-worn riding clothes leaning over the sink, cleaning something off. Her skin was like porcelain, and her chestnut hair was thick and lush.

"Ah," Patrick exclaimed happily, "Janet, I want to introduce you to Anne."

"You may want to address her as 'Your Highness,'" our host broke in with a side whisper, before I had had a chance to say anything.

I was a little flustered, so I said, "Pleased to meet you, Mum."

"No, no," the two men teased in unison, "that would be the Queen Mother or the Queen."

"Now, gentlemen," the Princess said and then turned to me. "Did you have a good ride?"

She put me at ease with her fluid, polite conversation. We were just two women chatting, while the men were off mixing drinks and slapping each other on the back.

It was a lovely day, and I felt privileged to have gotten this glimpse into a world I had not seen before. When Patrick and I got ready to leave, our host walked us out to the car and said in parting, "Well, Janet, you must be pleased to have met Princess Anne. It is quite an honor."

"Yes," I said in my most polite manner, "she is a lovely woman."

As we drove off, I contemplated his remark, with growing indignation. I know he did not mean anything by it other than commenting on our American tendency to be worshippers of royalty. But I kept hearing Dr. King's words about what it means to be a queen.

I had to endure racism, poverty, sexism, and the government projects, I thought, *and my ancestors even had to be dragged across the Atlantic just so I could have the privilege of doing so. All she has done is come out of a royal birth canal.*

I meet famous, privileged, successful people all the time, I thought, continuing my silent monologue. *She probably hardly ever meets anyone like me. She should feel honored to have met me.*

I was not railing against Princess Anne, who had been charming and gracious to me. I was just outraged by the presumption of class. I was again seeing how it claimed privilege for itself on the basis of nothing other than wealth and lineage, the same way racists claimed superiority on the basis of skin color.

Shortly thereafter, I returned to Boston. I had learned a lot about horses, and I realized that Delta, the polo pony with whom I had trained, was not being properly treated. She was old and heavy. She was beginning to get lame but was willing to do anything you asked. The woman who owned her kept her in a very cold stable and did not vet her or shoe her as often as she should have. She was just using Delta up to make money.

I approached Delta's owner and offered to buy the pony. I paid her two thousand dollars, which is not a lot of money for a pony, but truthfully Delta was worth no more than eight hundred dollars. Delta was a roan. She looked a little like a mule, because her ears were bigger than they should have been, and she would always fold them back. I still do not know if she was good by nature or just beaten down. There was a sadness about Delta that troubled me. She reminded me of the stories about slaves who were so broken and afraid they just surrendered their spirits and did whatever the master told them.

I often worried about Delta. I was afraid that I was not caring for her well enough. A friend I knew through polo told me that I might consider keeping her at the Palm Beach Polo & Country Club. "Are you kidding?" I said. "If I can't keep her here in this poor little stable in Boston, how can I afford to keep her at the Palm Beach Polo & Country Club?"

My friend explained that in Florida the horses did not need to be housed the same way, because the weather was so good. All I had to pay for would be the feed, the vet, and the shoeing. In addition, there were a lot of people there who rode the ponies and kept them fit.

So Delta went to live in Palm Beach. I also bought a second pony, Cindy. He was actually male, but we named him Cindy because he was so pretty. He was wild, and I never felt truly comfortable riding him.

Not long after the horses had settled into their new home, I went down to a spa in Fort Lauderdale. As long as I was in Florida, I decided to go see my ponies. I had made all the arrangements for boarding the ponies by telephone, and I was eager to see the place for myself. I rented a car and drove the forty-five minutes from Fort Lauderdale to Palm Beach.

The club was lovely with beautiful small villas where some people lived year-round and others during the season. It was so nice, I persuaded Bob that we should buy one of the houses. "You love the sun," I said. "When you retire, we can move down there. You'll have the warm weather, and I'll have my ponies all year."

Bob agreed, and we bought a small villa. I was so happy, because I could spend more time with my ponies. The joy was fleeting, unfortunately. One day, I took Delta out on the polo track for a walk. I sensed right away that something was wrong. Her front right shoulder seemed to be giving way. Before I had a chance to jump off, she fell forward and then rolled over, pinning my right leg under her, my foot still in the stirrup.

I wasn't hurt, but I was afraid that Delta would panic, jump up, and take off, with me dragging behind her. I stroked her neck and said, "Delta, just calm down, just calm down. It's all right." Meanwhile, I had taken my left foot out of the stirrup. I then slowly eased her up and pulled my leg out from under her.

We stood there and caught our breath. "Are you all right, Delta?" I asked her, petting her face. "Are you hurt?"

I looked under her shoulder to see what had happened. Just then, she lifted up her right foot to show me a cut between the knee and the hoof. She had understood everything that was happening to us. She knew she had fallen, and she was showing me where she was hurt. It was not a bad cut, but for a horse the legs are everything. I walked Delta slowly back to her stable and called the vet.

The vet examined her, and I knew from looking at his dispassionate face that I would have to give up Delta. Once a horse begins to go lame, it is not long before something serious happens and the animal has to be put down. I could not bear the thought of that; I decided to give Delta away.

There was a man I had met around the stables who was looking for a pony for his two little daughters to learn to ride. I told him that I wanted to give him the horse, along with the tack, as long as he promised me that he would take good care of her. "Oh, ma'am," he said. "My nine-year-old and six-year-old are just going to ride her around the backyard. She'll have a good home."

I felt a little guilty giving Delta away. It seemed cowardly that I could not stick it out with her until the end, but I just could not bear to have to put her down. After that experience, I did not have the same zest for polo and riding. It was also during this time that Bob began to have problems with his health and started to slip into a depression, and my attention shifted to more serious concerns.

Another Storm Rising

Bob, like most men, especially doctors, defined himself through his work. He was a surgeon, a practitioner, an author, a teacher. It did not really sit well with him that he was also human.

By 1985, Bob was in his late sixties. He began to develop arthritis. His fingers stiffened and curled into the palm, making it impossible for him to put on his surgical gloves. His eyesight was going. He was diagnosed with skin cancer and could no longer worship the sun the way he had done all his life. His liver was a little dysfunctional, so he could not have his gin and tonics at night. In other words, he was aging.

The hardest thing for Bob was not being able to do surgery. I did not understand just how devastated he was by this loss and tried to encourage him.

"You are brilliant," I would tell him. "You can always teach. And write."

"I don't want to teach," Bob would shoot back. "I want to do surgery. That's what I live for."

I would lose my patience and tell him to snap out of it. I would ask his colleagues to talk to him and tell him to pull himself together. He was my rock, and I could not face up to the fact that he was sinking.

Finally, in 1986, Bob sold his practice and retired. I happened to be working on a local news show in Boston at the time, which began to create some friction in our relationship. Our roles were reversed. I was the one working, and he was at loose ends. It was sad, and he did not like it at all.

Bob hated Boston's gloomy weather, so he would go down to Palm Beach. At first, he would go for a couple of weeks and come back. Then, he began to stay there longer and longer. I wanted to encourage Bob to do what made him happy, as he had always done with me, so I suggested that he move to the house in West Palm Beach. I would come down every couple of weeks or so, and he would make the occasional trip up to Boston.

That seemed to work for a little while. Bob gardened, played tennis, and generally tried to stay active. He made himself follow a routine, but he was simply not cut out for retirement. It was the worst thing that ever had happened to him, and he just slowly dissolved into depression.

Even when he was in the best of health, Bob had talked about his fear of being incapacitated by illness. "I can't imagine anything worse than languishing on life support," he had told me once. "Promise me that you will not put me on life support."

I thought he was being a little dramatic, but said, "I promise."

He looked away and said, "It won't come to that. I have some pills put away, for when the time comes."

We never talked about suicide again, but I had the distinct feeling that he meant what he had said. So when I began to sense that he was battling a serious depression, I begged him to see a psychiatrist. Bob refused and just withdrew further and further into himself. He pushed his kids away. He pushed his sister away. And he pushed me away.

He did it methodically, and in the most cold-blooded manner imaginable. One day, I received a letter from him. I always looked forward to his letters, because he wrote so beautifully. I opened the envelope eagerly, but could not believe what I read.

"Janet," he wrote tersely. "I no longer love you. I want a divorce."

We had not been fighting. It just came out of the blue like that, so I knew something was really wrong. I did not even read further but immediately dialed our number in Palm Beach.

"Hello," Bob answered in a voice that to me sounded agitated.

"Honey," I said, "I just got a very strange letter from you. What is going on?"

"I cannot make it any clearer, Janet," he said vehemently. "I no longer love you, and I want a divorce."

I realized that it was no use talking on the phone. I had to see in person what was happening with him. I flew down on the next plane. As soon as I saw him, I knew Bob was not himself. I could not engage him in conversation. He did not want to go out. When I did drag him out to dinner with friends, he just sat there, not even making an effort to talk.

I took our friend Lenny, who was also a doctor, aside to ask him what he thought of Bob's behavior. "Janet," Lenny said, "Bob's really depressed. He doesn't do anything. He won't play tennis. Won't even come over for a drink."

When we got home that evening, Bob unleashed his anger on me. "Never come back down here again," he said, his voice hard and low. "I never want to see you again."

I began to cry, hurt by his harsh words, but also hoping that my tears would touch his heart so we could reconnect with each other.

"I can't stand the sight of you," Bob said with disgust. "If you want to know the truth, I am in love with someone else. And I don't want anything more to do with you."

I really broke down then. I knew he was deliberately hurting me to drive me away. There was nothing I could do, though, in the face of his cruel determination.

First thing the following morning, Bob said, "I want you out of here today. Just get out."

I knew that I could not help him at that point. I called all his children and his sister while I was at the Palm Beach airport and told them that Bob was in a bad way, that he was acting erratically and irrationally. "I can't get through to him right now," I told them, "so please keep an eye on him."

Although I knew Bob was driving me away because he was depressed, I was deeply wounded by the rejection. It was particularly difficult because I felt as if I had no place to turn to lay down my burdens. Being pretty much of an introvert, I had only three girlfriends at the time on whose shoulders I could lean. I am not a regular churchgoing person, so I did not have a faith community to support me. And worst of all, I was having serious problems with my mother.

We had always been very close, but it was often a tumultuous closeness. I was her rock, her provider, as she had been mine. But when she felt overwhelmed by life, she sometimes took it out on me. Over the years, it seemed that things got particularly bad between us when I came home for the holidays. Mother would just pick fights with me for no reason, and I would fight back. It was miserable.

Years later I understood that my mother's behavior was caused by an anxiety disorder. My brother told me how she would spend days fretting and making everything perfect for my visit. By the time I would get there, Mother would be so tired and high-strung, she would just light into me.

I was used to her moods, but it still seemed very unfair. I had done so much to win her love, yet it was with me that she fought all the time. The relationship was deteriorating. The fact that I needed her more than ever did not help matters. We had one last, terrible fight over Christmas, and I decided that for my own emotional protection I had to begin to cut the relationship.

A Journey to the Center

That is how I entered 1987. I was estranged from Bob and worried about his health. I was not speaking to my mother. And to round out the dismal picture, I was unemployed, and there were no job opportunities in sight. It felt as if my whole world was crumbling, and worse still, I was sure that somehow I was to blame.

It was, without a doubt, the darkest time in my life. I just crashed. I was not motivated to do anything. I stayed in bed with my two beloved cats, Tony and Cleo, all day. I would not take phone calls. I would not eat. I let the housekeeper in to take care of the condo and made sure the cats had food, that was it. I had practically buried myself at the Ritz, overwhelmed with sadness.

I had done enough interviews with psychologists and self-help authors to know that these were signs of depression. However, I fought the knowledge with denial. *I'm not depressed,* I insisted to myself. *I've turned lazy. I don't have any reason to get up because my husband is not here. I don't have to cook for him. I don't have to dress up for him. I don't have a job to go to.*

One morning I woke up, and a new inner voice said, *Well, you may not have any of these other people around you, but why don't you want to do things for yourself? Enough of this nonsense. Get out of this bed. Get up, and don't let any of this get you down. The world is kicking you in the ass, so you've got to kick back.*

I staggered out of bed, weak because I had not eaten a proper meal in days. My inner voice said, *Today you are going to do everything you hate to do.* It was a way of asserting my will, of fighting back and proving that I had the strength to persevere.

The first thing I did was have breakfast, and then I set to work. I proceeded literally to do the things I most hated to do. I shaved my legs. Then I changed the bed linens, something I usually left for the housekeeper. I cleaned the kitty litter. I groomed Tony and Cleo, a procedure neither they nor I relished. I cleaned up in the kitchen, put my clothes away, and organized my closets. Finally, I forced myself to get on the stationary bicycle that actor Yul Brynner had given me and worked out for the first time in weeks.

By the evening, I was thoroughly exhausted but exhilarated. I could start counting my blessings and all of my many professional accomplishments. I was so thorough, I even counted the bit parts in movies in which I had appeared, *Medium Cool* and *Blind Ambition*.

At the time, they seemed like nothing, but now, I was grateful for every little thing. I felt a sense of accomplishment. I had beaten back the darkness, at least temporarily. As I sat thinking about the well into which I had fallen, I remembered something Shirley MacLaine had said when I interviewed her after her book, *You Can Get There from Here,* was published in 1975. Shirley is a brilliant woman, very spiritual. She said that the most important and the scariest journey any of us can take is the journey into ourselves. I remembered asking her why it was such a frightening journey. Shirley replied that we were all afraid of what we might find—who we might find. "You may not like who you find," she had said, "but that is who you have to live with."

It was a moment of epiphany for me. "Go inside," I said to myself. "All the external stuff is not working. See if you can find the answers in yourself."

I took a pad of paper and made a list of the things that I thought I needed to do to bring balance and harmony into my life. First of all, I had to take care of my body. I had to eat well and to exercise. Second, I had to have order in my life. I kept thinking of the old Chinese proverb:

> *If there is light in the soul,*
> *there will be love in the heart;*
> *if there is love in the heart,*
> *there will be beauty in the person;*
> *if there is beauty in the person,*
> *there will be harmony in the home;*
> *if there is harmony in the home there will be order*
> *in the nation; and if there is order in the nation,*
> *there will be peace in the world.*

The following day, I went down to a bookstore that specialized in books on Eastern philosophy, holistic medicine, spirituality, and the like. It was so peaceful in there, I felt as if I had entered a temple, surrounded by an assortment of rocks and crystals. Soothing music floated through the interior intensifying the smell of burning incense.

From that day on, I read stacks of books on psychology, religion, ancient shamanic traditions. I felt as if some force was guiding me to the books that would give me the insights I needed.

I listened to Shakti Gawain's tape, *Living in the Light,* while driving in my car and while exercising. I reread Shirley's book. I thought about the difference between the things I could and could not control. I remembered the serenity prayer:

God grant me the serenity to accept the things I cannot change, the courage to change the things I can, and the wisdom to know the difference.

I also read *Chop Wood, Carry Water* by Rick Fields and learned to enjoy the process of performing an act rather than achieving its completion.

I purified my environment and myself. I ate only vegetables. I exercised regularly. I did not drink alcohol. I endeavored for purity in my surroundings, my body, and my thoughts. It felt as if I had entered into a monastery of self.

I began to share some of my feelings and insights with a friend of mine, Liv Heraty. She told me that there was a book she wanted me to read and sent me her well-worn copy of Ernest Holmes's *The Science of Mind*. It is a text based on Christianity, which goes far beyond, into creative visualization.

Curled up with *The Science of Mind*, I remembered an interview I had done with Rabbi Harold Kushner, the author of *When Bad Things Happen to Good People*. The message of the book is that we all have to face difficult times in life and that our job is to rise above them, to deal with them, to do the best we can. What had particularly struck me was that this man of God had found answers in himself, which connected him to his deity.

I thought back to that interview equipped with the new knowledge I had been accumulating and realized that all spiritual disciplines are virtually the same. There is one truth, and all the journeys into self or to God or to enlightenment are one and the same. I was so inspired by this thought, I decided to attempt to channel spirit. I wanted to experience a direct connection to the universe.

I had my book on channeling, and I attempted to follow its instructions to the letter. I lay down on my bed one early morning before dawn, looked out the window at the stars, and welcomed spirit to come through me. I was giving it my best shot, but I am not sure I really expected anything to happen.

Suddenly, I said out loud, "All you have to do is ask." I then remembered one of the first things I learned in Sunday school: Jesus said, "Ask, and it shall be given." It had been a long time since I had listened to my inner self—the self that I discovered came from the wisdom of my ancestors. I wasn't channeling; I was soul talking.

Our true, divine selves are always there for us to discover. I was blessed to have been knocked down and forced to look at my life differently. I had to let go of the plan I had laid out for myself and accept that there was a higher consciousness in control. I simply had to flow with life's invisible currents. It was one of the many lessons that I had discovered in riding my horses. I could feel myself getting stronger as I went through this process. All the baggage, the external expectation, and the labels that had taken me down, began to fall away. I had come from the bottom to the top, out of the darkness into the light.

7

Black Widow

During this period of introspection, I discovered that I had the inalienable right to be myself, to live life according to my own values and beliefs rather than societal dictates. It had taken me forty-five years to know my real self, and I was eager to see how life would unfold for me.

The circumstances of my life did not change, but I did. What you resist will persist, the saying goes. I realized that I needed to find the lessons in the challenges with which the universe presented me and to shape my actions accordingly. I saw myself as a cocreator of my life, responsible for living with integrity, passion, and courage.

There was much work to be done. I was at an impasse in my career and in my marriage. I knew that I had to let go of beliefs and relationships that kept me from moving forward and began to rethink what I wanted out of my work, my life.

I had struggled for nearly a decade after leaving *Good Day* to build my television career. As I told a *Boston Globe* reporter who wrote a profile of me for the paper, I was starving creatively. I did make several guest appearances on *Good Day* during the "sweeps" rating periods and ratings shot up immediately. My job as cohost, however, had been filled by another woman, and she had little interest in having me make substitute appearances. In fact, once during a lunch at my home, she begged me to stay away.

"You're rich. You don't need the money," she said. "I need this job."

I first thought, *what audacity,* then I realized that it was desperation.

"You don't need the work," she continued. "I do."

I shot back, "First, I do need the work. It's my passion. And second, don't count other people's money."

Opportunity did come knocking, however, but the rap on the door was not a welcomed one. WCVB had been seeking to gain the rights to promote the state lottery. Authority to televise the drawing of winning numbers was conditioned on their securing me to play the role of Lady Luck. The financial terms were more than generous—one hundred thousand dollars and a chauffeured ride to the station each evening. Even though I was living at the Ritz, I was still supporting my mother and refused to allow Bob to contribute to this effort. In short, appearances aside, I needed the money. It was an offer I couldn't refuse—but did.

My forte was conducting interviews, bringing out the interior side of public figures, actors, authors, and newsmakers. Turning a lottery cage and plucking out a number was demeaning. Admittedly, they were not offering me chump change, but my grandmother's voice continued to echo inside me from my childhood days: Don't ever sell more of yourself than you know you can buy back later.

I thought this offer would have been a complete sellout to the journalistic credentials that I had worked so hard to attain, having done interviews with important and prominent figures of my time such as Margaret Thatcher, President Jimmy Carter, and Barbara Walters. It was the thought of Barbara Walters that angered me most. Even though I was local, asking me to do the lottery would have been tantamount to asking Barbara Walters to do *Wheel of Fortune.*

Attempts to compromise me had been tried in the past without success. During an executive dinner, that same senior manager, a professed "family man" and respected community figure, had slipped his hand under the table and began stroking my leg. I thought of the time the man in the Lido movie theater in Indianapolis tried to rub my leg when I was just five years old. This time, I did not sense fear, only revulsion. Apparently the manager thought that I would submit to his authority, if not his charm. But I had no intention of following any custom of sleeping with the boss in order to hold on to my job. He did not take the rejection gracefully. The only thing that saved me from a pink slip were the ratings I was able to generate. No one had ever broken my spirit, and it was not going to be broken now. It was a Faustian bargain that I was not going to accept.

Unfortunately, the station's managers got out ahead of me and leaked it to the press that I was going to accept the offer *to* do the lottery. During a cocktail party at my apartment, a friend of mine asked whether it was true. In an unguarded, spontaneous moment, I confided with her that I had no intention of becoming anyone's "Vanna Black." It was a remark that she felt too clever to keep private. The next day on the front page of *The Boston Herald,* the headline story was, JANET'S NO VANNA BLACK While I never intended to publicly rebuke my former benefactors, they took it precisely as that.

I never worked in Boston television again.

I had come to trust the universe, and was convinced that if one door closed, another would open. The trust was rewarded when a new opportunity in the world of politics presented itself. I was approached by the Michael Dukakis presidential campaign and signed on as a media adviser. It was especially satisfying to announce this venture in my hometown at a press conference that we held in Indianapolis in May 1988. National politics was an exciting new field to be involved in, and even though my candidate ultimately was not elected, I was very glad to have contributed in some small measure to a critical aspect of our democracy.

The Long Good-bye

The relationship with Bob seemed frozen in a torturous silence. He refused to speak with me, insisted that he wanted a divorce, and yet did nothing to proceed. Bob had hired a divorce lawyer who initiated legal proceedings, but for more than a year that was as far as he went. I understood that he was deeply depressed, yet I felt that I could not allow myself to sink along with him. I was determined to find resolution, and I hoped to shake Bob out of his malaise.

I considered retaining my own lawyer to push the divorce along. "Look, Janet," my friend Colette Phillips told me, "Bob's down in

Florida, and whatever else it may be, Florida is the South. You are a Black woman whose White husband is suing for divorce. You'd better get yourself a lawyer who can protect you."

I did not want to appear overly aggressive, but it did seem like good advice to get the best lawyer possible. All my friends advised me to go to Monroe Inker, who was the quintessential divorce lawyer, a real pit bull. I wondered whether I had made the right decision, though, when I first met him.

We discussed the situation, and he said to me: "I am going to give you an assignment. Go home and write down everything you can think of that your husband has done in the course of the marriage that is especially peculiar or anything immoral."

I was so put off by the idea that he wanted me to dredge up dirt from my relationship with Bob. I've never had any respect for people who kiss and tell.

"You know," I said, "I really can't do that. First of all, there's nothing negative about Bob and nothing unsavory in our marriage, and if there were, it would stay there."

To his credit, Monroe Inker did not press the point. He understood where I was coming from and handled my affairs with utmost respect and professionalism. To this day, I am grateful for how nice he was to me during that very difficult time.

Even after I retained Monroe Inker, however, Bob did nothing to move forward with the divorce. The lawyers talked to each other, but that was all. Finally, I could not stand it any longer and instructed my lawyer to file a countersuit. I needed to extricate myself from the painful ambivalence of the relationship with Bob.

We were a prominent couple in Boston, so of course the divorce filing made it into the newspapers. It was unpleasant to have our private difficulties discussed in public, but I also felt a sense of liberation, having taken action. I was on record as not being willing to stay in a relationship that my partner claimed not to want. I did secretly hope that my filing would shake Bob out of his stupor and that we could work things out between us.

With that in mind, I went down to Palm Beach to see him again. I was shocked to see how much weight he had lost. Bob had always taken such special care of his appearance, and he seemed not to care even about that. He did, however, have a lady friend. I had heard that he was seeing a beautiful blonde who was a real-estate broker in the area. By this point, I was so concerned for Bob's health, I was glad that he had her. I preferred to think that he wanted to divorce me because he was in love with someone else, rather than think it was because he was chronically depressed. Sadly, I later learned that it was indeed depression that was pulling him away from those of us who loved him.

ET *Calls*

I was so preoccupied with worries about Bob, I could barely acknowledge what seemed like the beginning of the revival of my television career. During my campaign days with the Dukakis presidential run, I met Donna Brazile, Ron Brown, and Bob Johnson. Bob owned Black Entertainment Television (BET) and offered me the chance to have my own show. His offer was very attractive—I would be the principal with my name on the show and have a great deal of editorial control. I wanted to do Black television, to serve my community directly. I still believed, however, that succeeding in mainstream media was also important to promoting the interests of our race.

At the same time I received Bob Johnson's offer, I was contacted by *Entertainment Tonight* and asked to become one of their field reporters. One of the producers I had worked with was involved with the show and suggested me as a possible replacement for a reporter who had left. I was delighted with *ET*'s offer because that exposure would enable me to bring greater cache to BET.

Ironically, my husband had always encouraged me to apply for a job at *ET*. We watched the show together when it first went on the air, and he would say to me, "Oh, it would be great if you could be on a show like that."

"Not in a million years," I told him. "They've got their one Black guy. They are not going to put two of us Blacks on."

So when I did get the call from *ET*, I took it with a healthy dose of skepticism. Of course, I was also elated to get the opportunity and sent the producers a tape of the best interviews I had done. They liked the tape and asked me to come to Paramount in Los Angeles to audition. That also went very well, and they offered me a contract. I wanted the contract to be nonexclusive so that I could also work for BET. This arrangement was acceptable to Bob Johnson, but not to Paramount Pictures, *ET*'s parent company. I signed an exclusive contract with *ET* but still had reservations about the wisdom of doing so. I was not convinced that it all was not an elaborate charade to give the show "equal opportunity" cover. My experience had taught me that Black people had had their fifteen minutes, as far as the television industry was concerned, and I needed to protect myself from disappointment by curbing my expectations.

I was completely surprised when a producer from *ET* called in mid-September and said, "Is your passport in order?"

I said, "I think so."

"Well, you better make sure, because we want you to go to Russia. Julio Iglesias is doing a series of concerts in Moscow and Leningrad. You'll interview him in Moscow and fly to Leningrad with him to interview Sean Connery. He will be there filming *The Russia House*."

"You've got to be kidding," I said. "This is my first assignment? Sean Connery and Julio Iglesias in Russia?"

I decided that I had better take *ET* seriously. They were giving me a real opportunity, and I was determined to make the most of it.

Julio's first concert was scheduled for October 2, so the crew and I flew to Moscow over the weekend. I could not believe how bleak and dreary the city was. It was early fall, and yet it felt like winter. The light was gray and meager. The buildings were old and dirty. And the people all seemed terribly sad. I was filled with dread and wanted to leave as soon as possible.

We stayed at the Sovetskaya, which was the largest hotel in Russia. It was like something out of the movies: One lightbulb lighting a whole corridor and furniture so dingy, I did not want to touch anything. For me, it was real culture shock. I simply was not prepared for the poverty I saw in the Soviet Union. I could not believe that a superpower that spent so much money on weapons could not provide its people with the barest of necessities. It was a real cultural contradiction for me to see White people living in third-world conditions.

I still remember the sight of our Russian hosts eagerly reaching for the tired-looking, spotted fruit that was served at the reception held for Julio the night we arrived in Moscow. I had been nervous about meeting him all day and hungry because we could not find anything to eat other than lardy cold cuts. When I got to the reception, I could not believe my eyes. The tables were overflowing with caviar and champagne. All the Russians, however, were congregating around the fruit plates. Fresh fruit, as I found out, was not something that even the highly placed could easily get at that time.

Julio came into the room, tanned and well-dressed. He did not seem to notice the shabby furnishings or the moldy fruit. He was gracious and charming, a real star.

"I am delighted that you are here," he said to me. "I look forward to seeing you at the performance, and then we can talk over the next few days."

Julio had been named UNICEF special representative for the performing arts and was in Russia as part of a world tour to highlight his work on behalf of children. One of the concerts he was scheduled to give in Moscow was, in fact, a benefit for the children's project.

The following evening, the Moscow Sports Palace was packed for the performance. Julio came out and just communed with the audience. He is a marvelous entertainer. He sang only in Spanish, and yet, half the audience seemed to be singing along with him.

"The Russian people are really remarkable," I said to our Russian guide. "They know his songs. They're singing in Spanish."

"Those aren't Russians," she said. "They're Cubans."

"Oh, okay," I said, amused by this cultural reminder of the dynamics of geopolitics.

After the concert, everyone—the men, the women, the young kids—rushed the stage. They just adored Julio. And he stood there and signed every autograph, even though he had to be exhausted. I had been a fan of Julio's before I met him; however, seeing him behind the scenes, I was really taken with his genuine sweetness.

We did several interviews in the course of the few days we were in Moscow, including some stand-ups in Red Square, with the beautiful St. Basil's Cathedral in the background. This was at the height of *perestroika* (economic reform) and *glasnost* (free speech) when the Soviet empire was beginning to collapse. In fact, the Berlin Wall would come down in a little more than a month.

We were filming in Red Square, when suddenly the gates to the Kremlin swung open and a column of big black cars came speeding toward us. Raised on Cold War movies, I was sure they were coming to arrest us. There was still this ominous air in the country, despite *glasnost*'s promise of unrestricted speech. And with all the unrest in the Soviet Union and its satellites, there was a heightened sense of danger. I was relieved when the motorcade passed by us. We finished the interview and retired to the Western-style comfort of the bar at Armand Hammer's hotel.

The following day we hitched a ride to Leningrad on Julio's jet. His was the first private plane to have been allowed into Soviet air space. He was going to Leningrad to do several more concerts, and we were trying to coordinate schedules with Sean Connery. Principal photography on *The Russia House* was scheduled to have begun on October 2, and *ET* wanted to do an interview with him on location.

We joined Julio on boa:d his plane. It was a beautiful caramel-beige jet that seated about twelve people and had a private bedroom. Julio's initials were etched on the glass and embossed on the leather. It was so luxurious, especially after the Soviet accommodations.

Julio was the perfect host. As soon as we sat down, he began to offer us champagne, eager to make sure we were happy and comfortable. Julio's father, who is a gynecologist, was traveling with him. The more champagne Julio poured, the better my Spanish became, and the more detailed our conversation about gynecology became. I finally explained that my husband was Robert Kistner, and Dr. Iglesias exclaimed, "Ah, that is why you are so knowledgeable."

By the time we landed in Leningrad, I was exhausted. I had had quite a bit of champagne and had taxed my Spanish beyond its limit. Fortunately, we did not have to work the next day, and I got some much-needed rest. While I wandered through the beautiful streets of Leningrad, I was amazed that I was still in the Soviet Union. To this day, I regret not having taken the tour of the famed State Hermitage. Leningrad was so different from dreary Moscow. I was especially taken with the light. The city is far north, across the bay from Finland, and the light has a magic quality to it, illuminating the pastel-colored buildings with an even, cool glow.

I enjoyed the visit, even though we did not manage to do the interview with Sean Connery. The schedules got all confused, and I did not meet Sean until several years later, at a reception at the State Department when he received the Kennedy Center Honors. I was so excited to meet him finally. All those years, I had regretted that I did not get to see him in Leningrad. As thrilled as I was about interviewing Julio Iglesias, Sean Connery was the one on whom I had a crush. He is the kind of man whom men want to be like and women want to be with. I was overjoyed to find out a decade later that I was sitting next to Sean at a State Department reception. Unfortunately, he was more interested in discussing politics with Bill Cohen than in hearing my story of how I had missed him in Leningrad in 1989.

A Death in the Family

Despite my disappointment at not having met Sean Connery, I returned from Russia in a euphoric state. I was working again, and it looked as if I might find a place on national television after all. But the shadow of tragedy continued to stalk me. In early January 1990, my husband followed through on the vow he had spoken of to me and attempted to take his life with pills he had put aside for that purpose. The woman whom he was seeing, alarmed by the fact that he was late for a date, went to the house and found him in time to save his life. I learned later that he was furious at her for interfering with his plan.

When I got the news, I was completely distraught. I had tried for days to speak with Bob on the telephone, but he refused to take my calls. I wanted to go down to Florida to be with him, but my lawyer warned me that I could put myself at serious risk.

"You are in the midst of a divorce," Monroe Inker said. "If your husband really does not want you there, he can press charges. Do not go down there."

"But he needs me," I said.

"He may need you, but he is the one who initiated the divorce. I am not a psychiatrist; I am a lawyer. And as your lawyer, I have to insist that you not go to Florida."

Reluctantly, I abided by his advice and stayed home. I did, however, speak to Bob's four children and asked them to make sure that someone would watch over him. My relationship with his kids had always been a good one. We were not super close, but we were a family. The oldest son, Skip, even jokingly called me Mom, having fun with the fact that his father married a woman who was close in age to his children.

After Bob's attempted suicide, however, I noticed that they were distancing themselves from me. They did not call to let me know how Bob was doing. And when I called them, they were, at first, not forthcoming with information and, eventually, simply unavailable to me. The only one who continued to take my calls was Stephen, who lived near us in the Boston area and with whom I had the closest relationship. But even he just gave one-word answers to my inquiries about Bob.

I resigned myself to the pattern of alienation that had placed me beyond the family circle and tried to focus on my work. By February 1990, I was living in New York, preparing for my next assignment for *ET,* the Academy Awards, which were to take place in March.

Bad news always comes late at night, and I was sure something terrible had happened when the phone rang at midnight of February 6. Even so, I was not prepared for what I heard.

"Is this Mrs. Kistner?" a man with a slight Southern twang asked when I picked up the receiver.

"Yes," I said tentatively, unaccustomed to being addressed by my married name.

"This is Mrs. Robert Kistner?" the man asked again.

"Yes," I said, now really alarmed. "Who is this?"

"This is the sheriff of West Palm Beach, ma'am. I have some bad news for you. Are you alone?"

"I'm alone."

"Well, please sit down."

"I'm fine," I said, even though my heart was pounding. "What is it?"

"Mrs. Kistner, I am sorry to have to tell you that your husband is dead."

"Are you sure?" I asked, unable to accept the reality of what I had feared for so long. "How do you know?"

"I'm here with him, ma'am. I am sure," the sheriff said, trying to spare me the gory details.

"Where?" I demanded. "Where are you?"

"I'm in your condo. In the kitchen." He described the room, and I knew that he was calling from our house.

"Put my husband on the phone," I said, irrationally clinging to the hope that Bob was alive.

"Ma'am, I just told you. He's dead."

I allowed the words to sink in and felt my heart tighten at the thought of the despair that drove Bob to kill himself. I had no doubt that he had committed suicide.

"How did my husband do it?" I asked the sheriff. "Did he take pills?"

"No, he didn't," the man answered but did not volunteer any information.

"Well," I said, "he doesn't have a gun. How did he do it? Did he hang himself? What did he do?"

"He was a surgeon, right?" the sheriff said. "He slit his wrists with a scalpel."

"Tell me," I entreated, feeling like I had to know every detail. "Tell me what he did."

"Do you really want to know?" the sheriff asked wearily.

"I have to know everything," I told him firmly and braced myself in my chair.

The scene the sheriff described was gruesome. Apparently, Bob had gone into my bathroom, filled the big Jacuzzi tub, got in, and cut open his wrists. He went into shock from losing blood, climbed out of the tub, and wandered through the house, leaving a trail of blood everywhere. Finally, he went into the bedroom, lay down on my side on the right side of the bed (my side), and died. There was so much blood the sheriff said, that it soaked through the sheet, the mattress cover, and the mattress, all the way to the carpet.

I kept pressing the sheriff for more details, until he finally told me that the coroner would send me the death certificate with the cause of death listed, and that if I had more questions I could call the coroner's office. I did speak with the coroner after the autopsy the following day, because I needed to know more, to be able to imagine Bob's last moments. *Did he suffer?* I wondered. *How long did it go on?* The coroner was very gentle but direct. He told me what happens to a person as they lose blood, the physical sensations and the physiological changes. It seemed a particularly horrible way to die.

After I hung up the phone, I played the scene that the sheriff had just described over and over in my mind. The sheriff must have thought me macabre for insisting that he relate every grisly detail of Bob's suicide. I couldn't help it. Even though we had been separated and had divorce proceedings pending, I was convinced that we somehow were going to reconcile.

I didn't believe Bob was in love with another woman. And I knew that he didn't hate me. He forced me away because he had hated how the final chapters of his life were being written.

I tried to imagine the depth of loneliness and desperation of his final moments. Bob's gift was that of helping others give life. He had saved thousands of women from infertility. The medical profession revered him. Time after time when we entered a banquet or lecture hall he would receive standing ovations for his work. Frequently, young men and women would come up to Bob to thank him for solving their fertility problems, enabling them to have children. On more than one occasion, grateful parents would thrust an infant into Bob's arms saying, "This is a Kistner baby." Bob was so happy with the contribution he made to their lives, that he kept a bulletin board on the wall in his office with photos of other smiling Kistner babies.

While he was not given to open displays of emotion, he cared deeply for the patients he treated. He was a great doctor. A good man. Even though his hands were no longer nimble enough for surgery, he could still have typed or dictated. And since he could no longer go out into the sun, why did he insist on remaining in Florida?

At first I was in a state of shock, then one of denial. Pacing in my hotel room, I found myself becoming angry. Suicide is such a selfish act. Bob couldn't live life exactly on his terns, so he decided to take it away from all of us. Didn't he consider how his death would affect his children? His friends? Me? Was the cloud of depression so thick that he just didn't give a damn?

The more I pulled these dark thoughts out into the light, the more they wrapped themselves up into a psychological Rubik's cube, eluding every attempt to make everything fit into a neat resolution.

I couldn't wait until morning. I had to talk to his son, Stephen.

I thought Stephen had been the last one to have seen his father, and I wanted to know what had happened.

"Stephen," I said, "he's dead! He did it."

I must admit, I was angry with Bob's children. They had promised me, after his first attempt, that they would take turns looking after him, but none of them had been there when he tried again. I attempted to hide my anger, but the feelings of grief and helplessness were too overwhelming, and I voiced my reproach.

"I thought you were going to be there, Stephen," I said and heard the silence on the other end of the line become more dense.

Stephen's voice sounded flat and distant when he finally spoke: "I was just there, Janet. And to tell you the truth, if people are going to kill themselves, you can't stop them. They are going to do it anyway.

"In any case," he continued, in an even harsher tone, "I don't want to talk about this now. My father has just died."

"But Stephen," I said, hurt by his dismissal, "he was also my husband."

After we hung up, I decided that Stephen's reaction was brought on by grief. *Everyone grieves differently,* I thought. *He's just lashing out at me.* However, I knew something else was afoot when Stephen called me the following day to tell me that they were making arrangements for the funeral. In so many words, he told me that the family would be viewing the body at a particular time, and that I was not welcome to join them. I was already numb, but this news stunned me.

This brutal rejection came as almost as much of a shock as the news of Bob's death. I had no reason to expect that kind of treatment. Bob and I had been having difficulties in our marriage involving his depression, but that had never affected my relationship with his children. I felt that we were all in the same situation, trying to prevent him from pushing us away. In fact, after I had talked to the coroner and understood that as the nearest of kin I was expected to make the decisions about the burial and the service, I had resolved that I would let Bob's children make the arrangements. I thought they would want to bury him next to their mother, and I knew that was the right thing to do.

I simply could not believe that they would be so dismissive of me. At the very least, they could have treated me decently in memory of their father. All they had to do was go through the motions, just be polite. Instead, they seemed determined to hurt me and to show their disdain publicly.

I called my lawyer and told him about what was going on. "You know what? Your husband is gone," he said. "Whatever is past is past. Just let it go."

I had to remind myself of Monroe Inker's good advice when I got another telephone call from Bob's son. "Janet," Stephen said, "would you mind calling the mortuary and giving them the address of the funeral home in Boston."

"Stephen," I responded, trying not to sound angry, "just call them directly."

Suddenly, Peter was on the line, even though he had not said anything up to that point, not even hello. "We've already called," he said, "and they told us that you are the only person who can release the body. It's a legal thing. They have to have instructions from the next of kin."

I was really furious when I hung up. *The law acknowledges me as the nearest of kin*, I thought bitterly, *and these people can't even be nice to me in our moment of sorrow. If I were really mean, I could have their father cremated and sent to them in an urn, or I could have him buried in Florida with no marker.*

My love for Bob and my own integrity won the day, of course. I gave the coroner's office the instructions for sending the body to the funeral home in Boston. I even called Stephen back and told him that I thought Bob would have liked to be buried in his favorite cashmere blazer. "I will have it sent up, a whole outfit. That's the only request that I am making: Please bury him in that jacket."

"Well, I'll have to consult with the rest of the family," Stephen said.

He did call me back, after the family had agreed to my request and I had sent the jacket up to him. "Thank you, Janet," he said. "That was a very generous gesture." It felt good to get even that little bit of tenderness and acknowledgment. It allowed me to do one last thing for Bob.

While I was unwelcome at the viewing, I did attend the memorial service, which was scheduled for Saturday, February 10, 1990, at Harvard's Memorial Church. The evening I arrived in Boston, I received a phone call from Elle and Joe, an elderly couple with whom Bob and I were friendly. They had embraced me during Bob's life and the years that followed.

"How are you getting to the church?" Elle asked me, letting me know that the dissension in the family was widely known. "Why don't we pick you up?"

"No, thank you," I said. "I really appreciate the offer, but it's not necessary. I will get there."

The day of the funeral, I hired a limousine and drove out to Cambridge with two of my best friends, Liv Heraty and Colette Phillips. It was hard to walk into that crowded church. I felt like we were playing out this melodrama, like something out of *Dynasty*, in front of all of Bob's colleagues, his patients, and his friends. It was terrible.

I was there for Bob, however, so I was determined to rise above it all and say good-bye to him with respect and dignity. I sat four rows back and on the other side from the family. Elle tried to get me to join them in the front pew, but I declined.

"You know they don't want me there," I said. "And I am not going to create a scene."

I sat on the aisle and marveled at people's awkwardness and cruelty. Doctors who had dined with us, sent us holiday cards, chatted with us at professional conferences, walked by me and averted their eyes. I could not believe that all these people who had been so nice to me while Bob was alive were shunning me.

Have they always felt this way deep down inside? I wondered. *Is the bigotry just coming out? Do they think I am a Black gold digger who had married above myself, drove the old guy into his grave, and now is going to get all the money, leaving his nice little White children with nothing?*

Not one of the doctors came over to me to offer his condolences. To them, I was suddenly the slave who had come in from the field and dared to stay in the house after having slept with the master. I was appalled by their hypocrisy and lack of courage and decency.

It only went from bad to worse. Skip, the oldest son, read the eulogy. I was hurt that he did not acknowledge me or the significance of our twelve years of marriage. I started to wonder whether the children, like the doctors, had resented me all along. *Are they angry at me because I stood in their mother's place?* I thought, *Do they see me as standing between them and their inheritance?*

At this point, the service ended and the family walked in procession toward the back of the church. It was like a movie, watching this column of mourners, which I as the widow should have been leading, move down the wide aisle. Bob's sister, Shirley, came first, then Dana, his daughter, Skip, Stephen, and finally Peter, with their spouses and children. As they filed past me, Stephen extended his hand and pulled me from the pew. He did not say anything, just escorted me the rest of the way, his wife on one arm, and me on the other.

I will never, ever forget that moment. It was a moment of one soul reaching out to another. In spite of everything, Stephen heard the call of his own conscience and acted with humanity and kindness. I will always be grateful to him for that wonderful gesture. I thought that if Bob were watching, he would have been very proud of his son.

The family lined up in a receiving line, and I stood off on the other side of the church doors. I wanted to show that I knew my appropriate place as Bob's wife and now his widow, even if his family excluded me and his friends ignored me.

I had never felt so invisible in my life. People I had known for years simply walked past me. Even Dr. Robert Knapp, the William H. Baker professor at Harvard, who was the medical director at Bob's hospital, avoided me. Neither he nor his wife, with whom Bob and I had socialized, had the decency to acknowledge my loss. When I saw Dr. Knapp several months later, I took the opportunity to tell him how surprised I had been at the memorial service by the depth of his grief.

"What do you mean?" he asked, taken aback.

"Well, after the many times we had all had dinner together, it could not have been anything other than your grief that prevented you from offering me your condolences."

The man just looked at me and did not say anything. It was satisfying to be able to speak my truth.

On the day of the memorial service, however, all I could do was watch in stunned silence as people I had thought of as friends shook hands with the family and ignored me. When I could no longer stand it, I went outside to look for my limo. The service had started at four o'clock, and it was already dark. The car was gone. I guessed that my girlfriends, thinking that I would join the family for the reception at the country club, went back to the Tea Room at the Ritz. We had agreed to rendezvous there later that evening.

I looked up at the dark, cold sky and said out loud, "Bob, can you believe this? This is so surreal. Where am I going to get a taxi in Cambridge?"

Then, as it started to drizzle, I went off in search of a public phone. I finally did find a phone and called Boston Cab, a company with which I had had an account. "This is Janet Langhart," I said. "I need a cab."

"Where are you?" the dispatcher asked.

"I don't really know," I said. "I don't see any street signs. I just left Memorial Church in Harvard."

Not surprisingly, I waited in vain for a cab to find me. I just started walking, having decided that I would walk back to Boston. Fortunately, I did see a Boston Cab taxi. I flagged him down, and to my relief he stopped. It was highly unusual for a cab to stop on the street, especially for a Black person.

I told the driver where I was going and settled back, thinking about how terrible it had felt to be so unwelcome at my own husband's funeral.

"You just lost somebody really close to you, didn't you?" the driver said.

"Yes, how did you know that?"

"You lost your husband, didn't you? I read in the paper that Dr. Kistner killed himself, Ms. Langhart, and I am real sorry."

I was overwhelmed with gratitude for the kindness and compassion of this man I did not even know.

"Thank you," I said. "I can't tell you how much your words mean to me."

Outside of the rancor in the immediate family, there were many people who cared about Bob and me. His obituary was published by the *Boston Globe,* the *New York Times,* the *Washington Post,* and the Associated Press, among many others. Cards, telegrams, and condolence calls continued to pour in over several months. One of Bob's friends, Jane Stewart, who was married to a physician who served as a consultant to G.D. Searle Pharmaceutical Company, was the first to call. Like Joe and Elle, she had witnessed the depth of the love that Bob and I shared.

Among the people who called was my old friend Bill Cohen, who had read of Bob's passing in the newspaper. We talked briefly, but the connection that I had felt when we first met in the seventies was still there. We agreed to get together the next time he was in New York or I was in Washington. Although I was grieving for Bob, when Bill and I ended the conversation, I felt a stirring of hope. The universe is, I knew, infinitely benevolent, and joy would someday take the place of the sorrow that I felt at the moment.

In the meantime, I had a lot to do. I wanted to have our Palm Beach house cleaned. I could not bear the thought of Bob's blood spattered everywhere. I also needed to go there to get our papers together. The management company at the condominium association recommended a cleaning service. I explained to the man I spoke with what had happened, what they would find, and asked him to remove any traces of blood. I told him to do whatever necessary—rip out carpets, strip off the wallpaper, get rid of the furniture.

The man at the cleaning service was gracious and professional. He treated me with kindness and respect and did his job well. When I walked into the house a few days later, it looked as if nothing had happened. I had gone down with my brother, who had offered his support even though we have never been very close, and with a friend from Boston. I knew that I would need people on whom to lean. I was glad they were there when I went through the house for the first time. I was not really looking for blood, but I kept searching for some sign of his final moments. I could not rest until I found one little speck of blood on a baseboard in the bedroom. Somehow it helped to make Bob's death real for me.

I was amazed to see that all the papers were as meticulously organized as they had always been. Bob was a very precise person, but I had expected that in his depression he would have left things in disarray. However, everything was there, neatly arranged, as if he had left it for me to find. His will, the titles to our properties, and other papers.

As it turned out, Bob might, in fact, have wanted me to find those documents, because they became very important for me in protecting myself against the lawsuit that had been initiated by the lawyer representing Bob's children in an attempt to take control of the majority of his estate.

Divorces are always hard, even when "friendly." Family members are often touched as deeply as the principals. Frequently, they wrap up their grief in blanket accusations and cast blame against those they think responsible for their pain. Blood is almost always thicker than water, particularly when the suicide of a parent is involved.

Bailey for the Defense

Fortunately, the universe was looking out for me. Out of the blue, I received a telephone call from F. Lee Bailey, famous defense attorney. I had become friendly with him through his mother, Grace, who was a big fan of mine in Boston.

"What's going on, Janet?" Lee asked. "My mother called me and told me that the Kistner family is after you. I told her that I don't do estates; I am a criminal lawyer. But she was adamant: 'They are going to destroy our Janet. Go help her.' "

I told Lee everything that had happened up to that point, and he agreed to talk to the family's lawyer to see if we could reach a settlement. The thing that troubled me most was that they were coming after everything Bob and I had, so I would lose even some of the property I had brought into the marriage. I was perfectly happy to let them have all the things their parents had accumulated together, like the furniture Georgia had picked out for the house in Milton, but I was not prepared to part with things for which I had worked hard my whole life. Lee told me that by law I was entitled to as much as one-third of the estate if I elected to take action against the will. I told him that I thought fifty percent was fair under the circumstances.

With that, Lee went to see the family's lawyer. When he called me after the meeting, I could tell from his voice that he was angry. "We are in for a fight, Janet," he said. "This guy George Packard is out for your blood."

"Why are you talking to the divorce lawyer?" I asked, puzzled. Bob's divorce lawyer, George Packard, it turned out, had switched from the firm that was handling the divorce to a different law firm that was handling the estate.

"Is that common?" I asked Lee.

"No," he said, "it's highly irregular. He's got it in for you."

Lee proceeded to tell me about his conversation with Packard. He had laid out our proposal, saying "Janet is entitled to such and such, this is what we are willing to offer, and this is what we want."

"That Black bitch has gotten more than she deserved," Packard said. "She got the pleasure of being with Dr. Kistner, and she is not entitled to a damned thing. She's gotten all she is going to get. I took the case to make sure of that."

"He thought that because we were all White guys sitting around the table, it was alright to say that," Lee said indignantly. "I told him just what I thought of him, the unethical SOB."

"You know what," I said, my rage finally awakened, "I don't want to negotiate with these people anymore. Tell them that I've had enough of their dishonoring their father's memory and disparaging my name. I want the whole estate or nothing at all. Let the law decide who is in the right. Let's roll the dice."

"Are you sure?" Lee said. "It could go either way, you know. You might end up with nothing."

"I don't care," I said. "It's not about the money, anymore. It's the principle. Most of the money was Bob's anyway. He got it the hard way: He earned it. It should've been buried with him."

"Well, let's sleep on it," he said.

I did not hear from him again for a month. Finally, I called to find out what was happening.

"I just wanted to make sure you've had time to think about it," Lee said. "Remember, you are risking the loss of a lot of money."

"I've had more than enough time," I replied. "I am not changing my mind."

The case ended up going to court in Florida. Bob had asked me to sign away all rights that I had to his pension plan with the promise that he would draft a new will that would be extremely generous to me. He did draft a second will, but it excluded me from any share in his estate. We had to prove that my signature had been obtained by fraud.

Lee was brilliant in court. He used his skill at cross-examination to lead Bob's estate lawyer into referring to verbal discussions Bob had had with him, which then allowed us to use as evidence things Bob had said to me. It was a real courtroom drama.

Lee got Bob's lawyer on the stand and said: "You advised Dr. Kistner about restructuring his pension plan, correct? That required that Mrs. Kistner give up millions of dollars in inheritance. We're talking about a lot of money here. Did you think that it might have been necessary to advise Mrs. Kistner to have counsel represent her, since you were representing not her but her husband? Would you, if you were representing her, have allowed her to sign those documents, to sign away her rights? Didn't you have an ethical obligation to advise her she should have counsel at the table?"

"Yes," the lawyer conceded, "but Dr. Kistner said that he had talked to her about it."

"Judge Fine," Lee said, "at this point, I'd like to waive the Dead Man's Rule and bring into evidence what Dr. Kistner said to *my* client."

That was the turning point. I not only had a precise recollection of my conversations with Bob, I also had the papers that he left for me to find in the Palm Beach house, which backed up my version of events. The judge ruled in my favor. Mr. Packard filed an appeal, but it was only a delaying tactic. The game was over and he had lost, I had won, but the settlement would not be resolved for almost two years.

I was convinced that Packard was far more interested in the litigation than were Bob's children. In addition, I sensed that there was lurking below the surface of the firm that he was once with, the stench of racism. Bob had been a pillar in the medical profession and the White community. They considered his marriage to me to be a mere dalliance, an aberration in an otherwise stellar life. Had it not been for Packard's racist "Black bitch" comment, I would have accepted one-third or even less from the estate.

Lee came up to New York, and we had dinner at Café Diablo. We went over the details of the testimony and our strategy going forward. Even though I had won the case, I was determined to do the right thing. Bob and I had been married twelve years, and there were lots of assets that had been acquired by Bob and Georgia, which I did not begrudge their children. I had everything I needed. And now that the law had allowed the truth to be known, I wanted to be fair. I decided that I would divide the estate sixty-forty with Bob's children.

I told Lee what I had in mind, and he said, "That's why I love you. You've got brass balls, and you've got character."

"If I ever see Bob again," I said, "I want to be able to face him and say I did right by his kids."

Although I did right by Bob's family, it seemed that the world was not yet ready to do right by me.

I had acquired the real estate in Palm Beach and Boston because the two condominiums had been jointly owned. The problem was that I had also acquired their respective mortgages, and they were large. As a matter of pride, I initially refused to sell the condo at the Ritz even though I was living in New York. Pride does indeed goeth before he fall. The real estate market was down and I was forced to subsidize wealthy renters to keep the payments current with the bank. Then, when I could no longer carry the property and had to sell it at a substantial loss, I discovered that the city of Boston had placed a lien on the property several years earlier for back taxes.

When we had purchased the unit, the previous owner, Charlie Downer, the wealthy socialite who had introduced me to polo, had given the city a bad check for the taxes. Rather than pursue him for the misdeed, the city simply filed a lien in the registry of deeds.

In order to sell the property, I would have to pay the back taxes, accumulated interest, and penalties. I turned to the title insurance company, Lawyer's Title Insurance, but it denied any liability, claiming that the title was clear at the time of closing, which it was not if Charlie Downer's share of the taxes had not been paid. It argued alternatively that I had waited too long to alert them to the nonpayment of the taxes. When taking a thorough examination of the property tax statements from the City of Boston, I noticed an asterisk on the front of each page, alerting me to turn to the back. The explanation noted that "back taxes were due." Lawyer's Title Insurance representatives had assured us at closing that the title was clear. We had no reason to expect this asterisk represented any amount due, let alone, back taxes due. Therefore, we only paid the amount shown on the front of each statement. Further, Bob always paid his bills on time and in full.

My only option was to sue Charlie Downer, who was then living in Europe. All appeals to the city were fruitless. I needed to unload a very large albatross from my neck and was forced to use what little savings I had managed to put away to pay a rich man's taxes. I sent a check to the City of Boston.

So much for emancipation!

Celebrity Muscle

In the midst of all the turmoil in my personal life, my career seemed to be, for the first time in a long while, a bright spot for me. I continued to get interesting, high-profile assignments. In March 1990, I went to London for *ET*'s Oscars extravaganza. I did interviews with Glenn Close and other stars who were in England appearing in plays or filming movies.

Then in May, I went to Cannes to cover the film festival. On the way over, the producer discussed my putting more of an edge into my interviews. I was not sure how I was supposed to have an edge when my job was to read what the producers wrote. It had not been easy, weaned as I was on live television, to get accustomed to following a script, but I had trained myself to be disciplined. After all, the producers knew what "California" wanted and had the formula all worked out.

In any case, I agreed to infuse a little edge into the interviews. We had exciting people lined up. I had called Paul Bloch, an old acquaintance who handled major stars like Sylvester Stallone, Sharon Stone, and Arnold Schwarzenegger, and arranged to interview Stallone. *ET* booked Arnold and many others.

I was particularly pleased about getting the interview with Stallone, because he had refused to be interviewed throughout the festival. In fact, I had to talk to him in the kitchen of one of the hotels, so the rest of the media corps would not see.

The following day, I was scheduled to interview Arnold. I was in my hotel room, getting ready and thinking about what kind of an edge I could have with an action hero. *Larry King Live* came on CNN International. And as luck would have it, Larry was interviewing Arnold. They chatted a while about *Kindergarten Cop,* the movie Arnold was promoting that year. And then Larry asked him about a book that had just come out, *Arnold: An Unauthorized Biography.*

"The author talks in the book about Nazis . . ." Larry said. "How do you feel about that?"

"You know," Arnold replied dismissively, "I haven't read the book. I don't know this author. The book is just trash. She is going around talking to different audiences, but it's just trash. . . ." The author, Wendy Leigh, had written that Arnold's father had been a member of Hitler's Nazi Party in Austria.

It was not an out-and-out denial, but he handled the question skillfully. I had interviewed Arnold once on *Good Day,* when he was still just a bodybuilder, and promoting the film *Pumping Iron,* and had not been terribly impressed with him. Now, however, it seemed clear that he had matured and had become quite sophisticated. *Here,* I thought, *is an edge. I'll talk to Arnold about this book.*

The next day, we were out at Cannes shooting. I had just finished doing a stand-up interview with Grace Jones. Arnold came lumbering over, charming and sweet. He clearly did not remember me from Boston, but he hugged me and said, "Hello, *Entertainment Tonight.*"

We set up the shot, and I said, "Arnold, tell me about your latest project."

He gave me the prepared sound bites about the movie, and we moved on.

"On a personal level," I continued, feeling it was the moment to introduce some edge into the interview, "How do you feel about this book that's claiming your father was a Nazi?"

I suspected at that moment that my career in celebrity interviews just might be over. The look on Arnold's face changed from a friendly smile to an admonishing frown.

"We have an understanding with *Entertainment Tonight* that we are not to talk about that," he said.

"We do?" I asked, surprised. "Nobody told me."

Out of the corner of my eye, I saw Grace Jones slide away. Then my producer yelled "cut," and Arnold turned on his heel and stomped off.

"Why did you ask him that question?" the producer asked breathlessly.

"Larry King asked him the question last night on global television," I said, "and Arnold was very nice about it. You guys have been telling me to get an edge. I couldn't create one, so I borrowed Larry's."

By the time we got back to the hotel in Nice, there was a stack of messages from California. The producer was on the phone with them for hours, it seemed. Finally, when I saw her again, she said, "You know, you're going to get me fired."

"How am I going to get you fired? I did the interview."

"You weren't supposed to ask that."

"Wait a minute," I blew up. "When were you going to tell me I wasn't supposed to ask that question?"

"That's Arnold Schwarzenegger. *Entertainment Tonight* depends on their celebrities. We don't do anything to offend them. We're celebrity-driven. You ask a question like that, and we are liable to get locked out of the whole circuit."

The next morning, the word was out all over the festival. Arnold had made it clear that if I showed up at any press conferences or events, he would walk out, and no one would get interviews.

"You've got to be kidding," I said. "This is a major star doing an interview for a major celebrity show. I just asked him a question. Edit it out, that's all."

I sought out Paul Bloch and said, "Paul, do you know Arnold's practically banned me from the festival? He doesn't want to get sight of me. He doesn't even want me in the building at the same time he's in it."

"Look," Paul said. "You got your interview with Stallone. Don't worry about it."

"But what about Arnold?" I said. "How can he ban me from coming into a public place? I know this is France, but isn't it a free country too?"

"Janet, I can't deal with you on that," Paul said sternly and rushed away.

The next day, everyone in the crew was on edge, making sure that I did not come into Arnold's field of vision. Finally, the producer's walkie-talkie squawked. She listened, turned to me and said, "Arnold's on his way. You have to get out of this hotel."

I went out onto the terrace of the beautiful Hotel Cap D'Antibes and sat on the back step. I could not exactly enjoy the sights, but I did watch the people coming and going. A well-dressed older woman caught my eye as she stepped from her limousine. She strode in, carrying a small black poodle under her arm. I heard a commotion as she entered the restaurant, and even though I do not speak French, I surmised that there was a problem with the dog. Most restaurants in France allow dogs, but apparently not this one. Little CoCo was shown the door. In fact, she was tied up on the terrace near where I sat, with a bowl of food and water.

As the celebrities swept past us trailed by their fawning managers and paparazzi, I looked down at the little dog and just started laughing. *Here we are,* I thought, *two little black bitches not allowed inside.* We were in the South of France, but we could just as well have been in South Africa or the Deep South of America.

While I couldn't be sure, given our historical experience, I didn't think that Arnold's reaction was race-based. Rather, I thought it was a question of pure power. *Larry King* was live and carried internationally. Arnold had no choice but to respond in a manner that suggested a classic case of "more in sorrow than anger." Following that broadcast, however, he apparently had made it clear that he did not want to see the subject become a matter of routine interrogation. Discussion about his father's ties to the Nazis was to be strictly off-limits.

The problem was that no one at *ET* conveyed his diktat to me. I had simply assumed that if Larry King could discuss the issue of his relationship with his father, then surely *ET* would find it of interest. . . .

I knelt next to my little black companion and stroked her carefully groomed curls. I was angry, and depressed, and afraid that I would lose my job.

When Arnold had come and gone, I was allowed to re-enter the hotel. My little companion, I expect, went off to a sumptuous villa.

I was not surprised when *ET* began to find fault with my performance after I returned to the States. I had not had an assignment in several months. *ET* was still paying me but just not using me. Finally, I got a call from one of the executives. "We really have trouble with your English and the way you speak. You have a strange kind of accent. We want to send you to Magid Institute in Iowa to work on your speech pattern. It's way off."

"I'm speaking the same way as when you hired me. You did not have a problem with my audition tape, or the audition, or any of the interviews I've done until now. Suddenly you are having a problem understanding my English?"

Even Stevie Wonder could see what was happening. The studio executives wanted to fire me to pacify Arnold, but were afraid that I might institute legal action against them. Perhaps I would take the message and quit rather than go off to the Gulag and have some college graduate instruct me on the finer points of the English language.

I refused to accommodate them. Insulting and unpalatable as it was, I agreed to go to Iowa. I was not going to make it easy for them.

Off to Iowa I went and sat through basic media training conducted by a twenty-four-year-old blonde kid who had me say things like "How now brown cow."

I remember calling Bill Cohen and saying, "Bill, do I sound funny to you? These people are driving me crazy."

"They're setting you up so they can fire you," Bill said. "It's all a cover-your-ass strategy. They'll say that they did everything to help you, so you don't sue them for discrimination."

When the ax finally fell, they had all the big suits in the room. Now, you do not have the executive producer fly in from the coast to fire a lowly reporter. But when I was called into the Paramount Building in New York, the two top executives, David and Barry, were there.

"We want to talk to you about your language skills," one of them said. "We've sent you to Magid, and they just don't think there's any hope for you and your television career. You might consider doing something else."

"What is the real problem?" I asked, looking hard at them.

"Well, when we listen to the tapes, we don't understand you."

"Did you understand me when you looked at my tapes and when you auditioned me? What is the real deal? Are any of you man enough to tell me?"

"We've told you," one of them persisted. "At Magid, they concluded that you just don't have it."

It was truly laughable. I had been performing on television for more than twenty years, and I was being told that my English was imperfect, that I had a strange accent? The irony was too much. I was being fired because I had offended an Austrian born body-builder-turned-actor whose thick accent had remained as prodigious as his biceps!

I knew that I could not win that fight, so I said, "Okay. All right. Thank you very much. I understand. I just want two weeks' severance."

"You *do* understand that it's because of your language skills?" they said.

"I *do* understand that it's not racism," I said. "I also understand that it's Arnold Schwarzenegger and not my language skills."

I left the room dejected. I had just been terminated by The Terminator.

After *ET,* I took a job with a show called *9 Broadcast Plaza,* which was produced and aired by WWOR-TV, a regional "super station." It was a national New York talk show based in New Jersey that started out with a format similar to *Good Day* but that was slowly turning into something more akin to *Jerry Springer.* Bill Cohen, who could see the show down in D.C., kept saying to me, "Why do you want to do a schlocky show like that?"

"I want to work," I said, "and *60 Minutes* is not calling."

One day, as I was getting ready in my dressing room, I received a call from Wendy Leigh, the author of the book over which I had gotten fired from *Entertainment Tonight.*

"The grapevine has it that you asked Arnold about my book," she said.

"How do you know that? The interview never got aired."

"Because we've been following Arnold. We know how he is. That's how he treats people. That's why you got fired, you know."

"I know," I said, "but, of course, they wouldn't own up."

"Of course not. That's actually why I am calling. He's trying to squash my book. He's trying to destroy my character. And he's got a whole machine working for him. Will you stand with me?"

"Are you kidding?" I said. "I don't want to take on the whole industry. I will have my say one day. I know that. But this is not the hill I'll die on."

My instinct for self-protection suddenly kicked in. I was so tired from fighting with Bob's family, with my family, with the people of Boston, with the people at *ET,* I did not want to fight anymore. I just wanted to work and go on with my life.

Over the next eight months, I threw myself into work at *9BP.* We were building an audience in a very competitive market and getting good ratings, but I started to become increasingly disenchanted there. When Rodney King was beaten by the Los Angeles police, I wanted to do some of the interviews on the subject of racism and police brutality. The subject was ruled out of bounds for me. Apparently, a Black could not be trusted to be unbiased or objective on the subject. It was a case of rank discrimination and sexism to boot. The station manager wanted me safely in the kitchen, doing cooking segments with Bill Cosby as light entertainment. It was déjà vu all over again. I knew it was just a question of time before I would leave the show.

I began to explore other options. I had gotten to know Steve Ross, the former chairman of Warner Bros. Steve was moving Time Warner into the cable business in a major way. He wanted to create a show for me and asked me to visit with his top executive in charge of programming. I was eager to have my very own talk show on a cable network and flew immediately out to Chicago to meet with his man, Jonathan Gilder.

I arrived mid-morning at the television studio owned by *The Chicago Tribune*. Jonathan was in the control room watching Jenny Jones do a pilot show before a live audience. He could not take his eyes off the Canadian-born comedian.

"Isn't she beautiful?" he asked me effusively. I acknowledged that she was indeed very attractive.

"And talented too," he said, his eyes still glued to the monitor.

No, I wanted to say, *but she is blonde, and that counts for a lot to the men who control our careers.*

Jonathan made it clear that he was too preoccupied to keep our scheduled meeting. "Why don't you go to the hotel and wait there. I'll probably be tied up for the rest of the day. When I finish up, we can get together for dinner."

I checked into the hotel and waited in my room until eight o'clock that evening. Finally, Jonathan called. He was running late. Sorry. Dinner was out so why not just meet him in the coffee shop. He was not hungry but I could eat there if I wanted. Charming.

In the coffee shop, he continued to gush over Jenny Jones. He finally asked what I had in mind for a television show. "Well, actually, a talk show much like the one Jenny was doing today."

He earlier had said he had been a big fan of mine and had admired the way I handled myself on *Good Day* in Boston. I was stunned when he immediately rejected the notion of such a show for me.

"A Black audience won't be able to relate to you. You're too articulate." He went on to say that he thought that I sounded a little too much like Sammy Davis, Jr. Apparently, he found Sammy's English to be a bit on the British side of the Atlantic, and was therefore, an affectation. I could feel my blood start to rise. Once again, all Blacks were cast in a concrete mold of prejudice. If we studied language and practiced diction so that we could articulate our thoughts as well as any White person, our speech was artificial, and affected, therefore, subject to question or ridicule. No, we must remain on the plantation, inferior in language skills as well as talent playing out our script with *dis* and *dat*.

When I argued that I had crossover ability and could relate to a far wider audience than the Black community, he countered by saying that I was "too beautiful."

"Too beautiful for whom?" I could barely contain myself. "Is Jenny Jones too beautiful? Is Diane Sawyer too beautiful? Is Jane Pauley too beautiful? Do I have to wear an Afro and mangle my vocabulary? Is that what you're saying?"

"White women would find you too threatening."

"I'm not planning to sleep with their husbands. I only want to work."

It was no use. I was whistling in the wind. The conversation ended and Gilder left. The next day I packed my bags and headed for O'Hare airport.

I had been caught in a vicious catch-22. For *ET* I did not speak well enough. For Gilder I spoke too well. I returned to New York in a state of rage, and one just short of despair.

Capitol Verse

Just as one door was slammed in my face, the universe opened another one. Life had begun to take an interesting new turn. More than seven months had passed since Bob's death and as I emerged out of my mourning, I began to be more open to a different kind of relationship with Bill Cohen. Bill had been divorced three years earlier. We were in regular contact and would see each other occasionally when he came to New York. It was clear that there was a spark, and with time we started dating.

I was concerned that I was on the rebound. However, Bill was such good company, and there seemed to be so much we had in common, I allowed myself just to go with it. It seemed as if our stars had aligned after so many years and we were ready for each other. I remember one particular incident that convinced me that there was something special afoot.

It was near Christmas, the end of 1990. I was down in Palm Beach trying to wrap up some tax matters. I was feeling blue and decided to call Bill to wish him a happy holiday. I dialed his office number and left a message with his secretary. About five minutes later, Bill called me.

"Oh," I said, "that was fast."

"What do you mean?" he asked.

"Didn't Cindy give you the message? I just called you," I said.

"I'm up in Maine for the holidays," he said, laughing. "I was thinking about you. Wanted to wish you a happy birthday, and I figured you might be down in Florida."

"You're kidding," I said, feeling like this was some sort of an omen. "I was thinking about you too."

Later in the winter, Bill came down to Florida to see me. I wanted to show off and took him to the polo field. I had dressed up in my riding britches and helmet. Bill watched me ride around, just doing a little stick-and-ball practice. I galloped and turned, and then had the horse rear on her hind legs. Bill was duly impressed.

That evening, I wore a gardenia in my hair as I prepared dinner. Bill sat in the living room jotting on a pad of paper. Later, as we sipped our drinks by candlelight, Bill said, "I want to read you something."

I knew he was interested in poetry and wrote some himself, but I was not prepared for what followed.

> *A cry,*
> *a gull song,*
> *wings white against*
> *a liquid sky;*
> *palm trees sway in a wind*
> *suddenly warm with rage;*
> *horses race*
> *in the distance*
> *polo fields shudder*
> *under hooves that whip and whirl*
> *in pirouettes*
> *of mammoth grace.*

Was it you,
the one with gardenias
in your hair
who reached out
and touched me?
Were those your tears
or mine that salt-licked
their way into an
invisible wound?

Or was it, instead,
imaginary horses
whirling now
wet with heat,
trackless in the
wild-headed sea

drowning me
in the perfume
of crushed flowers?

At that moment, I realized that I was falling in love. Life had again found a way to surprise me. I had found the strength and courage to stay true to myself in the face of all the challenges that I had had to confront, personally and professionally. Now, it seemed, it was time for the next phase of the journey to begin. I was ready for it. Or so I thought.

8

Matters of the Heart

One of the things that I found most appealing about Bill Cohen, in addition to his poet's heart, was that he was a kindred spirit, a person who had had to define his own place in the world. I recall a brief incident from our early days of dating that reminded me just how much of an outsider this brilliant, accomplished man is.

Bill came to see me in New York, and as we were strolling down Fifth Avenue, I invited him to one of my favorite places in the city, Our Lady's Chapel in St. Patrick's Cathedral.

"I love this building," I said. "Let's go in and sit in the chapel."

"Can I go in there?" Bill asked, visibly dismayed by the thought.

"Sure," I replied. "It's wonderful."

"But I'm half Jewish," he said, furrowing his brow.

"Well, I'm not exactly Catholic," I joked, suddenly aware of his discomfort at the thought of being someplace where he might not be welcome. "Come on. Everybody can enter here."

Ironically, each time I had brought someone that I loved there, religious denomination had reared its own special significance.

Bill and I shared the experience of having to carve out a personal identity in the face of societal conventions and expectations that were too simplistic and constraining. As a couple, we did not fit any mold either. Our life experiences and personalities created an unexpected blend of perspectives, beliefs, and aspirations.

Even though there were a handful of prominent interracial couples at the time, I worried that our relationship would damage Bill's political career. When the fact that we were dating became public knowledge, Bill did receive a letter from a couple who were major contributors to his past campaigns, calling his character into question and "professing to speak for a majority of his supporters."

"If the rumors of your involvement with a Black woman are true, the people of Maine have misjudged you. You are not the man we thought you to be and the one who we have so generously supported over the years."

Bill's response was immediate and unequivocal: "I am confident that your views are not shared by the people of Maine. Apparently, it is *I* who have misjudged *you*. Had I known you held such racist views, I never would have accepted your support. . . ."

For the most part, however, it seemed as if no one even noticed. We were just Bill and Janet, a couple falling in love and meant for each other, as all our friends kept telling us. The question of race, if it was there at all, was an unspoken one, except for occasional teasing on the *Imus in the Morning* radio show.

Bill and I have always been fans of Don Imus. At one Washington event, we had the occasion of telling him so. I was excited to meet him and found myself gushing like a fan. Don was cool and his wife, Deidre, was pleasant.

I thought nothing more of it until the following week when Bill and I heard him teasing on his show that I "ran up to him like a groupie," and indeed was "gushing all over him about being a fan." I thought it was funny, even the continued banter between Don and Bernard. I remember Bernard saying, "Oh, I know Janet Langhart. She's the one that looks like Tina Turner."

Hearing that, Bill was taken aback. I laughed and replied, "Well, at least he didn't say I looked like Ike Turner!"

The teasing didn't end with just that one day. Intermittently, we'd be the brunt of their jokes. I remember one morning some time later, Imus said, "Bill Cohen has to be the whitest man in America, but he's got some brown sugar." I really chuckled on that one. I don't think Bill found it as amusing as I did because several of his friends would tease him and say how Imus was really letting him have it.

I had a pleasant surprise when watching the show one morning while Tom Brokaw was on, hearing him tell Don a little about Bill and me as a couple. "Bill's a swell guy and Janet is interested in things he's interested in. They're doing a great job serving this country at the Department of Defense." That was a lovely thing that Tom said, something that only a friend would do.

That was the only experience I ever had with anyone openly discussing us as a racial couple. In fact we once had been invited to share President Ronald Reagan's birthday with him and his friends at Chasen's Restaurant in Los Angeles. I was seated between two white-haired octogenarians who were intrigued, not by my color, but that we had so much in common in our love of horses.

Occasionally, we would get a glimpse of our breech of the racial divide, as the time when a stranger came up to us at our favorite restaurant in New York, Bravo Gianni's. As we were leaving, the man who had been staring at us all evening from an adjoining table, came up to Bill and said, "It must be very difficult for you."

When Bill asked what he meant, the man said, "Being a politician and all. You must have to be careful about what you do in public."

"I still don't understand what you're talking about," Bill said, understanding full well what was on the man's mind. "I'm free, single, and over twenty-one."

The man stumbled about, tripping over his words. Finally, he glanced over at me and said, "Well, you know."

Indeed we did.

Several months earlier, I traveled to Los Angeles to attend a book party thrown for Bill at the Beverly Hilton Hotel by Ruth Singer, one of his longtime supporters. He had just published his latest novel, *One-Eyed Kings,* and Ruth wanted to give it wide exposure among some of Los Angeles's most prominent people. Entering the hotel room as a couple, we generated a considerable buzz. It was not unlike that moment when I stepped out onto the runway wearing a wedding gown as a Marshall Field's model. I asked Bill if he had warned the hostess that I was Black. He said that he had not. Bill had said only that he was bringing his date. Ruth did not know and could not have guessed "who was coming to dinner." After the initial shock, however, the atmosphere was quite amiable. One distinguished gentleman, in seeking to make polite dinner conversation, asked me, "What island are you from?"

The question was innocent and carried no edge. It was obvious that I simply did not conform to his vision of what an African-American woman would be like.

I smiled and politely said, "Manhattan."

For the man at Bravo Gianni's that night, however, it was clear from his racist audacity in speaking to Bill, that Riker's Island was more of what he had in mind.

As I was considering the next steps in what appeared to be a very limited career, out of the blue, I received a call from Byron Lewis, Jr., whose family owns *America's Black Forum,* a syndicated news and public interest show. He came up to New York from Washington and over an elegant lunch at Mulholland Drive restaurant, a Manhattan hot spot, offered me a job in the nicest of possible ways. "Would you please come to *America's Black Forum?*" Byron said, after having told me how much he admired my work. "Julian Bond is the other cohost."

"Work with Julian Bond?" I asked, not even trying to disguise my excitement. "That would be fantastic."

I have always admired Julian. Although I had never met him during my time in Chicago, I felt connected to him through the memory of Dr. King. Julian, who was one of the founders of the Student Nonviolent Coordinating Committee, was an effective and passionate leader. In 1968, at the Democratic National Convention, Julian was the first African-American to have his name placed in nomination for Vice President. I saw the chance to work with him as a wonderful opportunity to learn and to bring my own passion on the issues that were confronting our people.

In fact, Julian and I did have interesting chemistry as cohosts of *America's Black Forum.* He and I are only a couple of years apart in age, but we come from vastly different backgrounds. Julian is the son of a prominent Southern family—his father was a noted educator—and Julian grew up in a Black, academic environment. When we first started working together, I was reminded of what Dr. King sometimes said about the class and cultural differences between Northern and Southern Blacks.

It was a class distinction. Julian and I had different experiences because of our respective backgrounds. In the South, Blacks responded to segregation by building their own communities, institutions, and social structures. They could insulate themselves from oppression by confining themselves within their self-contained enclaves. In the "integrated" North, we did not have that option. We had to confront racism daily, because we were dependent on the economic and public institutions of the White society.

Therefore, the edge that we brought to the fight against racism was very different. On the one hand, there was the intellectual, moral struggle embodied by Dr. King's nonviolent movement. On the other, was the raw rage of young people who grew up in Northern ghettos, deprived of a decent education, economic opportunities, and even hope.

Julian and I were a microcosm of these differences. He is very bright, precise, and intellectual. I am more emotional and blunt. His anger toward racism is refined and directed. Mine is rough around the edges. Together, we made for a dynamic juxtaposition of viewpoints.

We interviewed a host of Black people who were involved in public life. In doing the show, I had the opportunity to talk to the many people I had admired all my life, to meet many old acquaintances, and to make new friends. Among the interviews I enjoyed most was one with Harry Belafonte. We reminisced about Chicago, Sidney Poitier, and Dr. King. I jokingly reminded Harry of the time in 1967 when I came to his house with Dr. King to attend a meeting and was met with a distinctly cool reception. "I thought we were going to keep it small, Martin," Harry had said when he opened the door and saw me. Twenty-five years later, we talked about what a difficult time that had been for people in the movement, about the constant harassment and surveillance. It was such a pleasure to exchange memories with a man who had been so close to Dr. King and whom I revered as an advocate and artist.

One of the people I interviewed for the first time on *America's Black Forum* was Ron Brown, who was the chairman of the Democratic National Committee at the time. We had met during the Dukakis campaign. The first thing that struck me about Ron was how much he looked like my brother. Then, after we started talking, I was really impressed by his polish. It became clear how he had managed to overcome all the obstacles and opposition to become the political star he was.

Ron had his eyes on the prize. He was cool, smooth, and focused. He was working to have Democrats, particularly Bill Clinton, elected, and no matter what anyone said to him, he would not be distracted or deterred from his goal. In the face of outright racism, Ron would say things like, "Jesse Helms, you're a great guy. I've always respected you. I know we can work together." And he would win people over.

I admired Ron, in part, because I could never be like him, in the way that I could not be like Dr. King. No matter what the ultimate goal, I cannot ignore bigotry and racism, I want to confront them directly.

In Washington, where I had moved to do *America's Black Forum* and to be near Bill, I never experienced overt racism. For the most part, though, people were too political and buttoned up to let their views on race be known.

I was working in Black television, however, and with that I had greater latitude to explore questions of race with both Blacks and Whites. *America's Black Forum* inspired me to delve deeper into the issues that have interested me all of my adult life. The show itself, unfortunately, provided a limited opportunity to do so. We were syndicated around the country, but in most markets the show aired once a week, on Sunday at two in the morning or even later. We had a loyal audience, but a small one. The show, however, stayed on the air, and I continued as its cohost for five years.

Personal Diary

We taped *America's Black Forum* once a month. So I had a lot of free time to pursue other interests. I wanted to work and looked for every possible venue to do so. On weekends, I traveled from Washington to CNBC's New Jersey studios to sit in as cohost on *Talk Live.* I knew almost immediately that I would not continue with it for very long. The program had a heavy emphasis on the sexual interests and appetites of the guests. I should have anticipated this when the producer suggested that I pick up a copy of a book entitled, *Vox.* It was an instructional guide to phone sex, something that this so-called happily married man attempted to play with me. He called me on three occasions, always early in the morning. I was on to him. The job be damned. I called him on it. He never called again.

I decided to approach Bob Johnson again about the possibility of doing a show on BET.

Bob was a little reluctant, at first. He was concerned about potential competition between *America's Black Forum* and whatever show I would do on BET. He did eventually hire me. Trouble was that even though I was getting paid, I was still not getting on the air. It seemed as if the thing I wanted most was the most elusive. I wanted a platform to serve my people, and every time I got close, it slipped through my fingers.

Frustrated, I went to Bob and said, "Why aren't you using me? I've got all these ideas. I can get interviews on Capitol Hill. I want to work.

"You didn't even use me in the ads for your Color Code makeup line, and I am the only one here with a fashion background," I continued before he had a chance to answer.

Bob had developed a makeup line called Color Code and had created advertisements featuring many of the on-air personalities at BET. The cosmetics were designed to work with the full range of skin tones of African-Americans, and the ads showed Black women of all shades, from the very dark to the very light.

"I didn't know you wanted to do advertising," Bob parried.

"Well, why not?" I asked.

"Quite frankly," he said, relaxing a little, "I've got a problem here at the studio. I'm getting a lot of criticism from viewers that I only use light people. I've got to use more dark people on the air."

Suddenly, we were talking about a very different color code. I flashed back to Stokely Carmichael's calling me a "yellow pinup girl" back in Chicago. What difference does it make what color I am? I'm Black.

I realized at that moment that there is another layer of feelings I have about race. White racism angers me; Black racist color-consciousness hurts me. I recognize that there are jealousies, and that plantation thinking continues to exist. But we are not on the plantation anymore, and I refuse to accept the mentality that keeps Black people in a self-imposed ghetto allowing the long-dead master to control us remotely with this devisive color coding.

Once again, it seemed to be catch-22 for me. Color coding was indeed back. But as Marlon Brando said in *The Godfather,* "It's not personal, just business." I just didn't fit the demographics.

To his credit, Bob Johnson did not hold the fact that my skin is light against me. He acknowledged my talent, skills, and experience by giving me the opportunity to become the principal of not one but two interview shows: *Personal Diary with Janet Langhart* and *On Capitol Hill with Janet Langhart.*

Personal Diary, which I began hosting in the fall of 1992, focused on the giants of the Black community and on ordinary people doing extraordinary things. I interviewed such people as Rosa Parks, Ramsey Lewis, Billy Eckstine, Betty Carter, Faye Wattleton, Quincy Jones, Shirley Chisolm, Barbara Jordan, Spike Lee, Geoffrey Holder, Carmen DeLavallade, Earl Graves, and Clifford and Adel Alexander, to name a few. It was phenomenal to meet and get to know all these remarkable people. One interview, however, stands out in my memory as especially moving.

General Benjamin O. Davis, Jr., came on the show in our first season to talk about his experience leading the Tuskegee Airmen. His father was the first Black man to graduate from West Point, and the first Black man to become a general in the U.S. Army. Ben Davis also attended West Point. He graduated in 1936 and supervised the training of the Black airmen of the 99th Pursuit Squadron. Until that point, African-Americans had not been trusted to fly military aircraft. The Tuskegee Airmen began escorting American bombers in the European Theater in June 1943. Although he had to document and defend his squadron's superior performance, Ben Davis was ultimately able to convince the military to allow him to organize a larger air unit, the 332nd Fighter Group. An accomplished aviator himself, Ben Davis was awarded the Distinguished Flying Cross for his contribution to the American victory over Nazi Germany.

We started out talking about his days with the Tuskegee Airmen, and General Davis recounted proudly how they had never lost any of the planes they escorted. You could see the satisfaction on his face as he recalled proving wrong the bigots who had said Black men could not fly airplanes because they are not smart or brave enough.

"Talk to me about the code of silence during your days at West Point," I said, moving to the next subject I wanted to cover.

Ben Davis's face totally changed. His eyes, which had been all twinkles a moment ago, took on a deadened, opaque quality. There was pain in them, showing more than a hint of rage.

"General," I prompted him, "tell me about that time. What was it like?"

"At West Point," he answered slowly, "we were divided into study groups. That was your unit. And in my unit, none of the other cadets would talk to me. No one talked to me except the teachers in class."

"How did you do it?" I asked, identifying deeply with his anger at being excluded in such a cruel way. "I mean, a severe environment like West Point is hard enough on a young boy. To be the only Black, on top of that. How did you cope with their not speaking to you?"

"I just did it," General Davis said, straightening up in his chair. "I decided to do as we were all taught, to try twice as hard. I had my pride and my heritage. I wanted to serve my country, and I was just determined."

"Who were some of the people who were in school with you? Anybody we know? Any other famous person come out of your class?"

"Yeah," he said hesitantly.

"Who?" I pushed him.

"Westmoreland," Ben Davis said, jutting out his jaw a bit. "General Westmoreland."

"General William C. Westmoreland didn't talk to you?"

"No," General Davis said. "He ignored me along with the rest. As though I was invisible."

"Well, now that you've both gone on to do great things as American heroes, have you talked about that time?" I asked.

"No," General Davis said, his body language making clear that he did not want to go deeper.

"Do you want to talk about this, General?" I asked.

"No." He shook his head, and we left it at that.

What shocked me was not the fact that General Westmoreland would have acted out of racist prejudice as a young man, but that as a mature adult he had not grown to the point of having the courage to say, "I am sorry." I realized that while I did not forgive racism, I was prepared to move on, as long as people were willing to grow, to rise above bigotry. What felt significant and tragic to me about that interview—and why it has stayed with me—was the realization that while most of America attempted to put racial hatred aside, it had not fully owned up to the suffering that had been inflicted on my people.

I was vividly reminded of this sad fact several years later when I interviewed Senator Trent Lott for *On Capitol Hill with Janet Langhart* for BET. Bill worked with Senator Lott, so I knew him and his wife, Tricia, socially. The tone was relaxed and cordial when we began talking in his beautiful office on the Hill. We were discussing what it was like to be from Mississippi. Of course, since this was BET, there had to be a Black angle to the interview. So I asked him,

"Did you know that when I was coming up, Black people were ashamed to admit they were from Mississippi?

"It was not only the poorest state in our union," I went on, "but it was the most racist state. Nobody Black wanted to admit they came from a place where they were treated so oppressively. Nobody was proud to be from Mississippi."

He had been expecting a "soft interview," one without hard edges. He was not prepared for my questions.

I knew that Senator Lott had been in his senior year at Ole Miss when James Meredith attempted to integrate the university in 1962. I decided to find out what his experience of that time had been. In my mind, I was giving him an opportunity to admit to having held some racist beliefs in his youth and to renounce them as the product of a different time and place. Senator Lott, however, was determined to keep the interview light.

Finally, I asked, "Where were you when Emmett Till was lynched?"

"Emmett Till?" he repeated as if he was hearing the name for the first time.

Senator Lott and I were born within a few months of each other, so I was convinced that it would have been impossible for anyone from Mississippi to be unaware of the lynching, which had commanded international media attention. I reminded him how Emmett, a boy of our age, was murdered in Money, Mississippi, in 1955, when we were fourteen years old.

His only response was, "I don't know where I was then."

In retrospect, it probably was unfair of me to assume that a murder that was of such significance was not high on Senator Lott's mind at that moment since he was expecting a very different kind of interview. But I was disappointed.

I wanted to delve deeper into his views about racial injustice when an aide suddenly came into the room and said, "Senator, there's a vote coming up."

"One more question before you go," I said. "How do you feel about the Confederate flag flying over some of the state capitols in the South? Do you think that Black people may see that with the same alarm as Jewish people would see the Nazi flag flying over anywhere in Germany?"

"You know," Senator Lott said, clearly uncomfortable with my persistence. "That's a complex question that I really can't take the time to answer right now. I've got to go vote."

The interview was over. As I said good-bye, I glanced over his shoulder and saw the Mississippi state flag posted behind his desk, the Confederate colors displayed in its upper left corner. I had hoped that I could have had a real dialogue about the era that had shaped both our lives. I had grown to see that the same walls that were built to keep me out also kept White people trapped inside. I wanted to break through the barrier to make real contact. I wasn't pressing the senator just to be mean, I was searching to see if he could justify the reasons people had for oppression, deprivation, and hate. Although Senator Lott had always been extremely friendly, courteous, even courtly to me, it was clear that the conversation that I wanted was not to be.

As I was completing work on this book, the country witnessed the decline of Senator Lott's star. During the celebration of Senator Strom Thurmond's one hundredth birthday, in a moment of exuberance, Senator Lott proclaimed that Mississippi had voted for Strom and that "we would not have had all these problems" if the Dixiecrats had won the White House in 1948.

Many in the audience were stunned. I was surprised that he could not recall a tragic event in 1955, but could distinctly remember an earlier time, 1948.

Several days passed before the full shock of his sentiments were felt. Then a tidal wave of pressure began to build demanding that he resign his position as the Senate's majority leader. Most Americans could forgive him for voting against Martin Luther King Day in 1983; but they could not absolve him for still holding, in 2003, the view that life in America would have been better if the racist views of the Dixiecrats had prevailed. No public appearances or apologies could dissipate the furor he had created. Mainstream America, including Senator Strom Thurmond, had moved beyond most of the racial intolerance of the past.

Much to my surprise, I had a different experience when I interviewed Haley Barbour, another Mississippi conservative, who at the time was the chairman of the Republican National Committee. I had never liked what I saw of Haley on television and was prepared to dislike him in person. I did not waste any time on small talk and launched right into the heart of the subject.

"From my point of view," I said, " 'conservative' has always meant racist, anti-Black, anti-woman, anti-gay. The term implies that you have something to conserve, that you want to keep the status quo. What does it mean to be a conservative Republican?"

Haley did not get defensive. He looked me in the eye and answered the question directly and skillfully, while toeing the party line.

"You know," I said, digging deeper, "up North we always say that Southern Whites like their Black people one-on-one but not as a group. And that Northern Whites will let Black people get ahead as a group, but they don't want anything to do with us one-on-one. Do you think that's true?"

Haley explained that he believed there was a historical bond between Southern Blacks and Whites. Blacks had lived in the homes of Whites, had nurtured their babies, taken care of their elderly.

"Did you have any Black people close to you?" I asked.

All of a sudden, Haley choked up, his face turned red, and his eyes filled with tears. I had only had that happen in an interview once before, with Teddy Kennedy, when I asked him about his brothers' deaths.

Haley stayed silent for a few moments, drew a deep breath, swallowed, and said, "When you said that about how we like Blacks one-on-one, there's some truth to that. I know we've had some problems in this country, and certainly in the South, particularly in Mississippi."

"What was it about my question that you found so upsetting?" I probed.

"It reminded me of a woman named Hattie, who was with my family from before I was born," Haley said, his face softening into a look of fond remembrance. "She was more my mother than my own mother. When my brother and I grew up, she chose to come and live with me. I was her baby, and Hattie wanted to be with her baby and his babies."

"Where is she now?" I asked.

"That's what makes me sad," Haley replied. "One day I was looking for her, and nobody could find her. I finally found her on the floor in my bedroom. She had just made my bed and fell on the other side, between the bed and the window. She fell dead making my bed. She was like my mother."

It was such a human moment. Hattie had penetrated to Haley's heart. At that distance, it is impossible not to love. It is only when we erect artificial barriers to keep ourselves separate from each other that it becomes possible to hate.

My interview with Haley reminded me of an experience I had in

South Boston when I was working for *America Alive!*. I was there to interview Peter Falk, of *Columbo* fame, and director William Friedkin, who were filming *The Brink's Job* on location. I was apprehensive about going to "Southie," especially given my outspoken denunciation of anti-busing protesters.

"You don't understand," I told my producer, "Black people don't just show up in South Boston."

When I got there, however, I was surprised to be greeted by a White woman with two children. She came up to me, hugged me, and said in a classic Boston accent, "Janet Langhaaht, why did you ever leave Boston? We miss you. We love you. You belong to us, just like *Old Ironsides* and Arthur Fiedler." I could feel my heart expanding in my chest, as tears streamed down my cheeks. I felt a homecoming and for the very first time, I loved Boston.

In Washington, I was equally touched by Haley Barbour's love for the Black maid who had become his second mother. When I saw him in a restaurant some time later, I sent over a note, saying, "I'll never forget our interview for BET."

I did not agree with his politics any more than I had before the interview, but I had seen another side of Haley Barbour, had connected with him on an emotional level. Increasingly, I understood that was what I expected of people, the willingness to open up and relate as human beings, in all our imperfection.

It seemed that people started asking Bill and me when we were going to get married from our very first date. Shortly after we started seeing each other, he invited me to the annual White House Christmas party. I was excited to go and also a little nervous. It was the White House, after all, and it was my first time. It would also be my first time meeting "George and Barbara Bush."

We had a wonderful time, dancing, chatting with people, enjoying each other's company. At one point, we were talking in the arch of a large doorway. A clergyman passing by, stopped, snapped a picture of us with his little Kodak camera, and said, "I now pronounce you man and wife."

"Oh, hello, Reverend," Bill said, sounding a little abashed. "This is Janet Langhart. Janet, this is Reverend Ford."

"Pleased to meet you, ma'am," James Ford said, smiling. "I am the House chaplain. I hope you don't think me forward, but you two look like you belong together." He laughed and pointed at the mistletoe that hung over our heads.

Days later, I would have another exciting but daunting experience. Bill wanted me to meet Katharine Graham, the owner and publisher of the *Washington Post,* who was a friend and a mentor to him. They had met during the days of Watergate and were very fond of each other. I had the feeling that if Mrs. Graham approved, it did not matter what anyone else thought.

I had not been so nervous since the time I first met Bill's mother, Clara—a stunningly beautiful woman who embraced me as if I were her own daughter.

It was another Christmas party, this time at Georgette Mosbacher's house. Mrs. Graham was there, obviously the grand dame, even though she did not carry herself in a haughty or aloof manner. Bill introduced me, excited and proud. Mrs. Graham very deliberately looked me over, starting at my feet and working her way all the way up to the top of my head, and then said, "Hello."

As I got to know Mrs. Graham, I realized that she liked to have her innocent fun, but at the time I did not know what to think. Had I passed the test? I wondered.

Mrs. Graham was a wonderful woman. It did not matter who was in the White House, she was always the First Lady of Washington. Everybody knew and accepted it, because she wielded her power so delicately, as with a butter knife.

I quickly grew to love her. She did not suffer fools, but she was so lovely and easy to be with. She reciprocated my affection, insisting that I call her Kay. No matter how comfortable I became with her, though, I could never bring myself to call her anything but Mrs. Graham.

When her book, *Personal History,* came out, Mrs. Graham would talk to me about how nervous she was about doing interviews, except the one with Barbara Walters. She fretted little about that because they were friends. I found it so touching that this powerhouse of a woman was still shy about talking about herself.

She was especially concerned about doing the *Imus in the Morning* show with Don Imus. I could easily understand her concern this time. His show, while funny, was sometimes funny at the expense of his guests. I assured her the interview would be fine, and that he would treat her with respect.

"Mrs. Graham, first of all, you *are* Mrs. Graham," I said. "You are a national treasure. Nobody would dare to be irreverent to you. Besides, it's your story. You're the expert on that. Who's going to dispute you on your own story?"

Mrs. Graham was such an inspiration, and her death has left a void in the lives of all of us whom she touched. I often look at the hand-painted, papier-mâché box sitting on my dresser, that used to sit on her vanity, given to me by her son, Donald, after she passed away, and recall fondly her strength, courage, and her grace.

Donald's generosity was moving. He said, "Mom thought the world of you and Bill. She would've wanted you to have this."

Lucky Dog

The universe, in its infinite wisdom and bounty, continued to present me with opportunities to grow. Two new friends walked into my life; both had a profound impact on me.

On Friday, August 13, 1993, I was taping at BET. It was a pretty hot day, and we were late in starting. I went out to get a soda and saw a large crowd out on the veranda looking down at something and laughing. I went outside to see what was causing the commotion, and there was this little dog chasing his tail. He was skinny and bald. He looked like a large, white rat. It still breaks my heart to think about what he must have been through.

He had a red collar on, so it was clear he must have gotten lost. I asked if anybody knew whose dog it was. It is just a stray, my colleagues answered and told me that they had called the pound, because he was begging and not letting them eat.

I had just lost my beloved cat, Tony, and my heart went out to the little dog. I knew that he would be put down at the pound and resolved to save him. I called Dr. Mark Brown, who was my cat's vet, as well as a loving friend. He agreed to come for the dog, but I had another dilemma. I had to go inside to tape, and there was no place to pen up the little stray. Finally, I handed my intern a towel and asked her to hold him until the doctor came.

When I was done with the taping, I called Dr. Brown. "He'll be fine," he assured me. "Although, if you had not picked him up, he would have starved in a matter of another day."

"What kind of little guy is that?" I asked, relieved that the dog was all right.

"He's got better pedigree than you or I," Dr. Brown said, laughing. "His lineage can be traced all the way back to Malta."

"You're kidding," I said. "What kind of dog is it?"

"He's a Maltese," the doctor said. "You know, those little lap dogs with the long white hair that people like to put up in barrettes."

"How do you like that?" I said. "Well, give the little pedigree pup all that he needs—x-ray him, give him his shots."

"He is close to a year old. He needs to be neutered," Dr. Brown said, getting serious.

"Of course," I said. "Do you think you can find him a home? The condo association in my building does not allow dogs."

While Dr. Brown tried to find him a home, I visited the little dog at the vet's office. I had named him Theo, because according to my research Malta was the land of God. I found him on Friday the thirteenth. He was a pretty lucky dog, saved by God. Theo seemed like the perfect name.

Dr. Brown tried everything to find Theo a good place to live. He even took him home. Unfortunately his cats did not want to share their territory. Finally, through the United Maltese Rescue, he found a woman who trained and rescued Maltese, and she agreed to take in Theo and to find him a permanent home.

I wanted to go see Theo. Dr. Brown gave me the telephone number and the address. "Her name is Marion F. Hutchisson," he said. "She is eighty-two. She served in the Navy, and she is a little gruff. But if she loves animals, she can't be that bad."

I called her the same day. When she answered the phone in her clipped, businesslike voice, I said, "Ms. Hutchisson, this is Janet Langhart. I am calling about the dog Dr. Brown brought you."

"Yes?" she said.

"I found him, Ms. Hutchisson, and I wanted to see how he is doing."

"Hutch," she said, lowering her guard. "Just call me Hutch. That's what they called me in the Navy. All my friends call me Hutch."

"All right," I said, warming up to this brusque but clearly good-hearted woman. "How is Theo doing?"

"Who?"

"Theo," I repeated.

"His name is not Theo," she said with disdain. "What kind of name is that for a dog?"

I told her the story of how I found him and named him. But she would have none of it.

"When you train a dog," Hutch said, "you've got to have a name like Lucky, Dicky, Spotty, something that they can recognize from the ring of your voice. He's never going to respond to Theo. I named him Lucky."

"Wow," I said, "what an appropriate name for him. I did find him on Friday the thirteenth."

"Oh, you did?" Hutch said, surprised. "I didn't know that. I just named him Lucky because he is lucky you found him and I saved him."

"Well, that's true," I said, laughing. "Can I come out and see him?"

I was so surprised when I went out to her modest home. I expected to meet a sturdy, military woman, and out came Mrs. Claus. She had beautiful blue eyes; rosy cheeks; and gorgeous, thick white hair. Then she opened her mouth, and the illusion disappeared. Hutch was a crusty, salty dog, with a voice that could crack a glass pane at fifty paces. She was Navy through and through.

That first day we met, Hutch told me all about her dogs and the Navy. She grew up in Ohio, in a big family of Scottish and German immigrants. A "modern Millie" before her time, Hutch joined the Navy. Hutch loved the service and was one of America's first Navy Waves.

"I served something bigger than myself," Hutch said. "And it reminded me of my family. Big, disciplined, and orderly. We stuck by each other."

Although she said her time in the Navy was the happiest in her life, Hutch gave up the service because of her cocker spaniel, Happy Girl. Near the end of World War II, Hutch was supposed to be shipped to Hawaii. That meant that Happy Girl would have had to spend six months in quarantine. "I had to give up the Navy," Hutch said, "because I wasn't going to put my little animal in a pound for six months."

I could not part with my little dog either, and I eventually convinced Bill to give Lucky and me a home in his new town house. To this day, Bill credits Lucky with my decision to get married. That is not entirely true, but we did become unofficially engaged at that time.

Hutch and I became fast friends during the short time she took care of Lucky. She had just lost her Maltese a short time before we met, and she was still grieving. She was so devoted to her dogs—she wanted to be buried with them.

One day I took her out to lunch at Po Folks, a fast-food family restaurant. "This is where I was Easter," Hutch said.

"You spent Easter here?" I asked, thinking that it was not a very festive place. "Who were you here with?"

"By myself," she replied as if that should have been self-evident.

"Well, and who were you with at Christmas?" I pressed her, beginning to get a picture of her lonely life.

"Myself," Hutch said again.

"What about your family?" I asked.

"I never married, but I've got an older sister in Ohio," she said. "Ohio's too far. Too complicated. I prefer to stay here by myself. When I had my dogs, it was just me and the dogs. I would put up a Christmas tree for them, bake a chicken. It was nice."

"Let me tell you something," I said, my heart going out to this independent, self-contained woman. "If you want, every single holiday that the Lord brings, I want you to be with Bill and Lucky and me. We need you, and I think you might enjoy it."

For the next nine years, Hutch spent every holiday with us— Christmas, Thanksgiving, Easter, Mother's Day, Father's Day, birthdays, Fourth of July. She became our family and brought us so much joy.

Hutch baked a cake for me every December for my birthday, and she didn't forget Bill's on August 28th or Lucky's on August 13th— the day we found him. She cooked us meals and knitted, crocheted, and embroidered gifts. I felt as if I had found a fantasy grandmother, the kind who waits by the door with hot chocolate chip cookies when you come home from school. I just adored her.

Hutch was much more than a surrogate mother, however. She became a real buddy, the thirty-year age difference notwithstanding. We went everywhere together—flower shows, horse shows, dog shows. She gave me recipes and talked about canning, and the hard but happy days on her family's farm on Marysville, Ohio.

I enjoyed sharing with Hutch some of the quirky and glitzy aspects of the official life of Washington. I took her to Capitol Hill for the famous Senate dining room bean soup. When she turned ninety, we threw a birthday party for her at the Pentagon. We even introduced her to Harrison Ford at the air show at Andrews Air Force Base.

One of my favorite memories of Hutch, though, is of going to the White House Christmas party with her. We were all dressed up and having a ball. Hutch and Bill danced, and I watched them, filled with satisfaction and joy. When they came off the dance floor, a young Navy officer came up to us and addressed Hutch, "Ma'am, I want to thank you for your service to this country and to the Navy."

"How did you know I served?" she asked, with her customary gruffness, but obviously pleased.

"We knew you were coming, and we did our homework on you, ma'am," the young man said, smiling broadly. "The work that you did saved a lot of sailors' lives. I just wanted to take this opportunity to thank you, Chief."

Hutch was one of the first WAVES to serve in the United States Navy. During her military career, Hutch had been promoted to chief of communications, the highest rank of the Navy's enlisted, and retired from the National Security Agency (NSA) twenty years later.

I was totally blown away. I knew that Hutch had remained in government service, but I did not know what she did. It was not until after her death that I discovered that she had worked for NSA after she left the Navy.

Well, if I was surprised by the young officer's speech, I had to pinch myself when Vice President Al Gore came up a few minutes later.

"Is this Hutch?" he said.

"Hello, Mr. Vice President," Hutch replied.

"Thank you for your service, Chief," the Vice President said. "We are mighty grateful for everything you've done for this country, and we are honored to have you here at the White House."

It was wonderful to see Hutch take in the acknowledgment that she so clearly deserved. She came from humble beginnings and was a self-made woman. I basked in the moment. It was nothing I could have planned, but I relished having had a hand in honoring my friend.

The one thing that bothered me about our relationship was that Hutch was so reserved about expressing affection. Whenever we said good-bye, I would say, "I love you."

"Okay, bye," she would reply.

One day I said, "When I tell you I love you, why don't you ever say you love me back?"

"*Love* is a cheap word," she said. "People change. They fall in and out of love. Love doesn't mean anything."

"You clearly feel something for me Hutch," I insisted. "What is it?"

She thought for a moment and said, "I cherish you."

"*Cherish* is better than *love*?" I asked.

"Yes, because when you cherish something, it is always a treasure to you," Hutch explained. "It will always mean something."

I accepted that, but in the back of my mind, I still wondered why she found it difficult to tell me she loved me. After all, she said she loved Lucky all the time. She would even occasionally say that she loved Bill. Why not me?

It was not until much later, when illness was carrying Hutch away from this world at the age of ninety-two, that she was able to bring herself to tell me she loved me. She was suffering from congestive heart failure. I was with her every single day. I bathed her, changed her bandages, and helped her eat. I wanted to be there with her to the end.

One day, I was transferring her from the bed to the commode. Hutch could barely stand. Her chin was resting on my right shoulder, near my ear, and as I lifted her up, she said, "I love you."

It was the most beautiful keepsake Hutch could have given me. I looked into her beautiful blue eyes and said, "I love you too. You have to promise me that if you go first, you'll find me when my time comes."

She looked back at me and gave me the okay sign, as she had done through all the years we had known each other.

The day she died, I had been with her for several hours. I knew she was in pain, but she had been in pain before and had gotten better. I thought it was all right to leave for a while. I fed her some vanilla ice cream and headed home. By the time I got there, a message on my answering machine told me she was dying. I spoke to the nurse, who told me that I would not make it in time to see Hutch one last time.

I rushed over and saw her body laid out on her bed. Her beautiful white hair lay softly on her pillow, and her skin had taken on the iridescence of pearl. She looked beautiful and at peace for the first time in more than a year.

Hutch was buried with her dogs. She could have been buried at Arlington, but even though she loved the Navy and her country, I knew she would want to be with her animal family. I held a service for her at the Navy Memorial. Admiral Barry Black, now the chaplain of the U.S. Senate, the first African-American to hold such a post, read her eulogy, with twenty Navy chiefs standing at attention while taps sounded. It was the final honor I felt she deserved.

Not long before she died, Hutch gave me the most peculiar gift, a four-foot-long bell chime. I had always remarked that I liked the sound of the chimes in her yard, but somehow it seemed odd that she would have chosen that as a parting gift. I hung it in my garden, near a rosebush and a clematis that she had also given me. Now, whenever I hear the chime's resonant voice, I imagine that Hutch is letting me know that she's waiting for me.

Lucky also hears her and barks his greetings. He is still with me, a faithful companion, who has been at my side while I have endeavored to set down in these pages the course of my life's journey, to pay respects to the many people I have known and loved, and to reflect on the lessons I have learned.

Washington life required a lot of stamina and composure. There were parties, openings, events, benefits, and more parties. I am not by nature gregarious. While socially at ease in crowds, I prefer to relate to people one-on-one.

There were occasions, however, when I genuinely enjoyed these outings. As when I had the chance to tell Arnold Schwarzenegger how much I appreciated what he had done for my career. Bill and I were attending a benefit for children born with spina bifida, organized by Washington's beautiful couple, Judy Woodruff and her husband, Al Hunt. Arnold was sitting a few tables away from us.

"There's that arrogant SOB who cost me my job at *ET*," I told Bill.

I was so angry, I could hardly eat. Finally, I said, "I'm going to get him."

Bill, ever the politician, said, "No, please. Just forget it. It's long ago."

"I haven't forgotten," I said, seething. "It was a crappy thing to do. And I'm going to tell him that."

When the lights came up and people began leaving, I stood at my table waiting for Arnold to pass by me. Bill stood beside me while the room cleared out. As the last of Arnold's admirers left and he headed toward the door, I put myself directly in his path.

"Arnold," I said, "it's wonderful to see you again. I never got a chance to thank you for all you did for my career."

Arnold was stunned. I wanted him to say, "What do you mean?" so I could really confront him. But he just glared at me and walked away. Regardless, I had had the pleasure of standing toe to toe with him, and I felt as much strength in my heart as he had in his biceps.

Matrimonial March

It was clear to me that the political life would not be one I would relish. Although Bill and I talked about marriage, I was reluctant to marry again.

In October 1995, however, Bill's father died, at the age of eighty-six, while mixing dough at his bakery in Bangor, Maine. Ruby, as he was known, was a major force in Bill's life. I found him to be a wise, plain spoken, yet sensitive man. His passing precipitated several months of deep reflection and conversation.

During that time, Bill and I created a vision for a new life for ourselves. Bill would leave politics, build a consulting practice in international business, and would return to writing. I would pursue television and media production. We would be home at five or six o'clock, and on weekends we would go to concerts and movies. We would travel and go up to New York to the theater and to see friends. Occasionally, we would have a Washington-style dinner party.

That was the plan when Bill announced in January 1996 that he would not run for reelection, also making it public that we were engaged. I wanted to have a small wedding, so I insisted that we not drag out the planning. Always a romantic at heart, I wanted to get married on Valentine's Day. Bill protested that it would be on a Wednesday and nobody gets married on Wednesday.

"If you don't want to wait till June," he reasoned, "let's at least have it on Saturday. We can celebrate our anniversary on Valentine's Day anyway."

"No," I insisted. I would like to have it on February fourteenth, Wednesday, notwithstanding."

We thought we would have the ceremony in the chapel in the

Capitol. I wanted it there to celebrate how far we have come as a nation. The building that was intended to serve as a temple of freedom was built by slaves, whose masters were paid sixty dollars a year for the labor of their slaves. I hoped our wedding would, two centuries later, pay tribute to the spirit of my ancestors who chiseled the words *freedom, equality,* and *justice* under the magnificent dome of the Capitol. Rights they would never enjoy.

Our plan was to have a handful of people in the small chapel. We wanted to invite Bill's sons, my friends, Hutch, and a handful of others. Well, word got around town that we were getting married, and suddenly we had people calling to say that they had not gotten their invitations. It was a little embarrassing, and we decided to move the wedding to a larger space.

I remember walking through the Capitol hand in hand with my sister, who was working for Senator Fred Thompson at the time. We looked around the building and spoke about our mother who would not be able to attend this occasion either, and said, "Here are Louise's girls choosing which room of the Capitol to have a wedding in. Who would have believed it?"

Finally, as the invitation list kept getting bigger, we settled on the grand Mansfield Room. We got married in front of the fireplace, under the portrait of George Washington. Reverend Ford, who had married us in jest five years earlier, officiated. Bill's sons, Kevin and Chris, were his best men. My sister, Myrna, was my maid of honor, and my girlfriend Millicent Proctor was the bridesmaid.

The ceremony was very eclectic and moving. We had traditional readings, one of St. Paul's letters to the Corinthians, and lines from Khalil Gibran.

It was very romantic. There were pink roses and orchids, candles, and a string-and-flute trio playing beautiful music. The people I loved were all around me. Hutch was sitting in the first row, the surrogate for both Bill's and my parents. Mrs. Graham was there right alongside her.

Somehow, I did not mind that our small wedding had turned into a real Washington event. I had decided to let go and allow whatever was going to happen to take its course. I knew something magical was afoot when the first face I saw as I was coming down the aisle was that of Strom Thurmond, beaming a wonderful, loving smile. Somehow, he had ended up sitting way in the back, even though protocol demanded that he sit in the front row.

We have, indeed, come a very long way, I thought, smiling to myself as I walked toward Bill, so handsome in his tuxedo.

I saw Katherine Graham look at me—head to toe—in the same scrutinizing way as she did when we first met. She nodded, signaling her approval and blessing.

Senator Trent Lott was there with his wife, Tricia, along with Senators Christopher Dodd, Claiborne Pell, Al D'Amato, Olympia Snowe, John Glenn, Don Nickels, Sam Nunn, and Warren Rudman. Andrea and Alan Greenspan came, as did Bob Johnson and his wife. Defense Secretary William Perry, CIA Director Richard Helms and his wife, Cynthia, and Dan Rather and his wife, Jean, were also among the hundred people who witnessed the exchanging of our vows.

I was so nervous when Reverend Ford finally said to Bill, "You may kiss the bride," I let out a big sigh, to the amusement of our guests, and threw my arms around his neck. It seemed like a fairytale. I was Cinderella and I had married my Prince Charming.

At that very moment, I thought of Dr. King's dream. "One day, little Black boys and little Black girls will be able to join hands with little White boys and little White girls and walk the streets as brothers and sisters." I don't think that even Dr. King envisioned that walk would take place in a ceremony on Capitol Hill.

The exchange of our vows became big news. Press came from everywhere. BET, NBC, CBS, CNN, and *People* magazine covered the wedding, and the story was on the evening broadcasts. We were on our way to becoming the country's most visible interracial couple.

Even more people showed up for the reception at the Hay Adams Hotel, across the street from the White House. Colin and Alma Powell, Ron and Alma Brown, Vernon and Ann Jordan, John and Christina McLaughlin, Senator Edward Muskie, and Admiral Borda were among the guests. It was a wonderful party.

Fallen Star

Bill used to joke that if I married him, he'd show me the world. That opportunity came shortly after our wedding on Capitol Hill. He didn't take me on a slow boat to China, but close to it.

Bill persuaded me to join him and Senator Fritz Hollings and his wife, Peatsy, on a trip to Beijing, Shanghai, Hong Kong, and Kuala

Lumpur, Malaysia. Although I don't enjoy flying—I hail from the "If God had wanted me to fly, he would have given me wings" school of philosophy—it sounded like a rather exotic honeymoon excursion.

Bill and Senator Hollings, by virtue of their seniority and influence on the Senate's defense and appropriations committees, assumed that the Defense Department would provide an aircraft suitable to accommodate a traveling delegation of fourteen people. The department either had other priorities or other motives in mind. We were offered a C-20, which could accommodate fourteen people—provided one of the Air Force stewards sat in the lavatory compartment throughout the flight.

In addition to the discomfort of sitting straight up (as if strapped in an electric chair), the plane had to be refueled every four and a half hours. By the time we arrived in Beijing. I was a prime candidate for chiropractic rehabilitation.

I wasn't sure of what to expect of China or its people. Over the years, I had read about "brutal Communist dictators," and "the Butchers of Beijing," and had seen evidence of that brutality in 1991 during the student-led rebellion that was visibly frozen in time by a young man bravely confronting a tank in Tiananmen Square. In short, I was prepared to dislike the country and its people.

Once we finally arrived in Beijing, those preconceptions evaporated. What I saw was something quite different from what Bill had described to me during his first visit to Beijing in 1978. Then, Beijing had only one hotel that he described as material for a Stephen King horror novel. Then, men and women—who were not allowed to hold hands in public—were dressed in drab blue-and-gray Mao suits. Private cars were in the hands of high-ranking party officials only. Cosmetics, even though unaffordable, were seen as a sign of Western decadence and officially verboten.

It was something of a shock to see a city that was as vibrant and dynamic as any in the Western world, with grand hotels, fashionable boutiques, and highways crowded with German- and Japanese-made automobiles. There were millions of bicycles as well; but clearly, this was a city and a country very much on the move.

Everywhere I could see in the eyes of the people we met, a sense of pride, determination, and destiny. We were treated with extraordinary courtesy and politeness. It may have been false and artificial, but it didn't smack of being calculated or obsequious. Rather, their tone and body language were the products of a culture that offered—

and demanded—courtesy and respect. It said we may not yet be your equal, but we have never been your inferior. We hope to stand with you as good friends and partners if possible, but formidable rivals if necessary. I recalled the old saying, "When China wakes, the world will tremble."

Going from Beijing to Shanghai was the equivalent of traveling from Washington, D.C., to New York City. Skyscrapers everywhere reached for the clouds. Not a building was without a construction crane on its roof, stacking floor upon floor in a pyramidal climb of glass and steel. The city of eighteen million people was so alive and dynamic it seemed to breathe and expand before our eyes. We would return some four years later when Bill was Secretary of Defense and the changes were even more dramatic.

By the time we reached Hong Kong, I was looking forward to a bit of downtime without formal meetings with local officials. We had planned to spend a quiet evening in the home of a close friend. But no sooner had we arrived at the Shangri-La Hotel than we learned that Secretary of Commerce Ron Brown's plane had crashed in the Balkan mountains. Ron had been leading a group of businessmen to explore how they might contribute to the economic development of the region. My heart sank. I broke down and began to sob.

Ron was the very best that any people had to offer. He had drive, charm, charisma, and he was brilliant. He was a strong, handsome Black man who could move among common people and corporate boards with equal ease, who could debate any issue with the clarity and power of a sophisticated lawyer, who could dismiss all of the political malcontents or racial bigots with lighthearted aplomb, who rose from the partnership of a powerful law firm to the chairmanship of the Democratic National Committee. Ironically, he had liberal detractors in the party who said he wasn't qualified to serve as the chairman. So he did what all of us have had to do—work twice as hard to get half as much. He went out and raised more money for the party than anyone had ever done previously. President Bill Clinton publicly acknowledged that if it hadn't been for Ron Brown, he would never have been elected President.

Ron Brown was the very antithesis of the slave, thug, pimp, rapper, or drug dealer that Hollywood had kept alive in its vicious policy of stereotyping and discrimination.

Our best and brightest had either been killed or disrespected. Dr. King had been assassinated. Muhammad Ali stripped of his title and robbed of his best years. Andy Young fired as U.S. Ambassador to the United Nations. And now Ron Brown, who offered so much hope to so many, had been ripped away from us. I remember after hearing the shocking news of Ron's death, reading a woman's comments: "It wasn't supposed to end like this."

I was flooded with conflicting emotions. Disbelief at first. Initial reports indicated that there may have been survivors. I prayed he was one of them.

I sat glued to the television set in the hotel room. With each report describing the remoteness of the crash site, the bleak weather conditions, the inability to move rescue teams to the scene, I knew that my prayers were not going to save him.

Grief turned to anger. Dark conspiracy spiders started to crawl across my mind. To this day I believe that J. Edgar Hoover was either directly or indirectly complicit in Dr. King's assassination. I know that this runs up against all odds and so-called evidence, but for me it remains more than plausible when placed in the historical context of how the federal government used Black people to experiment in treating syphilis, allowing us to be used as guinea pigs in the name of scientific inquiry. And the record books are replete with evidence of Hoover's fear of and hatred for Dr. King.

I fought back the urge to think that the aircraft had been sabotaged and would later reject allegations that surfaced that Ron had been shot in the head either prior to or after the plane went down. But the mere fact that I, and so many others, could even contemplate that Ron had been a homicide rather than an accident victim said more about Black people's collective experience of violence at the hands of White people and our distrust of them, than it did about dismissive charges of delusion or paranoia resulting in conspiracy theories.

The finality of Ron's fate cast a pall over our trip. Bill made plans for the two of us to fly directly back to Washington, but Senator Hollings would have none of it. He said, "We'll all fly back together. I liked Ron. I'd like to pay my respects, too. We'll leave early." A large formal reception had been planned for us in Kuala Lumpur. Bill called his friend, Anwar Ibrahim, the Deputy Prime Minister, to explain the significance of Ron's death and why we could not stay for the formal ceremony. Anwar understood completely. We agreed to make a quick, courtesy visit to the Malaysian capital and then began the long, slow flight back to Washington.

We arrived just a few hours before the funeral services were scheduled to begin at the National Cathedral, a breathtaking architectural marvel in Northwest Washington. I searched frantically for a black dress to wear for the occasion. Almost all of official Washington was present. Attendance for Democratic politicians was virtually mandatory. Sadly, high-ranking Republicans, with rare exception, felt it unnecessary to pay final respects to a fellow public servant. Decency and courtesy had fallen victim to the poison of rank partisanship.

As beautiful as the cathedral is, however, the pomp and ceremony that characterized the service did not reflect the essence of Ron's life or the profound impact of his death. Attempts were made to capture the substance, as well as some of the lighthearted moments of his career and what he meant to those of us who are so desperately in need of heroes, of leaders. I could not contain the tears as his coffin came down the aisle past me.

I felt it was all so staid and soulless. Adolescent voices soaring to the cathedral arches; thunderous organ music deep as the universe; people singing hymns, the words of which sought vainly to place the meaning of our loss into the fabric of an unfathomable plan. It had little relevance to the man I knew and admired. Ron was action, passion, laughter, joy, jazz, confident, classy, and fun-loving. The service—as high an honor as official Washington can offer—was more ceremony than celebration, more about the canonical traditions of the church than about the man. I left the cathedral that day, glad that Bill and I were able to arrive in time to pay our respects, but in no way relieved of the grief I carried like a stone around my heart. I thought of W.E.B. Du Bois's observation that, "Throughout history, the powers of single Blacks flash here and there like falling stars, and die sometimes before the world has rightly gauged their brightness." Ron was a fallen star, and right at that very moment, I felt that the political world had failed to gauge how he illuminated the horizons for so many.

I later learned that a different tribute had been paid to Ron the night before, one that really rocked, one to which Ron would have said, "Yes! Now that's the way to carry me home!"

9

A Call to Serve

In the spring of 1996, Bill and I were proceeding with putting into action the plans we had made for our married life. He was finishing his term in the Senate and preparing to launch his consulting firm. I continued to do television and also opened a media-training company, Langhart Communications.

There were rumors about Bill's name appearing on lists for various high-level positions in both Republican and Democratic administrations but then again, such whispers had been around since 1974, when *Time* named him one of America's 200 Future Leaders. In the course of his career, people had often speculated about Bill's ambitions, naming everything from the directorship of the CIA to the presidency.

Through the summer and the fall, as it became clearer that President Clinton would win reelection, the rumors grew louder. Finally, after the election, it became official. The President was considering Bill for a post in his new administration.

I remember very vividly walking into our apartment to find Bill and his chief of staff in the living room.

"I'm on a short list," Bill told me.

"For the CIA?" I blurted out, having known that he had been offered that job in the past.

"No," he said, shaking his head. "Department of Defense. Secretary of Defense."

"You're kidding," I exclaimed.

"Think I should take it?" Bill asked pensively.

"Absolutely," I said, surprised that he was even asking the question. "What an honor, to serve in the Cabinet."

"But I made the decision to get out of politics," Bill said. "This will set back all of our plans." He obviously wanted the job, but didn't want to disappoint me by stepping back into the political maelstrom. He also had just had his business cards printed and had signed a lease agreement for office space in downtown Washington.

"This is different from elected politics," I tried to reassure him. "Our plans can always wait."

At that moment, I saw images of my father in his Army uniform, my brother in his Navy whites, Richard Pepper, the sailor who took me out on my very first date, and pictures of Hutch in her chief's uniform. Bill would be serving the men and women who serve our country. There were few people who were more knowledgeable on defense issues, and it would be a wonderful way to complete a long career of public service.

While Bill was flattered by the prospect of being offered a Cabinet position, he remained skeptical about the wisdom of joining an administration whose national security policies he had openly criticized.

He also believed that it would be inappropriate to reject out of hand a request from the President of the United States. When he received an invitation to have lunch with President Clinton at the White House, Bill accepted it without hesitation.

When Bill returned from this meeting, he said only that he and the President had engaged in a broad philosophical discussion about foreign policy. It basically had been a get-acquainted meeting since he and the President had not spent any time together previously.

Their second meeting occurred several days later in Bangkok, Thailand. Bill had traveled there to address a United States–Thai Business Council conference while President and Mrs. Clinton were attending the celebration of King Bhumibol Adulyadej's birthday. Although he and the President had time to exchange only a few pleasantries, Bill was seated next to Sandy Berger, President Clinton's national security adviser, throughout a formal celebration in honor of the king.

Soon after he returned to Washington, Bill received a second invitation to the White House. The President was far more specific about issues he wanted to explore—whether NATO should be expanded and what steps could be taken for further reform at the Department of Defense.

Bill had been one of the driving forces behind the Goldwater-Nichols legislation that reformed the structure of the Joint Chiefs of Staff and had, along with Senator Sam Nunn, been the principal architect of the Special Operations Command that he pushed through Congress over the objection of the Pentagon.

Shortly thereafter, while we were standing in a reception line at a White House Christmas party, Vice President Gore approached Bill and quietly inquired whether he could take a call from the President the next morning. Bill nodded, not disclosing any reaction that might be interpreted by the many members of Congress and their spouses who were standing in line.

Later that night we discussed the significance of his brief encounter with Vice President Gore. He expected that President Clinton would ask him to serve as his Secretary of Defense. Yet, he didn't want to discount the possibility that the President had reconsidered the prospect of inviting a Republican into his inner circle and concluded that the political fallout made it too difficult to handle.

Bill still had his own doubts as to whether the Democrats would accept the need for higher defense spending and whether Republicans would consider him a traitor to the party and seek to undercut him at the Pentagon. Could he really produce a bipartisan consensus for a strong national security?

He was determined not to prejudge the President's decision or raise any false expectations. He seemed completely at ease with either outcome.

I was amazed that he could be so calm over what surely was such an important decision.

We continued to talk that night and the next morning waited for the President's call, which was scheduled to occur between eight and nine o'clock."

President Clinton is a little like Dr. King; he runs on Southern time, so he is always a bit late. Bill waited until about eight-thirty and then started to grow impatient. He said, "I'm going to go walk Lucky."

"But the President's going to call," I protested.

"Well," Bill said, putting on Lucky's collar, "if he calls, take a message. I'll call him back."

"That is not the right attitude," I chided him.

"Lucky's got to go," he said and walked out.

Of course, as soon as he left, the phone rang. "Mrs. Cohen," Bill's secretary said, "President Clinton is calling for Senator Cohen."

I did not understand why the White House would have called Bill's office when he was waiting at home, so I figured the staff was playing a little joke to relieve the tension.

"Sure, Stephanie," I said, laughing. "He's outside with Lucky."

"No, it really is the White House," she said urgently. "Please get him on the phone."

"Oh my God," I cried out. "Hold on."

I ran out onto the balcony and looked down the ten stories to the Navy Memorial. That is where we usually walked Lucky, but I did not see Bill.

I got back on the line and said, "Stephanie, can the President hold?"

"I don't know," she said.

"Well, Bill is not back yet," I said. "I guess he'll have to call back."

I was beside myself by the time Bill strolled back in. "The President just called," I said, rushing toward him. "You've got to call your office."

I stood in the living room and listened intently as Bill was patched through to the White House. "Hello, Mr. President," he said. "Yes, Mr. President. Yes sir, Mr. President. Subject to the conditions that we've discussed, I accept."

"What are the conditions that you mentioned?" I asked him as soon as he hung up the phone.

"That I have complete independence from any political considerations to run the department, and that the President never ask me to engage in any partisan politics as a member of his Cabinet."

"And he agreed?'

"Absolutely."

Instinctively I knew that this was the universe pointing out the way. I remembered what Dr. King said about fulfilling one's mission in life: "Everybody can be great. Because anybody can serve." I had worked for so much of my life to serve my people by attempting to break down racial barriers and to give African-Americans a voice in the mainstream media. Now, it seemed, I might have the opportunity to serve in a completely different and unexpected way at Bill's side.

Bill held me in his arms and said, "We are about to become the first interracial couple to stand at the head of America's military. Are you ready for that?"

I hugged him. "Yes, I'm ready."

In "The Building"

Bill had served on the Armed Services Committee throughout his eighteen years in the Senate. As Maine Senator Olympia Snowe wittily put in formally introducing him to the Committee at the confirmation hearing on January 22, 1997, "Introducing Bill Cohen to the Armed Services Committee is a little like introducing Cal Ripken to the Baltimore Orioles."

The hearing was, as expected, largely pro forma. Senators from both sides of the aisle respected Bill and applauded President Clinton's unprecedented move to nominate an elected official from the opposing party for a cabinet post. For his part, Bill, in his remarks, set the tone for his tenure at the Pentagon: "I pledge to you and to the men and women in uniform to do my very best to merit this most solemn trust. . . . The courage, the loyalty, and the willingness of our men and women in uniform to put their lives at risk is a national treasure that should not be taken for granted."

Two days later, on January 24, 1997, Bill was sworn in as the twentieth Secretary of Defense of the United States at a small ceremony in the Oval Office. I had been to the White House on several occasions, but never to the Oval Office. I have to admit it took my breath away to stand in this inner sanctum of American executive power, and not as a guest but as the wife of a man who was about to become a member of the President's cabinet.

At ten minutes past ten, President Clinton welcomed Bill and me, along with the small group of dignitaries to the swearing in.

"Good morning," he said, at his most presidential, "Mr. Vice President, Secretary-about-to-be Cohen, Janet, Secretary Perry, Deputy Secretary White, General Shalikashvili, General Ralston, Senator Inouye, Senator Levine, Senator McCain, Senator Stevens, Senator Thurmond, Senator Collins, Senator Snowe. I'm delighted today to be here with all of you for Senator Cohen's swearing in.

"I want to congratulate him on the swift confirmation of his nomination. It says a great deal about this extraordinary man that his Senate colleagues paid him the tribute of a unanimous vote of approval. In so doing, the Senate sent a strong signal of its intention to work in a constructive and bipartisan spirit to preserve and enhance our national security.

"Bill Cohen is the embodiment of that spirit. Throughout his years as a Senator and a Congressman, he's reached across the divisions of party to strengthen our defenses, shaping the START I arms control treaty, helping reorganize the Department of Defense, guiding the most important deliberations about our Armed Forces. He has never forgotten, as he said so eloquently in his testimony on Wednesday, that at the end of every debate stand our soldiers, sailors, airmen, Marines, and Coast Guardsmen, who look to us for leadership, not political strife. . . .

"In Bill Cohen, our military will have a Secretary of Defense with the vision, judgment, and dedication that our era demands. He has served the people of Maine with tremendous distinction. And now I'm pleased that all Americans will benefit from his leadership and wisdom.

"On their behalf, I now ask the Vice President to swear William Cohen into his new office."[1]

Bill faced Vice President Gore, raised his right hand, and placed his left hand on the Bible I held up for him. With immense pride, I watched the man I love receive this tremendous honor and assume the awesome responsibility.

Bill brought me back into the moment with his words of thanks: "President Clinton, Vice President Gore, Secretary Perry, General Shalikashvili, Deputy Secretary White, my colleagues from the Senate, and my dear friends, and most especially, my wife, Janet, thank you all very much for being here today.

"It's a great honor, Mr. President. I thank you for the trust that you've placed in me. We share a conviction that America can best defend her national security interests by uniting behind a bipartisan security policy at home. And your decision to reach across party lines for this appointment respects the desires of the American people for an approach to public policy that is free of political rancor. . . .

"Protecting and promoting America's interests require both wise policies and the military strength to back up those policies. We have today the finest military this nation has ever seen, the finest the world

[1]Transcript of Clinton, "Cohen Remarks at Swearing-In Ceremony," U.S. Newswire, January 24, 1997.

has ever seen. We must ensure that our successors, who will inherit the legacy of our decisions, can say the same. And, therefore, we must continue to attract and retain the highest quality men and women to serve in our Armed Forces, which means we must do right by them when it comes to pay, housing, health care, and other benefits for them and their families."[2]

This was the first time I heard Bill articulate the profound concern he held for the men and women in uniform that would become a hallmark of his tenure as Secretary of Defense. Although I barely noticed it in the excitement of the moment, his concern touched something deep inside of me. He suggested a different way of relating to "the military," not only as a fighting machine but as a group of human beings.

In the Oval Office, the ceremony had come to a close after a couple of questions from the press. It was now 10:21. In the space of eleven minutes, Bill and I had entered an entirely new phase of our lives. After all the congratulations, the handshakes, and other formalities were over at the White House, we climbed into the armored limousine of the Secretary of Defense and drove to the Pentagon.

I knew Bill had a full day planned, but I expected that there would be some pomp and circumstance, with Secretary and Mrs. Perry welcoming us to "The Building," as the Pentagon is known in military circles. We had spent time with them in the weeks leading up to Bill's confirmation, and I was looking forward to formally acknowledging their help and leadership.

I had no idea of what to expect at the Pentagon or what my role would be. I had passed the massive building on many occasions. It was stark and shorn of all exterior grace—simple, solid, enduring, the very nerve center and symbol of American military power. As we drove through the checkpoint at the River Entrance in the armored limousine that was to be Bill's for the next four years, the gravity of his responsibilities began to grip me. Two columns of honor guards stood at attention as we exited the limousine and started up the stone stairs. A team from the Protective Service Detail (Army special agents who would serve as Bill's bodyguards) placed us in a cocoon and escorted us from the front stairs to Bill's office on the E-Ring, the fifth and outer ring of the Pentagon. Their faces were fixed, unblink-

[2]Ibid.

ing, almost grim. I smiled at them to provoke some indication that if they were going to be that close to us, at least they could be friendly. No acknowledgment was forthcoming. They were strictly business. This, I thought, was not going to be easy.

I have a strong personality, confident of my talents and eager to make a contribution. Although not legally required to do so, I had already decided to suspend the operations of Langhart Communications, my media-training company, to avoid any appearance that I would benefit from Bill's position. But I wanted to do something in addition to being a loyal spouse to the Secretary of Defense. I have never been one to sit on the sidelines or fail to be productive. But it was clear that I had entered a male-dominated society and a woman's place was, well, secondary. Be silent, supportive, and of good cheer seemed to be the message.

We were greeted by a large delegation of civilians and military brass. Bill immediately went off for a short briefing, and I began to get acquainted with some of the staff and The Building.

When I returned to the second-floor office of the Secretary of Defense, I was surprised to see a brass plaque with Bill's name on it. I asked one of the aides where Secretary Perry was.

"He's gone, ma'am," she answered, sounding surprised by my question.

"Gone?" I asked, not quite understanding.

"Yes, ma'am," she said, adding with a touch of concern. "I called him a cab to take him home."

"You sent Secretary Perry home in a cab?" I was incredulous. "There's all these official cars."

"He is no longer at the desk . . . no longer SecDef," the aide said, straightening up. "He can't ride in government cars. It's against the rules."

Gee, I thought, *they really mean it. When you are out, you are out.* That was the first indication I had of what a different culture I was entering. As the civilian leader of the military, the Secretary of Defense is in a uniquely delicate position. As the wife of the SecDef, I would have to be highly attuned to the many layers of protocol that govern life in The Building. I decided that the best strategy would be to observe, listen, ask questions, and learn.

I quickly discovered just how much there was to learn. The office of the Secretary of Defense—that is, his immediate staff—comprised three thousand civilian and military positions. There is a deputy secretary, four undersecretaries, ten assistant secretaries, and six other statutory officials who help the SecDef manage an enormous complex of agencies that in 1997 employed nearly three million military and civilian personnel and accounted for fifteen percent of the federal budget.

That first day, I had my job cut out for me just keeping people's names straight. Honestly, I began to feel a little overwhelmed by the scale of it all, the huge responsibility. Even the furniture in Bill's new office was larger than life. The aide who was giving us the tour of the office pointed out the imposing desk and explained that it had belonged to General John J. "Black Jack" Pershing, who had been the commander of the American Expeditionary Force in World War I and subsequently Chief of Staff of the Army. He was known as Black Jack because he had commanded a Black cavalry unit in Montana after graduating from West Point in 1886. I thought my history was in this room.

Behind Pershing's beautiful, hand-carved desk hung a portrait of George Marshall, the five-star general who served as Secretary of Defense and later Secretary of State under President Harry Truman, and was the architect of the Marshall Plan.

I looked at Bill as he got acquainted with his new office and was filled with tremendous pride for him. He had worked so doggedly to overcome rejection and prejudice, to be his own man. He had succeeded beyond all expectations and without compromising his principles. I felt so blessed, and I felt scared. I was watching my husband, the man I love, the man I respect more than any other man I know take on the job of leading America's military.

Yet Bill appeared so calm. He seemed at home in this vast office. He had already displayed the picture of his military hero, Joshua Chamberlain, which he had brought with him from home. Chamberlain was a fellow Maine native and an alumnus of Bill's alma mater, Bowdoin College, who had won a reputation as a gallant hero in the Civil War. Bill especially admires Chamberlain for his chivalrous treatment of Confederate soldiers: At Appomattox, Chamberlain had his men salute Lee's defeated army as he received the formal surrender of their weapons and colors.

Bill had a long agenda for the day, and it was time for me to go. I learned in advance that I was not allowed to ride in his government-furnished limousine unless he was in the vehicle. The Secretary of Defense is presumed to be at risk, but his spouse is not. Rules are made to be kept, but at times they seemed quite absurd. I would discover, for example, that there were occasions when the threat level was so high that a decision was made to extend security protection to me.

I still was not permitted to ride in a government vehicle, so I would hail a cab (the identity and reliability of the driver being of little concern) and have armed security personnel following behind the cab in a chase car.

I called for a private driver and headed home. In the backseat of the car, as we made our way through Friday afternoon traffic, I thought about how unpredictable and wonderful life is. I pictured Bill behind his desk with the picture of Joshua Chamberlain on his wall. When I was a girl in Indianapolis, I never rooted for the cavalry in the movies; I always rooted for the Indians. The only time I would cheer the Union army was when they beat the Confederates. And here I was married to the Secretary of Defense. *What will this new adventure be like,* I wondered. *What will I learn?*

Over the weekend, my sister, who had been with us in the Oval Office for Bill's swearing-in ceremony, called me to recongratulate us. "Do you know what, sis?" she said. "You are the first African-American First Lady of the Military." This was a humbling realization. I had always been proud to hold up my race. Now I would have the additional honor of supporting our military and representing my country around the world.

While I was pondering the ways in which I could serve, an odd notion kept occurring to me. *I need a black dress,* I thought. I remembered how when Ron Brown was killed the previous spring I had scrambled to find a black dress to wear to his funeral. I wanted to be so proper and brave at his service in the National Cathedral. This time, I wanted to be fully prepared for the unfortunate circumstances of military service.

I wanted to learn the culture and code of our great military so that I would be appropriate in the face of great triumph and grave tragedy.

Bill's appointment as Secretary of Defense signaled the beginning of the most transformative four years of my life. Once the euphoria subsided, I began to absorb the fact that he was now sixth in the line of succession, should anything happen to the President. I also had to try to understand the demands Bill's new position would put on both of us. He was on duty twenty-four hours a day.

It was up to me to figure out how I could support Bill and the men and women he served. That was why I was especially grateful for the first congratulatory gift I received after Bill assumed his post. It came from Alma Powell, and it was *The Army Wife's Handbook.*

"I'm not trying to sway you toward the Army," she said, acknowledging the competition between the services and the Pentagon's emphasis on impartiality. "I know you have to be joint. But the book will tell you some of the history of how our military works, the rules and regulations, and the role of the wife and how critical it is."

Alma's gift meant so much to me. Of course, I have great respect for her husband. We might not agree on politics, but I respect Colin for his integrity. I remember asking him at a party once how he felt being in the Republican Party. His response was that you can do more to make change on the inside than by staying outside complaining. I thought that was a pretty good answer, and I was glad to see Colin stick to his guns as he has publicly reiterated his support of affirmative action in spite of opposition from his party. My hope is that he will be able to make the changes on the inside that he envisioned.

While I am proud of the unprecedented achievement of her husband, I look up to Alma Powell in a special way. I have always admired her for her accomplishments and her quiet, unassuming strength. She has stood by her husband, raised three lovely children, and has dedicated herself to making this country better for future generations. She managed to be a model "Army wife" and a powerful woman in her own right, and I was inspired by her gift to find an appropriate place at my husband's side while making a meaningful contribution with my skills and talents.

Ironically, the second gift I received was from Sheila Rabb Weidenfeld, who had served as Betty Ford's press secretary, it was a diary. Sheila suggested that I keep a journal, saying that it would be helpful when I wrote my book some day. *Oh, I am never going to write a book,* I thought. It would be some time still before I would see that I did have something important to say. In the meantime, I tried to adjust to our new life.

In the whirlwind of those early months, what truly came as a shock was the number of parties we had to host and to attend. When

Bill was in the Senate, we were invited to a lot of events, and we went to a good number of them. Attendance at social functions was no longer voluntary, however. We had to go, be charming, gracious, and exuberant. That is a hard thing to do night after night, especially for a person like me, who would much rather curl up at home and read a good book or watch an old movie.

The need to appear in public, however, gave me the opportunity to begin to understand the impact I could have as the wife of the Secretary of Defense. I remember seeing a picture of Bill and me at some function, with the American flag behind us, and being struck by the symbolic power we had as a couple. Together, we literally stood for the progress America had made in overcoming its painful racial past. At that moment, I decided that if I did nothing else, communicating that message to the rest of the world, as well as to the million and a half men and women in the service, was a worthwhile endeavor. The ceremonial role began to take on a meaning and a purpose.

In addition to fearing for his career, part of the reason I wanted Bill to get out of politics before we got married was because I did not want to be a Washington wife, the woman who smiles and waves from the shadow of her powerful husband. I see marriage as a partnership, and I was not interested in being relegated to the background, engaging in menial or make-work activities while my husband did work of national importance.

When I was growing up, we girls were always taught that if you had an idea, it was best to let the man think it was his. I never got that. Do men not have their own ideas? Or are they so insecure they cannot deal with the fact that women are also intelligent beings, who have good, often great, ideas?

I recently had an opportunity to get a male perspective on this question. I was talking with a very close and dear friend—a man of my generation—about the difficulties I have sometimes had in getting male business associates to treat me as an equal. I told him about my encounter with the man from *60 Minutes* and gave him a few other examples. He is an enlightened man, and I was sure he would have an interesting insight into the matter.

"Well, you think fast, and you talk fast," my friend said. "People see that as being aggressive, and many men find aggressive women threatening—emasculating."

I was stunned. I do care about dressing up my ideas to make them more palatable to someone who is not ready to hear them. However, when I get an idea, I move: What's Plan A? What's Plan B? What's our strategy? How do we manage the contingencies? How do we leverage the opportunities? That is how I think, and that is how I talk.

To hear that a man would find that emasculating was really disturbing. It means that while I am trying to engage him intellectually, he does not hear me because he is worried about protecting his privates.

"Emasculating?" I said in disbelief. "We're talking about ideas. What's that got to do with your you-know-what? I am trying to get into your head not your pants."

I had always known that fear was the driving force behind racism. I did not understand that it was also the fuel for male chauvinism. I once overheard one of Bill's staffers openly worry that my visibility might get higher than Bill's. There was that insecurity again, the dread of being overtaken, upstaged, outdone. In the face of it, I identified, more strongly than I ever had, with feminism. For the racist and the chauvinist, it's a zero-sum game. If I succeed, that means you fail? If I'm smart, that means you're dumb? Despite the law of physics, I do believe that two equal entities can exist in the same space.

Women are no longer confined by the narrow roles society once prescribed for us. More and more women are getting educated and stepping out of the shadows. We are thinking and doing and excelling. Even when it is our men who attain positions of power first, we are there to enhance them with our own contributions.

When Bill assumed his post, it was clear to me that was the kind of partner I wanted to be. I admired Hillary Clinton for her courage in defining the role of the First Lady as that of someone with a real mission in spite of all the criticism she received. There is too much work to be done in the world for a bright, skilled, committed woman just to stand there and smile and to serve as window dressing. Abigail Adams did not do it. Eleanor Roosevelt did not do it. Mary McLeod Bethune did not do it. And I was glad that Hillary Clinton refused to do it.

One could debate her politics and policies, but it was fitting that a woman of Hillary Clinton's intellectual stature, education, and experience should take an active part in addressing the issues that confronted this country. I, too, aspired to find a role at the Pentagon that would allow me to make my unique contribution.

Our military, with their lives on the line all over the world, was much too important for any of us to stand on the sidelines, stand on ceremony and not make a contribution, however small. I chose to lead with my strengths as a communicator to help reconnect America to its national treasure—its military.

Everywhere I went, I chose to remind America of the sacrifices of the military and their families. I focused most of all on the quality of life issues of our military: housing, health care, day care, education, pay and pension, and domestic issues. While exercising my passion and patriotism and need to serve, I did my best to obey protocol and stay in my lane. I wanted to make my contribution more than just symbolic.

"It's not easy being a symbol of any kind, let alone carrying the extra weight that race often packs," Kevin Merida wrote about Bill and me in December 1997, in a *Washington Post* profile entitled "In Defense of Love Beyond Race." "They host dinners for foreign defense ministers, travel the globe representing their country, tour U.S. bases to exhort the troops. In the process they have become the best advertisement for the kind of dialogue and interpersonal racial progress President Clinton is now pushing, the kind of progress that can't be legislated."

It was gratifying to have acknowledgment for the statement we were making about America simply by being ourselves. I must admit, every time we stepped through the doorway of that airplane with the words *United States of America* painted on its fuselage, it took my breath away because I knew we were saying to the world, "Yes, we Americans have our problems, but look at Bill and me, we're working them out."

Yet, I wanted to be more than a symbol, I wanted to serve. I remembered Dr. King's last sermon at Ebenezer Baptist Church, which he delivered two months before his death and parts of which were broadcast during his televised memorial service. In it he had said that he wanted to be remembered as a drum major for justice, peace, and righteousness. That image haunted me. I, too, wanted to be a drum major—a leader, an advocate, an inspiration.

The more Bill and I traveled to the various corners of the globe—from Bosnia and the Middle East to Japan and Africa—where American soldiers were stationed or were engaged in peacekeeping missions, humanitarian aid, and training exercises, the more I came to be in awe of them. They are young people, most in their late teens and early twenties, who have embraced the words *duty, honor, country,* and who voluntarily have committed themselves to safeguarding peace and democracy. That commitment reflected a biblical scripture that inspired a plaque hung within the Pentagon. The scripture is from Isaiah 6:8 which reads,

> *Then I heard the voice of the Lord saying,*
> *"Whom shall I send, and who will go for us?"*
> And [Isaiah] answered,
> *"Here am I; send me!"*

In their midst, I felt myself changing, and sensed a different world-view emerging. Just being around them was awe-inspiring and life altering.

When I was young, servicemen were revered in the wake of World War II. But the Vietnam War shaped much of my adult outlook. It seemed that the military was no longer the defender of freedom but an instrument of Cold War politics and geopolitical domination. To me, it seemed to be just another expression of racism and imperialism. Despite the lack of respect some Americans had for those serving in that war, I, like many Americans, loved the warrior but hated the war.

To see an army of volunteers—an army that is the most integrated institution in our society—forced me to look at my country in a different light. I saw America with the eyes of the young men and women who were prepared to serve and die for the nation, and I was infused with their patriotism. During my lifetime, I had watched the country struggle with its past, and we had succeeded, we had grown. I realized that in my heart I carried a deep love for America, and now I was able to say it out loud.

It was a transcendent feeling, almost a deep religious experience. I remember exactly the moment I felt it take hold. It was Christmas 1997. Bill and I had traveled to Bosnia to celebrate the holidays with the peacekeeping troops. It was cold and dreary. I saw mud caked on the boots of the young men and women and weariness in their eyes. I thought of the reports I had read of our soldiers befriending the thousands of children orphaned by the war.

I wanted to say something to them, to bring them a little warmth from home.

"Can I say Merry Christmas to them?" I asked Bill.

I hate public speaking, so I was literally planning to say, "Happy holidays and thank you." But when I took the microphone and looked into their upturned faces, I felt the spirit move me.

"I want to thank you on behalf of everybody back home for being here," I said, "for standing in the cold, standing in the mud, missing this Christmas at home."

Now, the Army has a tradition of call and response, just like the African-American churches. So when I said, "Thank you for standing in the mud," they said, "Whoo-ahh!"

"Thank you for being over here," I said, "just inches away from landmines."

"Whoo-ahh!" they responded in unison.

"I know you are missing your families, and I know they are missing you," I said.

"Whoo-ahh!" they shouted.

And with every response, I thought of more things to say on behalf of the rest of us back home.

"We haven't forgotten you," I told them. "We are grateful to you for keeping us safe and free and for taking care of the people over here, especially the little children. You know that when you are gone, they will remember you, and remember that you were here. They will tell their children, and their children will tell their children that because you were here, they have a future. Thank you, and God bless you."

The soldiers were cheering, and I was crying by the time I was done. I had finally found my passion. I was not exactly a missionary, the kind I had fantasized about being after reading Pearl Buck, but I was on a mission—to acknowledge the sacrifices of the men and women in uniform and their families and to make their life a little better.

From then on, when we visited the troops, Bill would call on me to be the last to speak, and the scene in Bosnia was repeated over and over. Bill was SecDef, their boss, and he spoke for the administration. I, on the other hand, could speak on behalf of their families, their loved ones, and their compatriots. If I was not yet a drum major, I had become a cheerleader. I would tell them that the American people had an obligation to see to it that their families are taken care of, and that they, our service members, have everything they needed to serve and survive. We have already equipped them with the best training, best equipment, and the best leadership.

The military just pulls you in. Once you get to know the men and women who serve, you cannot stand on the sidelines. When we would visit installations, I would wade out into the throngs of kids in uniform and talk to them. "Where are you from?" I would ask. "Anybody here from Indiana? Anybody here from Massachusetts?"

They saw that I was approachable and would talk to me. "How are you doing? How is your family coping?" I inquired. "What do you need? How's the host country treating you?" I was always curious as to what motivated them to join the military. Invariably, the answer was, "To serve my country, ma'am."

Pretty quickly word got around about the new SecDef's wife. Kids e-mail one another in the military; they have buddies all over the world with whom they have been on tours of duty. We would show up at a base in Eastern Europe, and I would be greeted with extra smiles and handshakes. "It's nice to meet you, ma'am," they would say. "You talked to my pal in Kuwait." Or, "My sister met you in North Carolina." Or, "My buddy in Germany wrote me after your visit."

I was so impressed with how the e-mails could connect everybody that I began to stay in touch with service members and their family by e-mail as well.

I remember an interview that Bill and I did with Barbara Walters on ABC's *20/20* where she asked me if I noticed if the Black service members related to me differently than the White service members. My answer was, "No, absolutely not. They don't see race and neither do I. They are all my children, and I love and respect them all equally."

I made a connection with each and every one of them. We all need that human connection, regardless of class, generation, gender, race, or religion. And I used my gift of connecting with people to reach out and embrace the young people who put their lives on the line in the service of our nation.

The military, with all its diversity, its mission, and its unique culture enabled me to reach past my rage and to embrace my country. Those kids gave me more than I could ever have given them. The military transformed me. In 1987, I had taken a journey inside myself and found my soul. During the years at the Pentagon, I journeyed all over the world and discovered the soul of America—the courage, strength, hope, and integrity of its people.

As I got closer to the men and women of the military, I became keenly aware of the fact that their mission is to put their lives on the line so you and I do not have to, so we are secure, so our interests here and abroad are protected. The first time I stood out at Andrews Air Force Base and watched a flag-draped coffin come home, I understood. And every time I saw families crying for another young person who had been killed in training or in battle, I vowed to serve them to the best of my ability.

The summer of 1998 was particularly difficult emotionally. Early in that year, at the insistence of his family, the remains of Lieutenant Michael Blassie were exhumed from the Tomb of the Unknowns in Arlington Cemetery and positively identified through DNA tests. Lieutenant Blassie had been shot down over South Vietnam in 1972. His remains—six bones—could not be positively identified, and in 1984 were buried in the Tomb of the Unknowns.

When the DNA tests became available, the families of the Unknown Soldier faced a difficult choice. Some had found closure and did not want to run the risk of finding out that the remains in the tomb were not those of their loved one. Others wanted confirmation that it was their son who was buried at Arlington.

The Blassies were among those who wanted—needed—to know. After Michael's remains were exhumed for testing, I spoke to his mother. "How are you going to be if it's not your son?" I asked.

"I'm going to be fine," she said, "but I really feel it's Michael. I just know it."

Mrs. Blassie's maternal intuition was right. The tests showed that the bones were Michael's. And so, Lieutenant Blassie was buried for the second time. The family had a choice of burying him at Arlington or at a military cemetery in St. Louis, where they made their home. They chose St. Louis, and several hundred of us assembled in the Missouri heat on July 11, 1998.

It was a beautiful ceremony. A squadron of F-15 fighters flew over in missing-man formation as Michael's casket, draped in the American flag, was placed by the honor guard at the feet of his family. I kept looking at Mrs. Blassie and thinking how difficult it must have been for her to wait twenty-six years to bury her twenty-four-year-old son.

It was all I could do not to sob out loud. And the more I tried not to cry, the more the tears welled up in my heart. When I heard Missouri Congressman Richard Gephardt, who was standing right behind us, struggle to contain his emotions, I thought I would collapse. But I looked at Mrs. Blassie and told myself that I had to bear up.

And I did, until I got in the car, where I just let go. Bill was very quiet; he was hurting too. He handed me his handkerchief and said, "It's okay. Don't cry. We've got to be strong for them."

"You've got to let me grieve," I said, sobbing. "They can't see me now. I need to cry, for them and for me."

I did not realize how much crying I would do that summer and in the years to come. Just four weeks after Michael Blassie's funeral, the American embassies in Kenya and Tanzania were attacked in nearly simultaneous bombings. Scores of people were killed—twelve Americans among them—and hundreds were injured.

On August 13, 1998, the bodies of the fallen Americans were flown to Andrews Air Force Base. We joined the families, the President and Mrs. Clinton, Secretary of State Madeleine Albright, other Cabinet members, the Joint Chiefs, and members of Congress at a ceremony to honor the dead.

This was the first funeral I attended where we were burying people lost in combat during our service. We were assembled in one of those enormous hangars, looking out toward the tarmac. A C-130 Hercules, a gigantic transport plane, was parked right outside. One by one, the coffins were brought out by the honor guard, placed into hearses, and brought into the hangar. It was such a ritual, done with such surgical precision and formality and grace. I had a lump in my throat from the moment I caught sight of the first casket.

Then Bill got up to the podium and gave a speech that has stayed with me to this day:

"This is a moment of profound sadness and grief," he said, "Justice Oliver Wendell Holmes, Jr., once spoke words that give us strength today. 'Alas . . . we cannot live our dreams. We're lucky enough if we can give a sample of our best and if in our hearts we can feel it's been nobly done . . .

"This tragedy has cost us precious lives and there's no expression of grief and no vow for justice that can lift the pain of this day, but we can never allow terrorists to diminish our determination to press on with the inspiring work of those who have been taken from us. Their sudden loss must only strengthen our sense of purpose. They did not serve and they did not sacrifice, they did not give their lives so that we could walk away from this new world that they were helping to build for others. We must ensure that the torch of freedom always burns brighter than the fires of hate; and that we continue to be an America worthy of the ultimate price that they have paid."[2]

I was particularly moved by the notion of "an America worthy of the ultimate price." I thought of Dr. King and the sacrifice he had made to ensure that this country was "worthy." He had often talked of saving the soul of America, and finally I was beginning to understand what he had meant.

I realized at that moment that although I was enraged by my country's racist past, I was being transformed by the men and women of the military into a patriot. They were the "good people" Mrs. Cass had spoken about. They were the "worthy" America.

As a symbol of my dedication to the people of the military, I began to wear a POW/MIA bracelet. It was for Bobby Jones, an Air Force flight surgeon whose plane was shot down on November 28, 1972, on a noncombat mission over Da Nang. Although emergency signals were heard, rescue teams could not get to the area of the crash for three days because of monsoons. Lieutenant Jones and his copilot, Jack Harvey, were never found.

The bracelet was given to me by Bobby Jones's sister, JoAnn Shirley. It was during one of our ceremonies at the Tomb of the Unknowns when afterward, I walked over to shake the hands of veterans and family members, and I noticed JoAnn wearing a button with a picture on it. I asked who he was, and she said, "It's my brother, Bobby." She told me about his plane going down that November 1972 and removed a bracelet from her wrist, handed it to me, and asked me to wear it out of remembrance for him. It was, without a doubt, a moment I will never forget, and an honor I'll always treasure. We've stayed in touch. I've even had the pleasure of meeting her mother, Mrs. Jones. She not only gave the country the gift of her son, but was kind enough to give me a china plate that she had hand painted. God Bless all the Gold Star Mothers.

I wanted to honor every person who has put on a uniform and served. I wanted to reach out and embrace the young people in the

[2]Albright, Cohen Remarks at Andrews AFB, August 13, United States Information Agency, August 13, 1998.

services to thank them. There were so many beautiful moments of human connection.

One of these moments in particular is dear to my memory. On December 23, 1998, I joined Bill, Senator Daniel Inouye, Congressman John Murtha, comedian Al Franken, singers Carole King, Mary Chapin Carpenter, Jon Caroll, and David Ball on a Holiday Tour to visit our troops in the Persian Gulf. After departing from Prince Sultan Air Base in Saudia Arabia, we landed on the *USS Enterprise* (The "Big E").

On the night of November 8, shortly after the *USS Enterprise* had departed from Norfolk, Virginia, on its way to the Persian Gulf, it suffered a major accident. An EA-6B Prowler crashed into another aircraft (an S-3 Viking) on the flight deck. A fire broke out in both planes. All four of the Prowler crew perished, with the remains of only one recovered from the sea. The two crewmen of the aircraft that was struck were injured, but survived. Bill had been briefed on the accident before we arrived. It was important for us to lift the morale of the sailors.

After we had formally greeted the crew and the entertainment began, I went out into the crowd to mix with those on board. I was doing my usual handshaking and picture taking when I noticed one young Black sailor standing off by himself leaning up against a pipe. He was wearing a red shirt, signaling he was a fireman.

I went over to him and said, "Hey, how are you doing?"

He said, "I'm okay."

"Are you really alright?" I pressed. "Why aren't you dancing and singing with us?"

"Oh, ma'am, thank you for coming," he said, "but I'm just not up to it right now."

"Are you physically sick?"

"No."

"What's the matter, then? Talk to me."

"Ma'am, I'm not supposed to talk about it."

"You can talk to me. I'm not your commanding officer."

"The other day," he said lowering his voice, "we had a plane go off."

I said, "Yes, I know about that. I'm so very sorry. That's one of the reasons we came out here, to give you guys a lift."

"Well, my job was to go out there and try to retrieve the crew from the water," the sailor said in a near whisper. "I couldn't get the pilot, ma'am. I did everything I could."

"That's all you can do."

"I was scared," he continued. "I was just so scared."

And I said, "What were you afraid of?"

"There were flames like I'd never seen. I've never felt so much heat. Never."

"But you tried, even though you were afraid."

He was silent for a few moments.

"Well, ma'am, you know, I really shouldn't be talking about this."

"Yes, you should be talking about this."

He said, "Ma'am, we are briefed when we come on board that if we have a mishap we are not to be in a maudlin, mourning mood. We have to snap out of it because if something else happens, that mood could prevent us from doing our job and saving another life."

"Oh, all right, I understand," I said. "We never had this conversation. But is it okay if I hug you? Because I need a hug."

He held his arms straight out and let me hug him. I could feel his hurt in the awkward posture, the tense muscles. It was such a profound moment for me. I felt I had done something truly worthwhile in offering a small measure of comfort to that one grieving sailor.

10

First Lady of the Pentagon

As I got to know the men and women in the service, I was also learning to see the military not as a world unto itself but in the context of civilian life and society. It was a young airman who got me thinking about that on that first Christmas visit to Bosnia. We were having breakfast in the mess hall the morning after the big holiday gathering. I was all pumped up and probably gushing just a little.

"I am so in awe of you all," I told him.

"Thank you for coming over, ma'am," he said, uncomfortable with my praise.

"Thank you," I continued. "I get to go back home after this, but you have to stay and miss out on Christmas with your families. You have to take all these risks, make all these sacrifices. You're all so brave and committed. You're our heroes."

"Thank you, ma'am," he said, "but we are not angels. We are not saints. We are just people like you. You know, ma'am, as civilians, we come from you, we serve our country, and when our duty here is done, we come back to you. We become civilians again."

It was important for me to hear that, to be reminded that all heroes are also flesh and blood. The young people who flew off at a day's notice to do their duty for the country also worried about their kids' schooling, their spouses' health, their parents, their relationships, and their futures—all the things that the rest of us think about. The difference is that it is much harder to tend to those kinds of concerns when you are thousands of miles away from home and bound by the strict regimen of the military.

I remembered a conversation I had had with my predecessor, Mrs. Perry, as we were making the transition into the Pentagon. I had asked her what I would be expected to do as the wife of the Secretary of Defense.

"Well, whatever you want," she had said. "There's no real role, but you might find an interest."

"What was your interest?" I had asked.

"I worked on quality of life," Mrs. Perry had said.

"Quality of life?" I had repeated, my eyes glazing over. I had no idea what that meant.

As I grew into my role as First Lady of the Pentagon, I began to understand the critical role quality-of-life issues played in recruiting and retaining volunteers and allowing our men and women to perform at peak capacity.

As I discovered, there was a long tradition of generals' and admirals' wives working on quality-of-life issues. I learned from these women, many of whom had spent most of their lives in the service, bringing their strengths and experience to our men and women. I wanted to bring my unique strengths and experience during my time as well. It was my empathy that would enable me to accomplish that mission.

Several things worked in my favor. I grew up in a government project. I know about discrimination, what it is like to feel invisible and powerless because you're young and poor. I could identify and understand what it was like to be an underdog.

I never missed an opportunity to ask how they were and if there was anything they needed. I made it clear that I could not promise anything, but that I could make sure the right people heard their views. I was in a position to raise questions that a private could not ask of a general, if ever he or she got near one.

I also began to rely on the spouses for information. Traditionally, while Bill met with base commanders and other brass, I would meet with the spouses. At first, these were little gatherings to welcome and entertain me. However, I began to send out word in advance of my visits that I wanted more than tea and crumpets. I wanted to know what their concerns were. I learned so many things, like how difficult it is for many families to make it on military pay.

I saw it as a noble obligation, to use what strengths I had and the access I had to make life better for the men and women in uniform and their families. I was not telling the generals or Bill or the president anything they did not know. Quality of life, recruitment, retention, morale were all issues that they thought about and endeavored to address. What I gained was a different perspective on those issues. It is one thing to sit at a briefing and listen to statistics and projections, and quite another to learn about a private serving in Kosovo who is worried about his wife coping without child care back home or an Air Force pilot who is reluctantly considering resigning his commission to take a job with the airlines for better pay.

I had the honor and the privilege to spend time with the people who do the fighting and the dying for this country. And I saw it as my duty to help their voices be heard by the people who had the power to make life better for them.

Finding a New Home

I am very fortunate to be married to a man who encourages me to live up to my full potential. Bill recognized the passion and commitment I brought to serving the military and supported my efforts in every way. With his support, I organized the first Military Family Forum, a one-day conference that included representatives from military families from all parts of the country. Bill opened the meeting, setting forth the need to have complete candor on what family members saw as their most pressing needs.

The chairman of the Joint Chiefs of Staff, General Hugh Shelton and his wife, Carolyn, were present, as was General Joe Ralston and his wife, Dede, the former vice chairman of the Joint Chiefs, who was then serving as the Supreme Allied Commander, Europe (SACEUR). General Ralston had flown back from his headquarters in Brussels to lend his support to the conference.

After several officials concluded their remarks, the sessions were closed to the media. This was not going to be a griping session but an open and candid discussion on what issues needed to be addressed in order to ensure that we continued to recruit the best people to serve our country and then did everything possible to retain them.

The conference proved to be a great morale booster. Once the families understood that The Forum was not a public relations exercise, they relaxed and then dove into the sessions with great enthusiasm. Perhaps for the first time, they felt that their voices were being heard at the very top of the chain of command.

As I became more and more involved in the quality-of-life issues, I was even afforded the use of a separate office.

Situated around the corner from the SecDef's office, this was a room designated as a place to entertain visiting dignitaries and top brass. I was allowed to keep my files there, however, and could use the round table for meetings and as a desk. Soon, my unofficial office had become a command center for working to secure better housing, schools, and support services for the enlisted, the people for whom it was difficult to advocate for themselves within the rigid structure of the military.

I began to feel very much at home in that imposing building despite the rigid structure of the military. It was a very diverse community with nearly twenty-four thousand employees. I used to take long walks and got acquainted with the Pentagon, and the more I learned about it the more I felt a sense of kinship. Its construction began the year I was born. (The actual date—September 11, 1941— did not acquire its terrible significance until the year we left the Pentagon.) And it was built in the same solid, government way as Lockefield Gardens, the Indianapolis projects where I grew up. The doorknobs were the same. So was the paint caked on the window frames. Even the heat coming up in the radiators reminded me of home.

I would walk down the long corridors, listening to the sound of my heels on the granite floor, and think about how far I had come from Lockefield Gardens. How many great people walked down these same corridors? I wondered. How many stories are within these walls?

Often, late at night, I would wander through the many exhibits: African-Americans in Defense, Buffalo Soldier Exhibit, Hall of Heroes, Hispanic Medal of Honor Display, Military Women's Corridor, Native American Display, Navajo Code Talkers Display, POW/MIA Corridor. So many heroes.

I felt very proud of the Black heroes, although I did find it ironic that we still separated our heroes by race. I also had a special place in my heart for the Native Americans, especially the Code Talkers. I remembered my great-grandfather preserving a part of his Shawnee culture out in the backyard during his morning prayers, and I felt proud of that part of my heritage too.

*   *   *

Synchronicity is a New Age word that suggests that there are meaningful relations between events that are seemingly coincidental. I have found it interesting, for example, that the initials of my name, JLC, are those of Bill's hero, Joshua Lawrence Chamberlain. Bill's, in turn, WSC, are those of the person I admire most, Winston S. Churchill. It all, no doubt, signifies nothing more than sheer coincidence, but still, I find it curious that I became the sponsor of the USS *Winston S. Churchill*. A nine thousand ton, Aegis Class Guided Missile Destroyer. This ship was the fourth in our history to be named after an Englishman. It was a special treat for me to have Sir Winston's youngest living child, Lady Mary Soames, join me as the honorary sponsor.

Serving as the "mother" of a mighty warship is an honor few enjoy. It is customary for the Navy and the contractor, after spending years of hard labor and millions of dollars, to send it off into the waters with a good deal of pomp and ceremony. On April 16, 1999, Bill and I flew to Brunswick Naval Air Station in Maine and then drove several miles to Bath, the home of one of our great shipbuilders, Bath Iron Works, a subsidiary of General Dynamics. That evening we attended a party hosted by Duane "Buzz" Fitzgerald, the CEO of BIW and one of Bill's closest friends. Scottish bagpipers, performing in honor of the British Defense Minister George Robertson, set the celebratory mood. Following dinner, a team of British Marines performed a silent drill exercise for all the VIPs in attendance, including Lady Soames, Admiral Jay Johnson, the U.S. Chief of Naval Operations and his British counterpart, Admiral Sir Michael Boyce, First Sea Lord and Chief of Naval Staff. John Dalton, the former Secretary of the Navy who had selected me to be the ship's sponsor, and his successor, Richard Danzig, were both present.

The next day, the shipyard was filled with thousands of BIW employees and their families, along with those of Commander Michael Franken and some of the officers and enlisted crew aboard who numbered more than three hundred and forty.

Because of the manner that BIW used to launch its ships into the tidal waters of the Kennebec River, the ship had to be released at a precisely, predetermined moment. All of the formal speeches had to be brief and tightly controlled, because the ship was going to be released at the ringing of a bell, whether or not the speeches were completed. The tides wait for no man. Or woman.

Fortunately, I didn't have to make a speech. My role and that of
Lady Soames was to smash a champagne bottle against the bow of
the ship at the signal of the ringing bell. I was somewhat nervous,
fearing that the bottle would not break and I would have to flail
away a second or third time. Bill calmed me. He had attended dozens
of ship launchings as a member of the Senate Armed Services Committee. "Just pretend you're hitting a baseball and you're swinging
for a home run. Don't tap it. Swing it. Trust me, the bottle will break."

At the appointed moment, the bell sounded. While I had not intended to say anything, I spontaneously shouted into the loud-
speaker system, "On behalf of my husband, the Secretary of Defense,
and the United States of America, I bring you, USS *Winston S.
Churchill,* to life. As you go forth to sail the seas in the defense of
freedom, I pray for your safety and that of your captain and crew."
Then Lady Soames and I swung for the fences. Both magnums shat-
tered; as champagne spewed out the crowd roared its approval. The
Churchill began its rapid slide down the greased wheys into the
Kennebec, amid a band playing "Anchors Aweigh."

I had given birth, not to a child, but to a full grown "Man O'
War." I wept tears of joy in the knowledge that I had become inex-
tricably linked to an indomitable leader whose courage and will
would help save the twentieth century from the forces of evil. Call it
coincidence or synchronicity. It has remained for me, a moment to remember.

Two for America

Another aspect of my role as First Lady of the Pentagon was to
serve as a goodwill ambassador to the countries that hosted our
troops. As we traveled and Bill met with defense ministers of the various nations where our soldiers were stationed, I would meet with
their wives and ask how our service memebers were behaving on their
soil. Were they respectful? Did they contribute? Was there more we
could be doing? Was there more the hosts could do for our people?

In places where there were problems, such as Okinawa, I would
try to find out what was contributing to the tensions. Could we fos-
ter dialogue? Were there resources in the community to address some
of the underlying issues?

Sometimes, these conversations would lead to more probing interchanges about American foreign policy, our moral authority, and global politics. On more than one occasion, my hosts would ask me how I felt representing a country where my people had been oppressed for so many centuries. I was thankful for these questions, because they gave me an opportunity to use my own experience to talk about the greatness of America, a young country determined to conquer its baser instincts and to strive for justice and equality.

"A country where I could go from the projects to the Pentagon," I would say, "is one I am proud to represent."

I felt very grateful to Bill for having the courage and vision to give me the opportunity to take on "a role that is almost unheard [of] for a Cabinet spouse," as *New York Times* reporter Elizabeth Becker wrote in "'Two for America' Beat the Drums for the Military" in March 1999.[1] As that article recognized, Bill made room for me to be a partner with him in boosting the morale of the troops, in making the case for the military to civilian audiences, and in improving recruitment and retention.

Of all the stories that were done about Bill and me during our time at the Pentagon, I am particularly fond of that one, because of a quote in it by Kati Marton, author of a book entitled *Hidden Power: Presidential Marriages that Shaped Our Recent History* and wife of then U.S. Ambassador to the United Nations, Richard Holbrooke. The *New York Times* quotes Kati as saying about me: "What she's doing is very much in keeping with that activist engaged role that Eleanor Roosevelt pioneered. She is essential to her husband's well-being and his job, and she is taking a full role in both." To be recognized as following in Eleanor Roosevelt's footsteps felt like a major achievement and a validation of what I was attempting to accomplish.

And a full role it was. Bill and I traveled nonstop. By one estimate, Bill flew more than 800,000 miles during his four years as SecDef, and I was by his side for many of those miles. Often, that would be the only time we would have to spend with each other.

As demanding as the travel schedule was, it was also very rewarding. We met incredible people everywhere we went, and I had unlimited opportunities to learn and to grow. I especially enjoyed the frequent reminders that came my way about how interconnected all of life is.

---

[1] "'Two for America' Beat the Drums for the Military," Elizabeth Becker, the *New York Times*, March 21, 1999, section 1, page 34.

On our first trip to the Middle East, for example, we went to Egypt and then Israel in April 1998. In Egypt, as I had done in many countries, such as Bulgaria and Bosnia, I wanted to see how the people lived, what they needed, and express goodwill on behalf of my country. As part of my tour, I visited several hospitals. On one such visit, I struck up a conversation with an Egyptian gynecologist. I asked him where he had studied and learned that he trained in Boston.

"My late husband was Dr. Kistner, a surgeon and infertility doctor," I told the man, thinking he might have heard of Bob.

"Oh, ma'am," he said. "This is such an honor. Dr. Kistner was a great man."

It turned out that the doctor had studied with Bob and could not say enough wonderful things about him. He invited me to his office and showed me a copy of Bob's book on the general principles of gynecology. It was such a beautiful gift from the universe, in the midst of this unexpected phase of my life, to meet someone who remembered and respected my late husband.

Several days later, we flew to Israel. Yitzhak Mordechai, the Israeli defense minister, met us at the airport and invited us into his car for the short drive to the hotel. On the way, his telephone rang, and he answered.

"Excuse me," the minister said, hanging up after a short conversation, "that was Topol."

"Topol the actor?" I exclaimed. "The one who was in *Fiddler on the Roof*?"

"Yes," he said, delighted by my enthusiasm. "He is a good friend."

"Oh my God," I said, losing my cool demeanor. "I met him when I was first starting out in television. Mr. Minister, please tell him I said hello."

"I'll do better than that," Minister Mordechai said. "I'll have him come to the Knesset tonight."

That evening we were the guests of honor at a gala in the Knesset's Chagall Hall, named for its beautiful tapestry by the great artist. All of Israel's political establishment turned out to pay their respects. I was sitting next to Ariel Sharon. Shimon Peres and Mrs. Rabin sat at neighboring tables. But for me, the most exciting moment came when Topol took the stage and dedicated an a cappella performance of "Buddy Can You Spare a Dime" to me.

Afterward, Topol and I talked about that interview that I had done with him in Chicago nearly thirty years earlier. It was so wonderful to see my life coming full circle and to see how far I had traveled and who I had become.

Of all the world leaders we met, none was to be more impressive and inspiring than Nelson Mandela. On a long trip to South Africa, we stopped first in Rabat, Morocco, to visit with King Mohammed VI, the young, progressive new ruler whom we had met on several previous occasions. He is wise beyond his years and spoke passionately to us about the challenge he faced in trying to reconcile the need to maintain the traditions of his country with the pressure and promise of economic and social globalization. I felt a special kinship to the people of Morocco, who were warm and openhearted. The King, who was fluent in Arabic, English, French, and Spanish, indulged me by conversing with me in Spanish. It was so kind of him to do that.

Once we arrived in Cape Town, South Africa, however, I experienced an entirely different emotion—that of coming home. While I believe that my lineage runs back to West Africa, I had the sensation of an ancient rhythm beating in my heart for all of Africa.

After we dropped our luggage at the hotel, Bill arranged for us to travel by military helicopter out to Robben Island, where President Mandela had spent so many of his twenty-six years in prison.

Upon our arrival, a tour guide gave us a briefing on the history of the prison and the years that Nelson Mandela and his fellow freedom fighters had spent there.

During the course of listening to this oral history, I reflected on the very first time that I saw Mr. Mandela. It was the day after Bob's memorial service in Cambridge. I had returned to the Ritz Carlton where Bob and I had spent happier days. I happened to look out of the hotel room and found myself staring into the bedroom window of the condo that was now occupied by renters. At that moment, the telephone rang. It was my friend Colette Phillips. I could hear the excitement in her voice.

"Are you watching this?"

"Watching what?" I suspected that something tragic had just happened, and after the previous day's experience at Bob's memorial service, I was simply too drained to absorb any more horrors.

"It's Mr. Mandela. They're letting him out of jail any minute now," she said.

I clicked on the television and sat glued to the story that was unfolding on the airwaves. Colette and I talked intermittently of joy and expectation. We also could not escape a sense of anger that roiled inside us over the thought of how another group of Europeans had come to Africa to enslave, imprison, and oppress African people in their own land. A roar from the crowd interrupted our conversation. The world was waiting for a glimpse of the man who was a hero to so many of us.

Then he emerged, a towering, forceful figure. He was much older than the photo we had cherished for so many years. The Afrikaners had refused to allow his visage to be seen over the years. They thought that by keeping him in isolation and invisible to the public that he would be forgotten. They were as misguided and mistaken as those who thought they could end Martin Luther King's inspiration and legacy by terminating his life.

Striding with his wife, Winnie, by his side, he broke into a smile that created a virtual aura around him. I had interviewed Winnie previously and she had told me that, "One day, he will be free." That day had come. February 11, 1990.

Several months later Mr. Mandela traveled to Boston to deliver a major speech. Colette was handling the public affairs for the event, and she arranged for me to meet him backstage after his speech. I was awestruck. He was a man bigger than any myth. He seemed to be in a state of grace, free of rancor and bitterness over the injustice he had had to endure.

I thanked him for coming to Boston and praised him for his inspirational and heroic fight against oppression. He, in turn, thanked me and all the African-Americans who had supported the struggle by demanding an end to the vicious policy of apartheid and a release of all who had wrongly been imprisoned in South Africa.

In the following months, I would see Mr. Mandela twice more in Washington, D.C. Bill had arranged for me to join him for separate lunches hosted by Senators David Boren of Oklahoma and Bob Dole, the Senate Majority Leader.

When we entered his cell on our visit to Robben Island, and I looked out through the bars of his prison cell, I lost all composure and began to cry. All of those years spent cracking rocks because he wanted freedom from the brutal, racist policies of the White minority, the Bull Connors and George Wallaces of South Africa. It was unconscionable.

And yet, Mr. Mandela emerged from prison unbowed and unbroken. The words of Jesse Owens about Adolph Hitler flashed through my mind: "I'm still here and he's not." Mr. Mandela's years had not been wasted on self-pity. He used the time that was not spent on senseless, mind-numbing labor, to study the law and language of his slave masters. Eventually, he turned both against them.

What was most inspiring about him was the absence of hate in his heart. He sought not vengeance but freedom, justice, and opportunity for his people. Like Dr. King, he appealed to the moral voice of the universe and made the world ashamed of its tolerance of brutal institutionalized bigotry.

The next day, when we traveled to his modest home in Qunu, I found myself sitting in the living room of a man who stood ramrod tall as a warrior, but who spoke with the wisdom and gentleness of a great diplomat on world events. I was in the presence of greatness, that of a man who had the courage to speak truth to power and who, in doing so, broke the physical and mental chains of millions the world over.

Even though I had previously met Mr. Mandela, I found myself, on this occasion, speechless. I embraced him and fought back the tears.

I would see him once again, this time in New York City in the home of United Nations Ambassador Richard Holbrooke and his wife, Kati Marton. I sat between Kofi Annan and Mr. Mandela who spent much of the evening talking to Oprah Winfrey. At the next table, Bill sat talking with Harry Belafonte. I thought of Dr. King. There was royalty all around me.

Pentagon Pops

Bill was working hard on a campaign to "Reconnect America to Its Military." One of the very first things he did during his first few months in office was to visit the major public relations firms in New York that were handling the advertising accounts for the military services. With the exception of the Marine Corps, the services were not meeting their recruiting goals. Bill was convinced that we had to do a far better job in our advertising techniques and placements if we hoped to compete successfully against the private sector for the best and the brightest in our society. He was surprised to discover that the firms all had five-year contracts and appeared overly satisfied with their work product. He insisted that all future contracts be of limited duration and far more competitive. I had accompanied him on the visit, and based on my experience in the world of television, agreed completely with his analysis that the firms had become far too comfortable and complacent. Competiton usually proves to be the mother of all creativity, and creativity seemed to be precisely what was missing.

We also discussed the important role that Hollywood had long played in shaping society's attitude toward our military. The *Sands of Iwo Jima, A Bridge Too Far, The Longest Day,* and *Stalag 17* came quickly to mind. But following the war in Vietnam, the military was cast in less than heroic light. With few exceptions (*Top Gun* being one), military officers were portrayed either as overstuffed buffoons or amoral megalomaniacs; the enlisted caricatured as psychic misfits. *Platoon, Full Metal Jacket,* and *Apocalypse Now* all contributed to a harsh and negative image of the military. Excesses can be found in any of our institutions, and the military is surely no exception. But the negative was being allowed to overshadow the positive. The American people were not seeing the incredible service and sacrifice that was being made by talented, patriotic men and women who were wearing our nation's uniform.

We thought we should make an effort to meet with some of the major producers and directors in Hollywood. We had no intention of trying to discuss the content of the movies being made, but wanted to suggest that the persistently negative and dispiriting stereotypes appearing on the big screens bore little relationship to the people who were making extraordinary efforts and sacrifices to defend our freedoms.

Steven Spielberg, Jerry Bruckheimer, and Peter Guber were all gracious and receptive. They were strongly committed to looking at our military through a lens that was free of ideological cataracts and cynicism.

In addition, Bill arranged for the Fox Sports team of Terry Bradshaw, Jim Brown, Howie Long, and Cris Collinsworth to broadcast their color commentary for two NFL games from the deck of the *U.S.S. Harry S. Truman* aircraft carrier that was sailing in the Mediterranean. A huge audience had the opportunity to see our sailors and Marines performing their daily missions.

During my years in Boston, I had enjoyed a wonderful relationship with maestro Arthur Fiedler, conductor extraordinaire of the Boston Pops Orchestra. After traveling with Bill on his Annual Holiday Tour to the Persian Gulf in 1998, I thought we should establish The Pentagon Pops, a musical tribute to our military. And where better to hold it than Constitution Hall? I was fully aware of the irony involved. The Daughters of the American Revolution had barred opera singer, Marian Anderson, from performing there. Hazel Scott, the wife of Adam Clayton Powell, Jr., had met a similar fate. Now, just a few decades later, a Black woman would host an annual event that would be broadcast globally over the Armed Forces Network. It was more than irony that touched me that evening. It was the exhilaration in recognizing just how much America had grown in such a short time.

We had asked NBC's Tom Brokaw to serve as master of ceremonies. We wanted to showcase the incredible musical talent of our military men and women that ranged from big band and country vocalists, to opera and the 104th Airborne Chorus. In addition, jazz spiritualist Phil Driscoll blew his trumpet with the power of Gabriel; R&B singers Peabo Bryson and Ruth Pointer infused the hall with soul; and keyboard genius Jon Caroll rocked it to the rafters. But the real stars were the Medal of Honor recipients whom we paid tribute to each year. When our heroes walked onto the stage, the audience burst into a standing and sustained ovation that brought tears to my eyes.

On Special Assignment

Among the many things I was able to achieve during our time at the Pentagon, I am especially proud of the level to which I elevated my advocacy for the troops by using my skills and experience. In 1999, we launched *Special Assignment with Janet Langhart Cohen,* a television show that was broadcast worldwide over the Armed Forces Network and was designed to show the rank and file the Pentagon's commitment to their well-being.

I wanted to use the power of television to demonstrate to our men and women in uniform, in the name of the Secretary of Defense, that they were heard and understood, that their problems were being considered at the highest levels, right up to the Commander-in-Chief.

That is why I decided to launch the program by airing a thirty-minute interview with President Clinton. He agreed, and we taped the interview on February 25, 1999, aboard Air Force One, en route to Tucson, Arizona. Although I had interviewed hundreds of prominent and powerful people during my thirty years in television, I was a little nervous in preparing to interview the President. After all, he was not just the leader of the world's only super power, he was my husband's boss. And I was planning to have a very frank discussion with him about some difficult issues involving budgets, military pay, family policy, and recruitment challenges.

I worried needlessly. We had a wonderful conversation, covering everything from pay increases and tuition reimbursements to mission and morale. The President demonstrated his deep commitment to our troops and his profound understanding of the issues that were uppermost in their minds. He was especially eloquent on the subject of mission:

"Well, first I would say that they're really the first generation of American troops to serve a United States that is both the dominant military power in the world and without a dominant military opponent, like the Soviet Union; that for the past ten years now, we've been trying to work out how we can fairly fulfill our responsibilities to promote peace and freedom and prosperity, consistent with our ability to afford it, and the need for our allies to assume their fair share of responsibility. . . .

"And it's sometimes dangerous [for the troops], sometimes boring, sometimes disruptive because of the rapid number of deployments that we have. But all of them should understand that they're part of a profound historic transformation in the world. And if we do this right, when we get through, the United States will share responsibilities for security with other democracies in a balanced and fair way, and will be doing it in a way that is quite effective."

The President and I also talked about the changing composition of the military, with women taking on more and more frontline roles. When Bill and I had celebrated Christmas aboard the *U.S.S. Enterprise,* I was proud to note that there were several female combat pilots among the crew taking part in operation Desert Fox. I remember once asking a commander how many female pilots he had on board. He said, "I don't know, ma'am. We don't see them as women, we see them as sailors."

"They worked for a long time," President Clinton said about the female pilots. "They trained for a long time, they waited for a long time. And when their chance came to do their job, they did their job without making a big deal of it, and they did it very, very well.

"We gave the Fourth Star to Benjamin O. Davis not very long ago in tribute to the Tuskegee Airmen," the President continued, seemingly anticipating my train of thought. "I think that looking backward is really a way of—in this context—is a way of ensuring you'll continue to go forward. It's a way of reminding us how far we've come and what we missed when we deny any group of people who wanted to contribute to our military the chance to do so."

He spoke from his heart about his commitment to diversity, and as we were concluding the interview, I was truly moved as he described growing up around his grandfather's little grocery store in a predominantly Black part of the small town in Arkansas where his family lived.

"We never believed it was right to keep anybody down," the President said. "And we were all raised, all of us, never to build ourselves up because there was somebody else to look down on. . . . In my family, we always had sympathy for the underdog."

I felt a special sense of kinship and gratitude toward President Clinton. He had honored the men and women of the armed services by giving to them so generously of his time, and he had honored me with his candid discussion of gender, race, and our common history.

Nothing could have prepared me, however, for the honor the President bestowed on me eleven months later, during his final State of the Union address to a joint session of Congress. When the President singled out my contribution to our military, I was overwhelmed with emotion.

I took a bow and thought of Rosa Parks, who had also been acknowledged in that very room. I thought of what my mother and my father would think. And finally, I thought of my dear friend, teacher, and mentor, Dr. King.

"I'm taking a bow for America, and for the race," I said to him in my heart. "So what would you think? Have I claimed my throne?"

Afterward, on the way to the White House for the reception, I kept thinking about Dr. King. I imagined how proud he would have been; how he would have teased me about blowing a kiss to the President.

I had actually intended it for Bill, but it did look a bit like I had sent it to Bill Clinton. Jay Leno actually made a joke about it on his show, having edited the tape to look like there had been a moment between the President and me. They showed him looking up adoringly into the gallery, after he had thanked Hillary. But instead of showing the First Lady taking her bow, they showed me mouthing, "Thank you, Mr. President" and blowing a kiss.

I felt euphoric for weeks after the State of the Union. To have the President's acknowledgment was one of those moments of illumination, when, in a flash, you can see how your life had led to this particular place. All the struggle, the rage, the striving seemed to fit into a pattern that brought me to the mission I was serving.

It was wonderful, when we went overseas a short time later, to have people all over France and Germany tell me they had seen me receive the President's thanks. The most surprising response, however, was waiting for me when we returned home. It was a letter from Bob's Kistner's oldest son, Skip, with whom I had not been in touch since the disposition of the estate.

"Dear Janet," he wrote in his beautiful, cultivated hand, "I saw the President acknowledge you at the State of the Union. Congratulations, and thank you for all you've done for the troops. I have always been a fan of Bill Cohen's, and when he looked up at you that night, I saw on his face a familiar expression of pride and love for you that I had often seen on my father's face."

And he signed it, "Love, Skip."

I delayed writing back for a long time. The resentment over how I had been treated by Bob's family had not fully dissipated. Finally, I did respond. "Dear Skip, I am sorry to be so late in writing you back. I wanted to say all the right words and not be filled with anger. Your letter was so beautiful. Your father would have been proud of you for having risen to acknowledge me. I hope you and your family are well. Love, Janet."

Later, as a further gesture of goodwill, I wanted to see Skip's children, so I invited Robbie and Katie to visit us in Washington. Bill and I showed them around the Pentagon, took them to a couple of museums and out to dinner. In parting, I gave Robbie Bob's gold watch fob, which had been Bob's father's. And I gave Katie an antique emerald ring, the first present Bob had ever given me. It felt good to pass a memento or an heirloom of Bob to the next generation. Life had allowed me to complete another circle.

As excited as I was about contributing to the morale of our forces and their families, the universe, once again, had another mission in mind for me. That mission was the care of my mother who had suffered a massive stroke.

I received a call from home, telling me that Mother was in the hospital lying in a coma, completely paralyzed on her left side. When I hung up, I was in shock, hurt, and anxious. I wanted to act, but did not want to act too fast, as it had been such a painful estrangement. I knew I wanted to be with my mother, but I needed to give myself a moment to allow everything to sink in.

It was a delicate reunion. I had steeled myself for what condition I might find my mother, as well as the aloof indifference my brother had always shown me. Sometimes his coolness had cut like a knife. I was so glad to have Bill's support and comfort at my side.

Much to my surprise, my brother seemed generally glad to see me, but the importance of that soon faded when I entered my mother's room in intensive care and saw her lying there on life support, her head shaved. I thought back to the last time I saw her robust and proud. Now she looked so small and lifeless, it was as though the bed was swallowing her up.

I went over, kissed her on the forehead, and spoke lightly into her ear, "It's Janet. I'm here, Mom." I held her hand, and I sat there for what seemed like forever.

Later when speaking with the doctors, I was told there was no chance of her regaining control of her left side, and that if she lived, she would be paralyzed for the remainder of her life, and that we should brace ourselves for another stroke at any time.

Somehow I summoned all the strength and courage I had seen my mother display at difficult times throughout my life. It was my turn to care for her. The roles had truly been reversed.

Mother regained consciousness a few days later. Through her dazed eyes I could tell she knew I was there. Although she didn't speak for almost two months, she did mouth, "I love you very much. Are you happy? I've missed you."

She was released from the hospital after about a month's stay. My brother had worked tirelessly to find the right nursing facility that could care for her, as taking her home was not an option. I would make frequent trips back and forth from Washington, D.C., to Indianapolis, and I was never happy in either place.

When I was at her bedside in Indianapolis, it grieved me to see her so helpless. This is the woman who never asked her children or anyone to so much as get her a drink of water. I remembered also, she had always said, "I never want to be dependent on my children." And here she was, at the mercy of her children and of strangers.

It was the thought of strangers caring for my mother that troubled me when I would leave her and go back to Washington that caused Bill to offer, without my asking, "Let's bring your mother here. We can take care of her here. She'll be better off, and you will be more at peace." That act of generosity is just one of the reasons I love Bill Cohen so deeply.

Bill arranged for a plane, a doctor, and all of the ambulances to transport my mother to Washington with every comfort. For the next four years, I would be her advocate, her therapist, her arms and legs, and always, her loving daughter.

While Mother's condition was painful and tragic, in a strange way, it was a gift to our relationship. For during that time, I learned that the difficulties we had had as mother and daughter had more to do with an anxiety disorder that had plagued her her whole life than any resentment she had of me. She also learned that beyond the material things I had shared with her, the greatest gift of all was my undying love.

I was incredibly inspired by watching my mother deal with her illness over the next four years. She had endured the stroke and the indignity of being dependent with such courage. It showed me another side of her. In this moment of her greatest need, Mother coped with grace and dignity. Incapacitated for years, she still insisted on having her hair done, her nails manicured, and her makeup applied, and took interest to every last detail down to the arch in her eyebrows. I especially remember her preparation for the day I took her to meet President Clinton in the Oval Office at the White House. She dictated thank-you notes for me to write to the people who visited or sent her cards or flowers. She also wanted to stay in touch with all of her friends back home and her beloved Mount Olive Baptist Church. She insisted on living her life as fully as possible, and I continued to learn from her every day about strength and grace.

11

A Farewell to Arms

On January 17, 2001, Bill and I, riding in the Secretary of Defense armored limousine, arrived at Comny Hall at Fort Myer with very mixed emotions. A new President had been elected, a new Secretary of Defense nominated. In just three days, we would pass the torch. It was time for us to step aside. We were prepared to do so, confident that we had both done our best to uphold the honor of serving the finest military in the world. Yet, even that satisfaction could not compensate for the loss we would feel at taking our leave.

The ceremony at Fort Myer was much like the one that had been organized for Bill's arrival four years earlier, the only difference being that we would exit stage left. I sat in the bleacher seats in the Hall, shrouded in darkness, as I watched my husband stand behind the podium and deliver his valedictory speech to the parade units of the respective armed forces and the large audience assembled there.

It was as though the time of our last four years flashed before me. There were so many special moments. It was curious that the only one that stood still in my mind was the worried and sleepless night Bill had for the lone pilot who had been ordered to fly over Iraq in an U.S. Air Force U-2 unarmed aircraft. He felt as though that was everybody's son in that cockpit. He remained cool and quiet but he stayed by the secure phone until the mission was successfully accomplished.

During his speech, he was, as always, profoundly eloquent. I looked on in silence, admiring him for his quiet courage—as a Congressman, Senator, and as the nation's twentieth Secretary of Defense. At that moment he looked years younger, almost boyish. It was apparent that the weight of responsibility of his office had been lifted from his shoulders.

Bill is a terribly modest man who studiously passes up every opportunity to sound the trumpet of his accomplishments. In all the years that I've known him, I've never heard him use the word *I* when discussing his thirty-one years of public service. He has the remarkable ability to function on just four and a half hours of sleep each night. Not once did he ever complain about being tired or about the pain in his arthritic hip that he refused to repair for fear of missing a day of work. He worried needlessly. Shortly after becoming a private citizen, he had a total hip replacement operation performed by Dr. Paul Pellicci at the New York Hospital for Special Surgery. He spent five days in the hospital and then returned to work the next day without using crutches or even a cane.

As he stood behind the podium in the darkened hall, I thought of all that I had witnessed during his years in the Senate and then as Secretary of Defense.

Time after time, he had been called upon to make tough decisions. On every occasion, he confronted the challenge with intelligence, integrity, and fairness. On a much more personal level was his courage in taking me as his wife, and his willingness to accept me as his partner.

He had one more secret in store for me. When it was time for him to "troop the line"—to pass in front of the honor guard units and inspect them—General Hugh Shelton, the Chairman of the Joint Chiefs of Staff, called me to come forward and to troop the line with him. Never before had a Secretary's spouse been given such an honor.

As I walked along beside General Shelton, I looked into the handsome faces of the young men and women. The faces were black, white, brown, and yellow in color. They were proud, patriotic faces. They were the faces of my children, my family, our future.

I was walking—no, gliding—along the grandest runway in the world, one for which no modeling or finishing school could ever have prepared me.

In his final comments, Bill remained true to his poet's heart:

"We have loved this job," he said, "knowing that this day would one day have to come. We have loved not this job, but this opportunity to be in the presence of heroes—to walk, to sail, and to soar with eagles . . ."

He closed his remarks by paraphrasing Rabindranath Tagore:

"When one comes and whispers to me, 'Thy days are ended.' Let me say to him, 'I have lived in love and not in mere time.'

"And he will ask, 'Will thy songs remain?'

"And I shall say, 'I know not, but this I know. That often when I sang, I found my eternity.' "

In the darkness, I whispered, "Amen, Bill. Amen."

Shortly after the transition, I invited Joyce Rumsfeld, my successor, to tea at the Four Seasons. I wanted to pass the baton to her directly. I thought hard about what to give her as a gift that would be meaningful. Finally, the same instinct that had told me four years earlier to order two black dresses guided my choice. I bought some beautiful lace handkerchiefs.

"These are for all the tears of joy and sorrow that come with this job," I told Joyce. "They will be precious tears because they will be shed for heroes."

12

Citizen Patriot

During our years at the Pentagon, I had become deeply involved with the USO, the nonprofit organization that had been entertaining the troops for sixty years.

As our time at the Pentagon was coming to an end, I wanted to create a legacy for Bill and to find a way for me to stay engaged in supporting the troops. I thought the USO would be the way for me to continue serving.

I had had all kinds of romantic associations with the USO. My mother and father had danced their first dance at the USO canteen in Indianapolis. Bob Hope was, of course, irrevocably linked with the organization. To me, it was a real symbol of patriotism.

I was also aware that the USO's past was not unblemished. Years earlier, when Lena Horne had traveled with the USO to entertain American troops during WWII, she refused to perform when she discovered that Black soldiers were moved to the rear of the audience, while German POWs were seated near the front. The USO, rather than alter the clearly racist and unpatriotic seating arrangement, essentially banned her from the organization. She was never invited to travel with the federally chartered and Congressionally funded organization again, but she continued to entertain the troops, funding the trips herself.

But that was then, and this was now, I reasoned. When the former commandant of the Marine Corps, General Carl Mundy, who was then the president of the USO, approached me to join the board of the organization, I accepted.

Afterward, on our overseas trips, I would ask the troops what the USO did for them, and they would enumerate a list of support services, like help with relocation, classes for families, e-mail access, and of course entertainment.

I worked with the USO to develop some innovative ideas for entertainment tours, like the Pentagon Pops and the Secretary of Defense's Annual Holiday Tour. My big idea, however, was to create a corridor dedicated to the USO that would be the capstone of a Pentagon tour. I wanted Bill's legacy to be something tangible that would help connect civilian society with the men and women who serve in uniform.

I got very excited about adding a USO exhibit to the rest of the exhibits that celebrate our victories and honor our heroes. It would allow people to see, after they had learned about the sacrifices of the men and women of our military in the name of freedom, what they could do for people in the service.

Trouble was that the USO, as a private organization, was forbidden to be in the Pentagon. I had to fight very hard to change the memorandum of understanding to have a USO exhibit in the building. My greatest champion was David O. Cooke, affectionately called Doc, the unofficial Mayor of the Pentagon.

Finally, when we had secured the space I had wanted and installed the exhibit, we organized a celebration. We called it a "ribbon joining," to signal the theme of the military and civilian society coming together. Bill presided over the ceremony, with actors Mickey Rooney and Gerald McRaney, football great Terry Bradshaw, former Navy Lieutenant Ross Perot, and other celebrities joining the event. It was a big success thanks to the support from Sgt. Major Marshall Williams and his wife Terri.

I wanted to continue to do the kind of high-visibility events we produced when Bill and I created the Citizen Patriot Award. We gave it to Jack Valenti, who was President Johnson's press secretary and a decorated World War II hero. He is the head of the Motion Picture Association, so we presented the award in Los Angeles, and all of Hollywood turned out. Steven Spielberg, Jerry and Linda Bruckheimer, Kirk and Michael Douglas, Angie Dickinson, Charlton Heston, Robert Stack, and Terry Moore all came to pay tribute to Jack. Quincy Jones was also in attendance, conducting the military band.

I had interviewed Steven Spielberg for the Armed Forces Network after *Saving Private Ryan* was released. He told me that he had made

Shindler's List for his mother and *Saving Private Ryan* for his father. Steven became and remains a generous supporter of our efforts on behalf of the military. As have Jerry and Linda Bruckheimer, who traveled with us overseas.

My association with the USO provided me the platform I needed to continue with events such as the Citizen Patriot Award after we left the Pentagon.

I followed through on that plan and created the Citizen Patriot Organization, a nonprofit entity whose mission is to support those who serve and defend America at home and abroad. It was particularly important for me to continue my efforts after we suffered the attacks of September 11. I wanted to look the young soldiers I had gotten to know over four years of travel in the face and say, "Yes, we have been attacked. Yes, we are scared. But we are strong and we're here for you and your families. We are going to support you. All the way."

I had hoped to continue my work with the USO. But my instincts told me to beware. During the four years at the Pentagon I had learned that despite Bill's position, there were landmines that lay in wait all over the landscape. Certain staff members were overly turf conscious, ready to treat any idea or act that did not originate with them as trespassing. Career civil servants had cautioned me to "stay in my lane." I could understand the need for rules of the road, so to speak, but those rules seemed to be open to rather arbitrary interpretation. At one point, for example, an attorney in the General Counsel's office suggested that my mere presence on the USO board of directors could be construed as a criminal offense under a strict interpretation of the law that prohibited conflicts of interest! How a nonpaying position on the board of an organization whose mission it is to promote the morale, welfare, and well-being of our military could possibly be construed as a crime remained mystifying. Something more than the law, I thought, was at work.

In addition, the Pentagon, for all of its rigid codes of honor and discipline, remains a very human institution. Many of those who worked there, particularly the civilian political appointees, had their own agendas, which too often included jealousy, and backbiting. I vividly remember what I'd overheard one staff member say to my husband after reading a small general quote attributed to me in the *New York Times*. He warned Bill not to let "my I.D. get higher than [his]." His comment reinforced what I had intuitively known: oppressors were determined to hold themselves up by holding others (in this case, *me*) down.

While playing polo years earlier, I had learned why it was important to develop all-around vision. The military, of course, has the same goal. Success depends on possessing total battlefield awareness. I discovered that watching one's back could prove as critical to the art of survival in the halls of the Pentagon as it was on the battlefield.

During the summer of 2001, I had been asked to serve, for the fourth time, as a judge in the Miss America pageant. The pageant itself was scheduled to take place in Atlantic City during the third week of September. After terrorists struck the World Trade Center and the Pentagon, doubt was cast on the advisability of proceeding with the pageant. I felt strongly that it was important to send the signal that the terrorists could not bring America to its knees and stop public events that were so much a part of our culture. Fortunately, the officials responsible for the event and a majority of the contestants decided that the "show must go on."

It was during the weeklong judging process that the answer to the question of how my Citizen Patriot Organization might assist the military and their families came sharply into focus.

As I interviewed the pageant's contestants, I became convinced that it would be important for the new Miss America to become actively involved in helping to bind up the psychic wounds that we had suffered at the hands of the terrorists. The young lady chosen to wear the crown would serve as a symbol of the youth, beauty, and talent of women throughout America. But she should also use her position to inspire others, to lift up their spirits, to say "Yes, we're hurt, but we're still here. You cannot break us."

Soon after Katie Harman was crowned Miss America I called her and asked her to join me in the effort to support the families of those who had been killed or wounded in the attacks. She was eager to help.

I instituted the first Citizen Patriot Homeland Tour and arranged for Katie to visit Ground Zero in New York. I personally accompanied her to the Pentagon to meet with the Secretary of the Army, Tom White, and to the crisis center that the Pentagon had set up in Crystal City, Virginia, to help the victims' families cope with their grief and loss. The families we encountered there were profoundly sad and full of quiet rage. It was heartrending to see how they were dealing with the murder of their family members. In addition to wanting justice, they insisted that under no circumstances should the remains of their loved ones be mingled with those of the terrorists. Lynda Carter, of *Wonder Woman* fame, was there with the families every day offering her support and a listening ear.

We then traveled to the Arlington National Cemetery and visited the Tomb of the Unknowns. Later, we drove to Dover Air Force Base in Delaware, where the remains of those lost in the attack were stored. We spent time there talking to the personnel responsible for the difficult task of sorting through and identifying the remains.

I began to call friends in Hollywood to ask their assistance in securing celebrities to travel abroad to visit our troops. It was during this time that I received a series of phone calls from USO officials indicating that I should discontinue any activities involving fund-raising or the solicitation of celebrities on behalf of the USO. Furthermore, I would not be allowed to travel with the USO on any future troop visits.

"Why?" I asked.

"Because your husband is no longer in office. The king is dead."

"Yes, but the queen isn't," I quipped. "Just because Bill isn't in office, it doesn't mean that I've stopped being a citizen and a patriot. . . ."

The conversation continued in this vein, all quite civilly, for a few more minutes, but I knew that I was not going to change anyone's mind. It was clear that the decision had already been made. Several days later, I received a letter from the USO, stating that my board membership had expired and would not be renewed. My good deeds in integrating the USO directly into the Pentagon were not to go unpunished.

But there has always been something about the word, *no,* that I've refused to understand. Rather than curse the darkness, I decided to light the fires of my own organization.

I knew from having negotiated the memorandum of understanding that created the USO corridor in the Pentagon, that the USO does not have exclusive rights to conduct tour visits to our military facilities, be they at home or abroad. Any citizen can visit our bases with the consent of the commander of the installation. I had spoken with General Joe Ralston, the commander of our forces in Europe. Getting consent was not going to be a problem. The biggest challenge was going to be securing transportation to Europe.

On October 11, one month following the attacks, I started working the phones, and within a few days was able to raise two hundred and fifty thousand dollars. I then called Hank Greenberg, the chairman and CEO of AIG, one of the world's largest insurance companies. Hank was a veteran of WWII and Korea and a strong supporter of our military. He was also a close personal friend. He agreed to help and put me in touch with executives at Canada's Bombardier. Yes, they could furnish an aircraft. More than one, if needed.

I called the top officials at Boeing. The company would also help provide transportation. I reached Paul Bloch, a dear friend, and super agent at Rogers & Cowan, the public relations firm based in Los Angeles. I asked if he could call on some of his clients to travel with me to Europe. Within twenty-four hours, country superstar Clint Black called and said he was eager to go. Comedian Al Franken joined us, along with singers Shane Minor, Phil Symonds, Jon Caroll and his wife Meredith, members of the New England Patriot cheerleaders, and Lorenzo Thrower of the Fairfax County Fire Department, one of the renowned elements of our nation's first responders.

Armed with money and aircraft, I, along with my executive assistant, Kari Lidgett, and Director of Security, Jeff Sorenson, organized a two-day Citizen Patriot Tour that traveled to bases in Germany, Bosnia, Italy, Macedonia, and Kosovo. *Entertainment Tonight* covered the entire tour. Ironically, they asked me to serve as their on-air correspondent, when twelve years earlier they had insisted that my diction was incomprehensible. We entertained more than fifty thousand troops and did four segments for *ET*. The tour was carried around the world on the Armed Forces Network.

The troops were enormously grateful for our effort. While working to support the war campaign to destroy the Taliban in Afghanistan, many of them expressed concern for the safety of their families back home. Lorenzo, dressed in his fireman's uniform, strode out onto the stage at each base carrying the American flag, thanking those who were serving our nation for their sacrifice. He assured all who were gathered: "Don't worry about your families back home. We've got the home front covered." In an emotionally charged gesture, he passed the American flag to a member of the military at each of the bases. They, in turn, said "Thank you. We'll take it from here." Even though I had written and produced the scene itself, I couldn't hold back the tears as we all joined in the singing of the National Anthem. A profound sense of camaraderie and commitment to the cause of freedom reinforced a sentiment since the days the Japanese had attacked us at Pearl Harbor: We are all in this together.

Several weeks after we concluded the tour, I received a letter from a three-star general stationed at Ramstein Air Force Base in Germany. He wrote that he had respected the effort I had made to help lift the morale of our forces while Bill was serving as Secretary of Defense. But that I was willing to do so now when no one expected it of me was an act of true patriotism.

To get a letter of such sentiment from one of the leaders of the finest military in the world took my breath away.

We are locked in a long and difficult battle against terrorism. With ongoing engagements around the world and a commitment to homeland security, we need a strong military that enjoys positive, sustained support from the civilian population—who is the greatest beneficiary of their service and sacrifice. We Americans get to sleep under a blanket of freedom every night because our military is out there with their lives on the line around the world 24/7.

I know that doing what I can to help those who are today's "greatest generation" is a noble mission, and I'm determined to do all that I can to help make *duty, honor,* and *country* inspirational words for all Americans.

Home at Last

The poet T.S. Eliot wrote that we are all explorers, destined to continue our exploration "until we arrive at the place where we began and know it for the first time." One of Bill's ceremonial acts during his final year in office involved attending the annual Indy 500 race held at the raceway in Indianapolis. Not only was he to address the five hundred thousand fans in attendance, but we both were to ride in the lap car that initiated the race that would be witnessed the world over.

Indianapolis was my birthplace. In my youth it had served as the home of the Ku Klux Klan. It was a city that had practiced segregation as a higher art form, one in which its top line modeling school advised me to cancel any aspirations I might hold. It was also the city that held the crown jewel of auto racing where I had met and interviewed the racing legends of our time: Al Unser, Mario Andretti, A.J. Foyt, Graham Hill, Johnny Rutherford and so many others. It was

Peter Revson who, in 1972, gave me a "first" while I had the show *Indy Today with Janet Langhart*. Race car drivers, like so many athletes are notoriously superstitious. At the time, they considered it bad luck for a woman to enter "gasoline alley," where the drivers parked their racing cars and made any last-minute adjustments before heading out onto the track. Peter Revson, whose family owned the Revlon cosmetics company, breeched the taboo and invited me into the alley where we conducted a brief interview. What truly amazed me was the courage that these young drivers possessed.

They traveled at speeds that allowed no margin for error, and knew that every second on the track they were in mortal danger. A miscalculation, however slight, be it theirs or that of a competitor, could send them spinning like a burning top into an unforgiving wall. Yet they faced that danger with a focus and fearlessness that I would later see, although under less life-threatening circumstances, in professional polo players.

I was able to gauge the scope of their passion in the person of Merle Bettenhausen, whose family is legendary in racing history. After having passed his rookie test at the Indy in 1972, Merle crashed on his opening lap at the Michigan Speedway and lost his arm while trying to escape his burning car. I interviewed him shortly after the accident and noticed that as he raised his arm it looked stiff as a club. He told me that when he realized during the escape from his vehicle that his arm had been severed and left behind, he sent one of his team members back to retrieve it. At the hospital the doctor informed him that he could reattach the arm but it would not have any function. The doctor offered him a choice of how he wanted his hand to be shaped.

"So what did you tell the doctor to do?" I had asked him.

"I told him to attach it in a way that I could hold a steering wheel," he said, raising his arm, which was fixed with a permanent, clawlike grip.

The following year he was back out on the tracks, aided by a steering wheel device improvised by his brother Gary. Courage, passion, tenacity, the will to win—the ingredients of what it takes to prevail in any profession or human endeavor.

As Bill and I moved through the crowd and approached the V.I.P. platform where we would be introduced as the honored guests of the Memorial Day race, we saw everyone suddenly gaze up at the sky.

One of the military's AV-8B Harrier jets flew over the center of the track, came to a complete standstill, then completed a slow, three-hundred-sixty-degree turn before zooming off.

The half-million fans in the stands stood in awe and cheered as the pilot lit the jet's afterburners.

"That's the sound of freedom!" shouted one man over the deafening roar, as tears streamed down his cheeks.

"Yes!" shouted another, pointing to the disappearing aircraft, his eyes turning watery. "And thank God, they're ours."

We finally made our way to the platform as television star, Florence Henderson, began to sing the National Anthem. I could feel the collective spirit of patriotism swelling up in the hearts of everyone there. My throat tightened as I fought back the tears.

After Bill was introduced and gave the briefest speech of his career, we jumped into the pace car to start the race. As we accelerated around the track, the race cars clustered behind us sounding for all the world like angry hornets, I thought how symbolic the moment had become for me.

I had come full circle to the place where I began nearly sixty years earlier. I recalled at that very moment Merle Bettenhausen's will to carry on against adversity.

Metaphorically, our life experiences were similar. I, too, had gathered up my broken parts and shaped them so that I could continue to drive on, to face the future without fear or thought of failure.

Once told by an intolerant society that dreams were not made for people like me, I continued to dream. Every fiber of my being, every ancient whisper told me that I could succeed in whatever I chose to do. I was never going to accept the limitations imposed by others and "stay in my place." No matter how many times I got knocked down, I was determined to keep getting up.

The faces of all those in the stands turned into a blur. The colors I saw were not black or white; they were red, white, and blue—just people who believe and revel in the spirit of being Americans.

For most of my life, because of the injustices that Black people had to experience and endure in this country, I never felt that America truly was *my* sanctuary, really *my* homeland.

My head was filled with ear-splitting noise. It was the sound and fury of freedom. *Thank God,* I thought, *it's ours. It's mine.*

I was home at last, not just in Indianapolis, but in America.

I had moved from blaming America, to claiming America.

Epilogue

My mother died on December 27, 2002, while I was working on the manuscript for this book. Surprisingly, while I grieved over her loss, I did not cry as I had fully expected to do. Somewhere in me, I felt crying would be a form of saying good-bye, and I never want to do that. I knew this person I had been born of who taught me so much, would always be with me in spirit. I felt a profound sorrow, but ever since her first stroke, I had been preparing myself for the inevitability of her passing. She had suffered greatly during her last four years. But throughout, she struggled to maintain a sense of grace and dignity that her body was determined to strip away. She had come to terms with her paralysis, and seemingly, with her coming departure from this world. During our last days together, she looked exceptionally beautiful, with a glow around her that was simply beatific. We spent the holidays together and she told me it was "the best Christmas ever."

It's been said that, "Life must be lived forward, but can only be understood backward." I have looked back over the past six decades in search of clarity and comprehension. I remain mystified as to just how much in my life has been the product of choice, chance, or the invisible hand of the universe.

I have traveled from a world of poverty and privation through those of modeling and television to the very center of power in Washington. I've accomplished much during this long and twisting journey, scaling mountains that I never aspired to climb, walking through valleys I had hoped never to find.

For so many of those years, I felt a red-hot coal burning at the very center of my being, an anger that was fueled by the blindness, bigotry, and inhumanity of others. Doors were closed, barriers erected, not because I lacked the right skills, but because I didn't have the "right" color.

Yet, I prevailed. I overcame. I refused to be broken, to be brought down by the inexplicable fear and hatred that resides at the core of racism. With success comes a measure of satisfaction, indeed, even serenity. But it is only a measure. I cannot claim the success as mine alone. I have stood on the shoulders of my ancestors who endured horrific suffering and humiliation on a scale unimaginable in a nation founded on the professed ideals of freedom, justice, and equality. I have been lifted up by the spirit of those who fought for racial equality during the long struggle for civil rights—Martin Luther King, Jr., Muhammad Ali, Malcolm X, Nelson Mandela, Frederick Douglass, W.E.B. DuBois, Rosa Parks, Andy Young, Melnea Cass, Eleanor Roosevelt, Angela Davis, Medgar Evers, Dick Gregory, Harry Belafonte, Arthur Ashe, Randall Robinson, Morris Dees, Mary McLeod Bethune, Andrew Goodman, Michael Schwerner, James Chaney, John Lewis, Ella Baker, Fannie Lou Hamer, Bill Baxley, Dorothy Height, Vernon Jordan, Madam C.J. Walker, Harriet Tubman, Thurgood Marshall and so many others.

There are moments when I look at the growing mutiracial society of today and think that the struggle for a truly "color blind" America is nearly over; when I think that the horrible murder of Emmett Till is but a faint scream from the past. But then the echo comes roaring back when news accounts describe how a Black man in Texas is chained and dragged behind a pickup truck, then slammed into a roadside culvert that beheaded him. The note of progress is that the defendant, unlike those in the Till trial held in Mississippi, was convicted of murder.

So the anger remains. But what prevents my anger from turning to bitterness has been the realization that America is still in its infancy, still growing. As I scan the world map and look at Northern Ireland, the Balkans, the Middle East, India, Pakistan, and Africa, I realize how much hate exists in the world, how much religious extremism and ethnic tribalism pulls us down into the lower depths of human existence. What rescues me from despair is the recognition, whatever our flaws and our faults, how blessed we are to live in America, to be American citizens.

If there is one word that captures the essence of this country, it is *hope*. The spirit of America is to always look up, to look beyond the horizon, to accept no limitations on our imaginations. What we can conceive, we can achieve. This is not a motto or mantra. It's the spirit that will power us to distant galaxies and to the more profound space in our souls.

Dr. King predicted that one day I would claim my throne. His prophecy has proved true. I have claimed a throne—not as a queen or princess, but as a patriot. Each day there is a new barrier broken, a new beginning made and the frontiers of the human heart expanded.

I truly believe that the two Americas that I have known will soon become one, and that the senseless fears and hatreds that have afflicted so many will remain a part of our history and not of our limitless future.

Index